THE CAMBRIDGE COMPANION TO
THE LITERATURE OF THE AMERICAN SOUTH

This *Companion* maps the dynamic literary landscape of the American South. From pre– and post–Civil War literature to modernist and civil rights fictions, and writing by immigrants in the "global" South of the late twentieth and twenty-first centuries, these newly commissioned essays from leading scholars explore the region's established and emergent literary traditions. Touching on poetry and song, drama and screenwriting, key figures such as William Faulkner and Eudora Welty, and iconic texts such as *Gone with the Wind*, chapters investigate how issues of class, poverty, sexuality, and regional identity have textured Southern writing across generations. The volume's rich contextual approach highlights patterns and connections between writers while offering insight into the development of Southern literary criticism, making this *Companion* a valuable guide for students and teachers of American literature, American studies, and the history of storytelling in America.

SHARON MONTEITH is Professor of American Studies at the University of Nottingham.

A complete list of books in the series is at the back of this book.

THE CAMBRIDGE
COMPANION TO

THE LITERATURE OF THE
AMERICAN SOUTH

THE CAMBRIDGE
COMPANION TO
THE LITERATURE
OF THE AMERICAN
SOUTH

EDITED BY
SHARON MONTEITH
University of Nottingham

CAMBRIDGE UNIVERSITY PRESS
Cambridge, New York, Melbourne, Madrid, Cape Town,
Singapore, São Paulo, Delhi, Mexico City

Cambridge University Press
32 Avenue of the Americas, New York, NY 10013-2473, USA

www.cambridge.org
Information on this title: www.cambridge.org/9781107610859

First published 2013

Printed in the United States of America

A catalog record for this publication is available from the British Library.

Library of Congress Cataloging in Publication data
The Cambridge companion to the literature of the American South /
edited by Sharon Monteith.
pages cm. – (Cambridge companions to literature)
Includes bibliographical references and index.
ISBN 978-1-107-03678-9 (hardback) – ISBN 978-1-107-61085-9 (paperback)
1. American literature – Southern States – History and criticism.   2. Authors,
American – Homes and haunts – Southern States.   3. Southern States – In
literature.   4. Southern States – Intellectual life.   I. Monteith, Sharon.
PS261.C336   2013
810.9'975–dc23   2012040136

ISBN 978-1-107-03678-9 Hardback
ISBN 978-1-107-61085-9 Paperback

This Companion *is dedicated to the many students who inspired it, and it is a tribute in memoriam to Noel Polk (1943–2012) whose scholarship on William Faulkner has been an inspiration to all and whose fellowship will be sadly missed.*

CONTENTS

CONTENTS

CONTRIBUTORS

MICHAEL P. BIBLER is Reader in American Studies at Northumbria University. He is author of *Cotton's Queer Relations: Same-Sex Intimacy and the Literature of the U.S. Plantation, 1936–1968* (2009) and coeditor of the essay collection *Just Below South: Intercultural Performance in the Caribbean and the U.S. South* (2007) and a scholarly edition of Arna Bontemps's 1939 novel *Drums at Dusk* (2009). He is working on a book project about the complete works of Truman Capote titled *Perversity, Conformity, and Truman Capote: A Parallel Identity Politics.*

DAVID A. DAVIS is assistant professor of English and Southern Studies at Mercer University in Macon, Georgia. He has published several essays on Southern literature, edited reprints of Victor Daly's *Not Only War* (2010) and John L. Spivak's *Hard Times on the Southern Chain Gang* (2012), and coedited a collection of essays on Southern literature and foodways. He is currently writing a book about World War I and Southern modernism.

SARAH GLEESON-WHITE is senior lecturer in American Literature in the Department of English, University of Sydney. She is the author of *Strange Bodies: Gender and Identity in the Novels of Carson McCullers* (2003) and essays on McCullers, Eudora Welty, Flannery O'Connor, Cormac McCarthy, and William Faulkner. She has become interested in the relationship of screenwriting and literary culture in the first half of the twentieth century, and is editing a volume of Faulkner's Twentieth Century Fox screenplays. Her essay "Auditory Exposures: Faulkner, Eisenstein and Film Sounds" was published in *PMLA* in 2013.

WILL KAUFMAN is professor of American Literature and Culture at the University of Central Lancashire. He is the author of *The Comedian as Confidence Man* (1997), *The Civil War in American Culture* (2006), *American Culture in the 1970s* (2009), and, most recently, *Woody Guthrie, American Radical* (2011). Also a professional folksinger and multi-instrumentalist, he tours the world with live musical documentaries on Guthrie (www.willkaufman.com).

JOHN T. MATTHEWS is professor of English at Boston University and, most recently, the author of *William Faulkner: Seeing Through the South* (2009) and editor of *A Companion to the Modern American Novel 1900–1950* (2009). He published *The Play of Faulkner's Language* (1982) and is the author of many articles on Faulkner, Southern literature, and modern American fiction.

PEARL AMELIA MCHANEY is associate professor of American and Southern Literature and Associate Dean for Fine Arts at Georgia State University in Atlanta. She is the editor of *Eudora Welty as Photographer* (2009), *Eudora Welty: Contemporary Reviews* (2005), and the journal *Eudora Welty Review*. She has lectured and published on work by William Faulkner, Barry Hannah, Alice Munro, Natasha Trethewey, and Tennessee Williams. Her current project is a book-length study of Eudora Welty's nonfiction and photography.

KATHRYN B. MCKEE is McMullan Associate Professor of Southern Studies and associate professor of English at the University of Mississippi. She is the coeditor, with Deborah Barker, of *American Cinema and the Southern Imaginary* (2011), and her articles have appeared in journals including *American Literature*, *Southern Literary Journal*, and *Mississippi Quarterly*. Her areas of research include the literature and culture of the nineteenth-century South, writing by women, Global South studies, film studies, and humor studies.

SHARON MONTEITH is professor of American Studies at the University of Nottingham, and was a Rockefeller Humanities Fellow at the University of Memphis. Her books include *Advancing Sisterhood?: Interracial Friendships in Southern Fiction* (2000); *American Culture in the 1960s* (2008); *Gender and the Civil Rights Movement* with Peter Ling (1999/2004); *South to a New Place: Region, Literature, Culture*, with Suzanne Jones (2002); *Film Histories* (2006); and *The New Encyclopedia of Southern Culture: Media* with Allison Graham (2011), as well as articles and essays on interdisciplinary Southern studies. She is completing *SNCC's Stories: Narrative Culture and the Southern Freedom Struggle of the 1960s* for the University of Georgia Press.

JUDIE NEWMAN is professor of American Studies at the University of Nottingham. She is a recipient of the Arthur Miller Prize and the former chair of the British Association for American Studies, and her publications include *Saul Bellow and History* (1984), *John Updike* (1988), *The Ballistic Bard: Postcolonial Fictions* (1995), *Alison Lurie* (2000), and *Fictions of America: Narratives of Global Empire* (2007), as well as many scholarly essays. She edited an edition of Harriet Beecher Stowe's *Dred: A Tale of the Great Dismal Swamp* (1992), as well as *Nadine Gordimer's Burger's Daughter: A Casebook* (2003), and, with Celeste-Marie Bernier, *Public Art, Memorials, and Atlantic Slavery* (2009).

GARY RICHARDS is an associate professor of English at the University of Mary Washington in Virginia. He is the author of *Lovers and Beloveds: Sexual Otherness in Southern Fiction 1936–1961* (2007) as well as essays in *Comics and the U.S.*

South (2012), *Faulkner's Sexualities* (2007), *Beth Henley: A Casebook* (2002), and a range of journals.

SARAH ROBERTSON is a senior lecturer at the University of the West of England, Bristol. She is the author of a number of articles, and her book, *The Secret Country: Decoding the Cryptic Fiction of Jayne Anne Phillips*, was published in 2007. Her current research centers on Southern poverty since the Depression, with a particular focus on poor white memoirists. She is completing a book titled *Locating Poor Whites in Southern Writing, 1970–2010*.

SCOTT ROMINE is professor of English at the University of North Carolina at Greensboro, where he teaches American and Southern literature. He is the author of *The Narrative Forms of Southern Community* (1999) and *The Real South: Southern Narrative in the Age of Cultural Reproduction* (2008). He has published widely in journals and essay collections on writers including William Gilmore Simms, Thomas Dixon, Lillian Smith, William Faulkner, Harry Crews, and James Wilcox.

ERNEST SUAREZ is professor and Chair of the Department of English at the Catholic University of America, and an occasional music critic for *The Washington Post*. His publications include *James Dickey and the Politics of Canon* (1993), *Southbound: Interviews with Southern Poets* (1999), and many articles on Southern poetry and music. He has been a Fulbright Senior Scholar in Spain and China, and he was named the Carnegie Foundation Professor of the Year for Washington, DC, in 1999.

NAHEM YOUSAF is professor of English and Head of English, Culture and Media Studies at Nottingham Trent University. He has published on new immigrants in the U.S. South in a number of journals and essay collections. He has written widely on postcolonial literatures; his books include *Alex La Guma: Politics and Resistance* (2001), a critical edition of La Guma's *A Walk in the Night* (2006), *Apartheid Narratives* (2001), *Hanif Kureishi's The Buddha of Suburbia* (2002), and *Chinua Achebe* (2003). He is editor of the Manchester University Press series of monographs on Contemporary American and Canadian Writers.

SHARON MONTEITH

Introduction: Mapping the Figurative South

Southern literature has comprised a myth-making as much as a place-making narrative – and a contested one as counter-narratives and competing stories intervene in its trajectory. The prevailing defensive symbolism of the "Old South," the "Lost Cause," generated in the nineteenth century assumed the image of a collective nostalgia for an antebellum South. Resistance to such myths was forged in the crucible of plantation slavery, in the Civil War, and in the Reconstruction era. African-American writers refused to concede a literary history filled with images of Civil War heroes, Confederate Dead, and martyred politicians, as canonized by Thomas Dixon in his Reconstruction Trilogy. This *Companion* examines the ways in which the region's writers have struggled over the dominant images of very different "Souths," nurturing and propagating them and resisting and rejecting them down the centuries.

It maps the southern literary landscape, taking different generic, thematic, periodized, and critical routes through regionally and nationally defined representations and their cycles and returns. Contributors pay attention to regional struggles that have taken place in a national frame because southern literature has played a key role in establishing a counter-narrative of exceptionalism to an industrializing North. Essays discuss the cultural multiplicity of the region's many constituencies that not only permits diversity into the traditional image of a racially bipolar South but also extricates the region from a national model and from a North-South binary. Southern literary culture now includes writing that engages the South even though it originates elsewhere, in the work of writers born on the region's borders like Toni Morrison in Ohio, or thousands of miles away like Monique Truong in Vietnam. The *Companion* closes by examining bicultural narratives that contribute to evolving regional identities.

Historical period is a determinant of the *Companion*'s line of inquiry, but genres do not maintain period boundaries, so essays make clear where a literary form established in one period has resonance in another. It is not possible to understand the revisionist neo-slave narrative without recourse to nineteenth-century originals or to the politicized aesthetic forged in the Black Arts Movement of the 1960s. Nor is it possible to appreciate literature about civil rights without considering that in the 1960s the era was often declared a "Second Reconstruction." C. Van Woodward keeps both periods in view throughout *The Strange Career of Jim Crow* (1957), and Edmund Wilson maintained comparative frames in *Patriotic Gore* (1962), his study of Civil War literature, locating the intransigent segregationist backlash of the 1960s within the white South's continual rebellion against the federal government, "never forgiven for laying waste to their country, for reducing them to abject defeat and for the needling and meddling of the Reconstruction."[1] The language used is evocative, and it is unsurprising that the same imagery-laden and transhistorical framework should animate much southern fiction.

By following different paths through the history of Southern literature, this volume tracks developments in literary criticism, from writing in periodicals that enjoyed a wide circulation before and after the Civil War and promulgated a romantic version of slavery, to the literary endeavor to facilitate the reconstruction of the nation that Scott Romine identifies in his essay as "the masterplot of Reconstruction, as both history and literature." As the nation modernized, key images of the South were of a retrograde racial system, with the cotton crop dictating the fiscal heath of the region – and its levels of poverty, as David Davis and Sarah Robertson explore from different perspectives, with Davis arguing that monocrop agricapitalism was so much more than a symbol because it "defined an elaborate system of race and class stratification that enforced the maintenance of a vast labor pool."

As agricultural laborers began leaving the South after World War I, so did many writers. The region's fiction travels further afield as Southerners and South-watchers reimagine the region from extrinsic vantage points. Literary movements, originally conceived to promote and sustain regional values and to canonize writers, have been expanded geographically, as well chronologically and ideologically, down the decades, but, as John T. Matthews notes of the Southern Renaissance label, "There are also good reasons to question its continued usefulness altogether." Pearl McHaney examines the category of "Southern women writers" and observes that "once its efficacy is accomplished, [a label] can occasionally be regrettable." The essays raise some knotty questions that readers may wish to examine when testing the parameters of the periods they study and the writers, movements, and genres they analyze. Judie Newman points out how many times the Southernness of the slave narrative, peculiarly American though the genre may be, has been ignored by critics, and she traces how that tendency continues in studies of the neo-slave narrative that overlook its fictionalization of the South in favor of other "master categories, under the general headings of history and memory, gender, and postmodernism." Can one understand a slave narrative without understanding the South? Certainly, when one consigns Southern history to background or takes it "as read," more is lost than gained. Essays that investigate a genre or cultural form benefit from elasticity, leading Ernest Suarez to combine poetry with song lyrics and Gary Richards to examine drama alongside musical theater.

What will not be surprising to readers is that "classics" such as *Uncle Tom's Cabin* (1852) and *Gone with the Wind* (1936) should texture very differently inflected discussions. Readers, as well as writers and critics, respond to such texts differently in each era, because the fictions function as barometers of changing values, beliefs, and ideologies. In 1943, for example, Langston Hughes imagined what would happen if Hattie McDaniel ("Mammy" in David O. Selznick's blockbuster film) played Harriet Tubman, the abolitionist who escaped slavery and helped other slaves to freedom via the Underground Railroad, in what he imagined could be a "sure-enough *Gone With The Wind* that shows how slavery was wiped out and how courageous Negro men and women helped to wipe it out."[2] Hughes neither wrote that screenplay nor saw it performed. Some sixty years later, when Alice Randall wrote a riposte to *Gone with the Wind*, the African-American writer's parody from the point of view of Tara plantation slaves was initially blocked by Margaret Mitchell's Estate. Other writers, among them Harper Lee and poet Yusef Komunyakaa, along with literary critics and historians, petitioned in Randall's behalf, rallying to her defense on the grounds of free speech. *The Wind Done Gone* (2001) was published after an Atlanta court's banning of the work – citing copyright infringement on the original – was overturned. Writer and critic Tony Earley enfolded Randall into Southern literary history when he endorsed the novel as the "connective tissue" binding "the fairytale of *Gone With the Wind* to the gothic nightmare of *Absalom, Absalom!*"[3] Familiar fictions mark the changing contours of Southern literary culture.

Kathryn B. McKee (Chapter 1) opens the volume by demonstrating the heterogeneity and fluidity of writing in the nineteenth century, an era typically understood as split rigidly along generic lines into sentimental literature, Southwestern humor, plantation fiction, reconciliation romance, anti-reconciliation literature, and local color writing. She begins in the 1830s, the decade that most scholars agree signaled the shift to sectional self-interest that promoted the South as a cultural, as well as a political, entity. Seeing the nineteenth century as "little more than a seedbed for the twentieth" was a dominant view until the end of the 1980s, and McKee unpacks how literary culture loosened that critical impasse as she investigates the extent to which Southern literature was crucial in fashioning the national story and "has much to reveal about how Americans made sense of their self-contradictory country at a crucial moment in its development."

Judie Newman's analysis of the slave narrative in Chapter 2 traces the cultural logic of the form via personal and fictionalized accounts by Frederick Douglass and Harriet Jacobs through many innovative revisions of the form. As she notes, "The story[of slavery] needs to be told anew to avoid it becoming familiar and our sympathies blunted – that is the risk of genre." Newman reveals how the genre was extended in a "reverse slave narrative" like Octavia Butler's *Kindred* (1979), for example, and in Edward P. Jones *The Known World* (2003), which explores the multiple (and contested) mental and geographical cartographies according to which slavery may be mapped. Newman also analyzes novels by white writers from outside the region and, indeed, the nation, which borrow from the slave narrative: Harriet Beecher Stowe in the nineteenth century, Margaret Atwood and Joan Brady in the twentieth, and Bernardine Evaristo in the twenty-first.

In Chapter 3, building on his work in *The Civil War in American Culture* (2006), Will Kaufman explores the "appeal to sentiment" that Civil War apologists harnessed to tell the story of the war. He shows how African-American writing critiqued "Lost Cause apologia" in the nineteenth century and analyzes writers who refined the antebellum South as a wellspring of pastoral nostalgia in the twentieth, as in *Gone With the Wind*, and Caroline Gordon's *None Shall Look Back* (1937) overlooked amid the hullaballoo surrounding Mitchell's Civil War romance. The war was a source of sensationalism in James Street's Mississippi-set *Tap Roots* (1942), and a revisionist fantasy in which the Confederate South wins in Ward Moore's science fiction story *Bring the Jubilee* (1952), but Kaufman also takes stock of quieter analytical fictions like Ellen Glasgow's *The Battle-Ground* (1902). Mapping Civil War literature across some 150 years, he concludes that "the war's end in the South's literary practice ... is not yet in sight."

Once the Civil War was over, Reconstruction was the period in which the idea of a "solid" white South was established as a monolithic bastion against black progress. Scott Romine's essay (Chapter 4) traces the role literature played on either side of the sectional conflict to shape images of Reconstruction. He examines writers students may discover here for the first time, like John William De Forest and Constance Fenimore Woolson, reading them alongside George Washington Cable and Frances E.W. Harper. Albion Tourgée sits between the writers who have been neglected and their much-studied contemporaries. Tourgée wrote the first major novel about

Reconstruction, *A Fool's Errand*, in 1879 and in tracing his career, Romine makes a case for (re)reading his works because "no writer had been more acute in critiquing Reconstruction's shifting position in the national consciousness." While Romine allows that historians have done more to blast partisan myths than twentieth-century writers, he closes by examining those modern fictions that do return to the era, notably Howard Fast's *Freedom Road* (1944), a novel that closes with Fast asserting that the eight-year experiment of Reconstruction was expunged from popular memory precisely because it had worked to forge an alliance between freed blacks and poor whites. It is not surprising, then, that it was studied in Freedom Schools in the civil-rights 1960s.

In Chapter 5, Ernest Suarez traces the relationship between Southern verse traditions. European verse influenced Edgar Allen Poe's and Sydney Lanier's poetics in the nineteenth century, but early in the twentieth, poets associated with *The Fugitive* magazine turned away from previous practices to develop a literary movement that morphed into the Southern agrarianism of *I'll Take My Stand*, which after 1930 crystallized as a model for literature that would hardened into conservative myth and ideology. Suarez examines key figures in Southern poetry and shows how John Crowe Ransom's lyric forms and local settings influenced another line of poets including Donald Justice, Charles Wright, and Ellen Bryant Voigt, and how Robert Penn Warren, Randall Jarrell, and James Dickey's narrative practices influenced Eleanor Ross Taylor, Dave Smith, and David Bottoms. Also in the late nineteenth century, another verse tradition emerged in the form of African-American spirituals and "field hollers," which melded into the blues ballad, a form that impacted the poetry of Jean Toomer, James Weldon Johnson, Langston Hughes, and Sterling Brown. Hughes and Robert Kaufman drew on Southern musical forms in jazz poetry. During the closing decades of the twentieth century, Suarez delineates, with close attention to aesthetics, how writers combined verse traditions from white and black "Souths" to create a new Southern poetry that emphasizes performance and is often set to music.

In Chapter 6, David A. Davis examines the fundamental irony of Southern modernism, the tension between the uneven development of modernity in the South and Southern writers' literary innovation. Opening with Faulkner's description of the buckboard as a cubist bug in *As I Lay Dying* (1930), he reads the works of a diverse body of writers to compare the urbanism, industrialism, and progressivism associated with modernity to the ruralism, agrarianism, and conservatism associated with the South. In this way, Davis examines how Southern writers negotiated the ideological gap that separated the South from modernity and also shows how reactionary conservatism played out in a number of ways in fiction between 1900 and 1940 through depictions of Prohibition, Jim Crow Laws, evangelism, lynching, anti-suffrage, and sharecropping.

The Southern states have been represented as the poorest and least progressive, with President Roosevelt claiming the South to be the nation's "No. 1 Economic Problem" in 1935 and Martin Luther King Jr., visiting an Alabama plantation in 1965, shocked to discover that sharecroppers had never seen U.S. currency because their commissary still traded only in "scrip" or credit. In Chapter 7, Sarah Robertson traces Southern literary responses to issues around poverty and social progress and investigates the ways in which epithets such as "redneck" and "white trash" – what Southerners supposedly became when they fell out of the working class into dissolution – have resonated in Southern writing, but also how some contemporary writers have rescued them from only being understood as terms of opprobrium.

John T. Matthews in Chapter 8 details the regional self-scrutiny that marked fictions published between the 1920s and 1945, when Allen Tate designated the period representative of a "Southern Renascence" according to which the South was a traditional antidote to a supposedly inauthentic industrializing North. Matthews demonstrates "how falsifying simple definitions of a Southern Renaissance may once have been, and how the complexities of Faulkner's writing correspond with much-expanded definitions of this broad event in modern culture." It is axiomatic to assert that Faulkner's fiction maps the primary themes of Southern literature, so much so that Michael Kreyling, in a paradigm-breaking text he boldly titled *Inventing Southern Literature* in 1998, observed with some irony that "if 'the South' is a cultural entity, then 'Faulkner' is its official language."[4] Here Matthews creates a taxonomy of the tropes through which Faulkner – and also many of his contemporaries – engaged the South – plantation, land and labor, race, desire, language – and through carefully wrought examples proves why it was difficult for those like Allen Tate to recruit Faulkner to their "traditionalist" concerns. In so doing, Matthews maps the history of Faulkner criticism and finally conjures a twenty-first-century Faulkner, who "in a maximized conception of the Southern Renaissance, might reveal how both figure in cultural representations of global modernity."

In Chapter 9, Pearl Amelia McHaney investigates the influence that Eudora Welty, Flannery O'Connor, Carson McCullers, and, in turn, Alice Walker and Toni Morrison had on younger generations of women writers. McHaney unpacks the "brand" that is "the" Southern woman writer and considers who lies outside the brand, left to thrive under labels of "African American, Latina, 'white trash,' lesbian, and/or feminist writers." Her essay endeavors to be inclusive in its reconceptualization of the breadth and heterogeneity of fictional and non-fiction writing by women, including Gayl Jones, Judith Ortiz Cofer, Natasha Tretheway, and Jesmyn Ward, who wrestle with labels and who reveal across a plethora of cultural forms why, as well as how, they continue to tell stories about the South.

Sarah Gleeson-White also intervenes in the category "Southern literature" to examine the Southern writer in Hollywood. While film scholars have introduced the "Southern" into discussions of Hollywood genres,[5] the presence of writers in Hollywood, and of Southern novels and stories on the screen, is an evolving area of research. In Chapter 10, Gleeson-White details how Southern writers and journalists carved out alternative careers as screenwriters. She shows that they were expected to bring a representative "Southernness" to bear on the movies, and traces the idea through the Hollywood sojourns of William Faulkner, Walker Percy, Horace McCoy, in the studio era, and Barry Hannah and others later. With a dual focus on the Southern Hollywood novel and the film screenplay, she examines how the region's writers' engaged Hollywood cinema and film production.

Chapter 11 argues that critics and reviewers in the 1960s overlooked fictions published in the era that represented the civil rights movement. I uncover fictions that depicted the courage of black Southerners and civil rights organizers, massive resistance to their initiatives, and racial terrorism – many of which were written by African Americans including Junius Edwards, Michael Thelwell, Alice Walker, and Henry Dumas. I analyze the cultural work typically undertaken to contain race relations within a more positively curated image of the region according to which, as Louis Rubin claimed in 1961, "important though the race problem may be, most people, even in the South, do not spend every waking moment thinking of it." This essay also examines depictions by those white Southern writers who thought about civil rights enough to reveal the troubled conscience of Southern gradualists, before it turns to contemporary writers. I conclude that: "Civil rights stories are as heterogeneous as their authors; they cross periods and genres and historical momentum and their continuing relevance carries them into the twenty-first century."

In a wide-ranging essay mapping Southern drama, Gary Richards (Chapter 12) begins by examining why the South has "rarely been scripted as central to the nation's history of writing, producing, and attending drama" in scholarly histories of the theater. He traces Southern performance from seventeenth-century Virginia and metropolitan theater culture in antebellum Charleston and New Orleans before tracking dramatic forms like minstrelsy into the twentieth century. He analyzes the South's acclaimed playwrights, like Lillian Hellman and Tennessee Williams, and explores stage adaptations of novels, including Erskine Caldwell's best-selling *Tobacco Road* (1932). Richards's research reveals the eclecticism of the Southern theatrical marketplace. Despite, and indeed because of, his conclusion that "the South's relation to theater remains a troubled one," his survey also points to possible avenues for further scholarship.

Building on his work in *Cotton's Queer Relations* (2009), and on Gary Richards's *Lovers and Beloveds: Sexual Otherness in Southern Fiction, 1936–1961* (2005), Michael P. Bibler in Chapter 13 explores homosexual and homoerotic readings of Southern texts in an essay that weaves across centuries to include discussion of domestic fiction, dime novels, and stage plays. Bibler locates a long tradition of homosociality in Southern writing because queering the South offers ways to understand "the complex deployments of gender, desire, and eroticism both prior to the invention of homosexuality as a category and in relation to the region's diverse cultural topographies." He follows the "interwoven strands of gothicism, humor, eroticism, and gender play" among which queer narratives may be uncovered. He examines Truman Capote and Tennessee Williams, as might be expected, but also Ann Allen Shockley who in 1974 wrote the first novel to explore an interracial lesbian relationship in detail to a very mixed critical reception.[6] Bibler's wide-angled critical lens reveals queerness in a plethora of popular cultural forms including the graphic novel.

In Chapter 14, Nahem Yousaf explores contemporary fictions that "project the regional studies model outwards to forge spatial connections across more fluidly conceptualized landscapes," particularly narratives by new immigrants to the U.S. South and writers of bicultural heritage, but also fictions by Southern writers, black and white, who open up to new scrutiny "typical" concerns, such as the plantation South and labor on the land, civil wars, and civil rights. These include Lan Cao, Susan Choi, Gustavo Pérez Firmat, Monique Truong, and Marcos Villatoro, as well as Robert Olen Butler, Cynthia Shearer, and even John Grisham. Characters of different ethnic heritages further dispel the myth of a static racial landscape, and Yousaf pays attention to the ways in which the New Southern Studies facilitates study of such fictions and closes by reading Monique Truong's novel *Bitter in the Mouth* (2010), which borrows from *To Kill A Mockingbird* but tells a very different story of a family in the small-town South.

Reading and studying Southern literature now, one enters a digital network of sites and cyberspaces, whether reading poems posted by locals post-Katrina on the Hellicane blogspot, downloading the latest edition of *New Stories From the South* to a Kindle, tweeting a review of a new novel, or evaluating a new essay collection on the region for H-Net Southern Literature (www.h-net.org/~southlit), the discussion forum that British critic Martyn Bone founded in 2007 and developed in conjunction with the Society for the Study of Southern Literature. This *Companion* encourages readers to take circuitous conceptual routes through Southern culture whereby analyzing the traditional motif of "a sense of place" is to recognize the region as polyphonic, and its stories as syncretic, not least when they cross borders in a hemispheric South. If a "global" and Internet South risks becoming less regionally distinctive, and less "real," it will not become less "Southern" – and, in any case, telling about the South has never been solely a regional affair. Contributors to this volume, from the South but also from the northern United States and from Australia and Europe, signal something of how Southern scholarship has always developed in national and international contexts.

Jon Smith's 2002 pen portrait of what he thought a New Southern Studies scholar would be like in the twenty-first century is a description that bears returning to periodically. She or he, Smith predicted, would need to be versed in postcolonial theory and local and global conceptual models, to demonstrate expertise in minority literatures, to be able to read French and Spanish, and to demonstrate a knowledge of the Caribbean countries that are the U.S. South's near neighbors, and of immigration patterns into and across the region.[7] While the ability to read foreign languages, especially because so many are spoken in the region, remains most difficult to evidence in contemporary literary criticism, other qualities Smith noted are not, as the essays which bookend this *Companion* show. Even when the critic casts back to literature produced in the 1830s, 1850s, and 1880s, as Kathryn B. McKee does, she discovers the "interlocality" in what she reads in the hemispheric concerns of a neglected woman writer, Sherwood Bonner, whose southern stories alluded to Persia and Madagascar as well as Europe. And, as Nahem Yousaf demonstrates, in contemporary writing, "stereotypes of the insularity of southern literature are proved untenable when fictions equate the region with other 'Souths'."

Literary texts, like historical moments, are neither static nor limited to their place or moment of production; our understanding of them evolves with a changing historiography and cultural geography. The literary-critical history of the U.S. South still contains unexplored routes, and this *Companion* does not pretend to be exhaustive. Instead, it was conceived and is presented as a series of interconnecting and thought-provoking sources for discussion and debate for students of literature and culture. Hopefully it also answers a question that one of my students asked recently. He was reading the short story that Monique Truong wrote while a student at Yale in 1991, based on her experience of living in North Carolina as refugee from Saigon in 1975; it is a story Truong tells again and differently in *Bitter in the Mouth*, as Yousaf explores. This short story led my student to inquire: Why is it that even writers who were not born there seem to have the same compunction as those who were, like Faulkner, to continually "tell about the South"? I hope that when he reads the essays in this *Companion*, he will find that its contributors answer his question in some detail.

NOTES

1 Edmund Wilson, *Patriotic Gore: Studies in the Literature of the American Civil War* (New York: Oxford University Press, 1966), p. xxi.

2 Langston Hughes, "Is Hollywood Fair to Negroes?" *Negro Digest* 1: 6 (April 1943), pp. 19–21.

3 Tony Earley, blurb for Alice Randall, *The Wind Done Gone* (New York: Houghton Mifflin, 2001) and deputation recorded by Randall's publisher at http://www.houghtonmifflinbooks.com/features/randall_url/pdf/Declaration_Anton_Mueller.pdf. Accessed 30 March 2012.

4 Michael Kreyling, *Inventing Southern Literature* (Jackson: University Press of Mississippi, 1999), p. 127.

5 See Warren French, "'The Southern': Another Lost Cause?" *The South and Film*, ed. W. French (Jackson: University Press of Mississippi, 1981), pp. 3–13, and for a critical overview, *The New Encyclopedia of Southern Culture: Media*, eds. Allison Graham and Sharon Monteith (Chapel Hill: University of North Carolina Press, 2011), pp. 1–30.

6 Monteith, *Advancing Sisterhood? Interracial Friendships in Contemporary Southern Fiction* (Athens: University of Georgia Press, 2000), pp. 173, 204, n. 21.

7 Jon Smith, "Postcolonial Theory, the US South and New World Studies," *Society for the Study of Southern Literature Newsletter* 36: 2 (Fall 2002), p. 11.

I

KATHRYN B. MCKEE

Region, Genre, and the Nineteenth-Century South

In classic formulations of nineteenth-century U.S. Southern literature, the region's output serves a variety of functions, none of them particularly admirable. In a broad context, "the South" delineates increasingly sharp political lines fracturing the antebellum nation, and residents express that sense of sectional difference through their participation in a literary civil war of words. According to this formula, writers of the postbellum era record the aftermath of the century-splitting conflict in memoirs and Lost Cause laments before rallying around a continued sense of local distinctiveness expressed in regional literature, populated by still rebellious, careworn Southerners trying to find their way into the twentieth century. A related approach is to cast the nineteenth century as little more than a seedbed for the twentieth. Combing through the considerable volumes of literature from the period becomes quick work, then, because the scholar seeks only precursors to the ambivalence of modernism, a South both hated and loved and never successfully left behind. Louis Rubin codifies this view in his introduction to *The History of Southern Literature* (1985): "[T]he principal importance of much of the earlier literature lies in the extent to which it contributes to the development of the literary imagination that would flower in the twentieth-century Southern Literary Renascence."[1] This should be, then, a short essay.

However, the field of Southern literary study has shifted dramatically since 1985, and as a result scholars are now better equipped than ever to engage the nineteenth century as a period of literary production that is provocative and significant in its own right. That they have not yet done so with the frequency and diligence devoted to Faulkner and the writers that surround and follow him attests not just to the obvious value of that study, but also to continuing habits of mind and accustomed ways of seeing. The reasons for this reluctance are several and only partially recounted here. Most prominent is the unpleasant necessity of dealing with sectional politics. The unchecked racism of much of the period's writing sits uneasily with a contemporary readership and is for that reason often excluded from anthologies of nineteenth-century U.S. literature and frequently given short shrift even in anthologies of Southern literature. Yet the result is also unsatisfying; Harriet Beecher Stowe sounds like she is shouting in an empty room, minus the genre of plantation fiction to absorb and contradict her imagery, and it is difficult for readers to understand the stakes involved in the abolitionism of the Grimké sisters from South Carolina without a sense of the rhetoric against which they fought. Yet to study that rhetoric also feels oddly to reanimate it, an unsettling move in a nation still struggling to live into the ideals of equality that guide it. A second discomfort extends from that first one: as traditionally conceived, the literary study of the nineteenth-century South has been unrelievedly white. Scholars have long located nonwhite literatures as enterprises parallel to, but not fully incorporated within, the study of "Southern literature," thus indirectly supposing that the place of "the South" figures very little for its Native American residents, its immigrant populations, and the four million slaves who lived there on the eve of the Civil War. The result is a primarily white, masculine story of defeat and lost honor that enables Quentin Compson to insist one had to have been born there to understand it, the exceptional South wound into a tight ball of regional particularity, at odds with the rest of the nation and glad of it.

Scholars of both the region and the nation have relied on a narrative so construed, and the South has functioned powerfully within the national imagination. As Jennifer Greeson summarizes, "A concept of the South is essential to national identity in the United States of America ... it is an *internal other* for the nation, an intrinsic part of the national body that nonetheless is differentiated and held apart from the whole."[2] For the twentieth-century Agrarians, looking back to the nineteenth century, this sense of difference is positive. Casting the region as an alternative to fast-paced industrialization and loss of connection to the concrete world of the land and the harvest, they position the South as an antidote to the alienation of the modern condition. For others, the region has provided a holding bin for all that counteracts the American way of life as ideally conceived – poverty, racism, inequality, intolerance. Even contemporary representations of the South in popular culture often vacillate among a number of prepackaged landscapes, ranging from a hospitable, genteel, slower-paced world to a land still benighted by its own failure to embrace progressive thinking. Those conflicting images do not begin in films like *Gone With the Wind* (1939), *Deliverance* (1972), or *The Help* (2011); they only gain new energy and wider circulation there. As Karen Cox points out in *Dreaming of Dixie* (2011), they begin in the writings of the nineteenth century, and understanding how and why they developed deepens our sense of the power of representation.

Recent approaches to the study of the U.S. South helpfully broaden our frameworks for reading and highlight interconnected themes winding throughout the nineteenth century. Scholars now regularly acknowledge that paying attention to the nation-state as a political construction, albeit one with far-ranging consequences, underscores the U.S. South's hemispheric positioning and reorients the North-South axis along which regional identity was long assumed to have been exclusively formed. Rather, scholarship of the last fifteen years considers the consequences of a nineteenth-century U.S. South whose face is turned farther South, rather than North, to Latin America and the Caribbean, where climate, growing conditions, and the need for a massive labor force were more familiar than a New England winter. Pointing out that literary study remains locked in nationalistic paradigms, George Handley in *Postslavery Literatures in the Americas* (2000) maps "a new hemispheric geography" that he terms "Plantation America." His focus on the Caribbean demonstrates "the interdependency of plantation cultures in the Americas in the construction of divergent national identities" by foregrounding the structure of "the plantation" as a unifying device reliant on colonization and the displacement of populations, including both those indigenous to the region and those brought to it from Africa.[3] Through the lens of hemispheric study, one of the region's defining moments becomes not an event that happened on U.S. soil at all, but the culmination of the Haitian Revolution in 1804. The specter of black rebellion, then, echoes down the long hallway of the nineteenth century and seeps repeatedly into racially anxious narratives from century's beginning to end.

Given the complexity of nineteenth-century Southern literature, this essay approaches its subject by focusing on three seminal decades: the 1830s, when white Southern self-consciousness shifted clearly into focus; the 1850s, when the literary civil war of words reached its height; and the 1880s, when Southerners and non-Southerners began actively constructing literary images of "the South" for the national marketplace. A survey of nineteenth-century U.S. Southern literature typically relies on a series of familiar categories: the historical novel, frontier humor, plantation fiction, slave narratives, the literature of reconciliation, the sentimental novel, and postbellum regional writing. Yet scanning across these three decades, we can recognize that generic fluidity, rather than generic fixity, characterizes the region's literary output. Understanding not just national boundaries as porous, but generic ones as well, means that postbellum women can write in the vein of southern frontier humor, that plantation fiction and fiction by African-American writers can share structural parallels, and that even within exemplary models of particular forms, moments of resistance sometimes undermine the text's more obvious goals, thereby suggesting that hasty dismissals of the period occlude its rich potential for study.

Although pinpointing an exact moment at which white Southerners begin to understand themselves as at odds with the national whole is difficult, most historians suggest that such an awareness comes during the 1830s. Beginning with Nat Turner's revolt in 1831, the period is shot through with racial anxiety, coupled with sectional tension enflamed by the Nullification Crisis of 1832 and the rhetoric of, among others, South Carolina's John C. Calhoun. Yet that same tension is present even in the literature seemingly most devoted to the continuation of the status quo: plantation fiction. John Pendleton Kennedy's *Swallow Barn* (1832), published shortly after Turner's revolt, is the most widely recognized early example of the form and establishes the tactics to which later writers will return. Set in Virginia, the plot consists of the narrator's account back to his New York family of his visit to a plantation he expects to disdain, but ends up admiring instead. Perhaps most telling is his chapter called "The Quarter" where he finds, not discontented slaves, but happy ones, satisfied with their lot and far better off than they would be in some unsupervised state of life. Yet as Lucinda MacKethan suggests in her 1992 introduction to the novel, unrest ripples beneath the plot in the form of several irrepressible African-American characters, most particularly the rebellious slave Abe who is eventually dubbed a hero for his acts in saving his white shipmates but is himself swallowed into the sea rather than reincorporated into antebellum society. Paul Jones, in *Unwelcome Voices* (2005), reads the novel as at odds with the ideology it appears to bolster, pointing out its relentlessly ironic treatment of the situations and personalities at its center. Thus built into the very progenitor of the fictional plantation are pockets of resistance, wittingly or unwittingly "creating a self-examining text that overtly struggles against the lure of romance in favor of the critical eye of realism."[4] If Kennedy's romanticized plantation appeals to postbellum inheritors of the form, it is because they manage to choose selectively among its components in an effort to quell later anxieties about race and power already brewing beneath the surfaces of 1830s writing.

Although critics have struggled to link geographically and historically the dreamscapes of Kennedy's contemporary Edgar Allan Poe to the U.S. South, some readings of his texts suggest a relationship to simmering racial unrest. For instance, Lewis P. Simpson, in *The Brazen Face of History*, reads Roderick Usher's house allegorically as signaling a flaw in the agrarian vision itself. Knowing of Gabriel Prosser's 1800 rumored slave revolt in Poe's own Richmond means that the repeated fear of blackness, darkness, and being buried alive throughout his stories of the 1830s and 1840s may signal submerged racial anxieties at work in his fiction.[5] Interestingly, it is a much later critical text about twentieth-century women's writing that proves especially useful here. In *Dirt and Desire* (2000), Patricia Yaeger is concerned with "radically dislocated surface landscape[s] filled with jagged white signifiers ... that bespeak ... a constant uneasiness about the meaning of whiteness."[6] Such a focus proves useful, for example, in thinking about Poe's novel, *The Narrative of Arthur Gordon Pym* (1838), in which white and black literally and repeatedly stand in high contrast to one another, the black residents of Tsalal threatening to eclipse white power in a naval standoff that anticipates the performances of Herman Melville's *Benito Cereno* (1856). The narrator at story's end appears to be subsumed into an unexplained, looming whiteness, and the hieroglyph, decoded to be "Poe," only mystifies rather than illuminates, suggesting Poe himself as trickster figure. But the novel's play between black and white arguably represents the decade's, and the nation's, central dilemma, gathering force in the 1830s to reach a crescendo in the 1860s and disrupt the hallmark binaries of the century: black/white, state/nation, North/South.[7]

Other writing of the 1830s more directly confronts these issues, at the same time that it reveals additional tensions characterizing the period. The number of white women writing accelerates during the nineteenth century, an increase that Mary Louise Weaks in *The History of Southern Women's Literature* (2002) attributes to more widespread literacy, more available printed materials, and greater amounts of leisure time. Enough of them had published material to warrant Julia D. Freeman's collection *Women of the South Distinguished in Literature* by 1860 and only a decade later *Southland Writers* (1870), edited by Mary T. Tardy and republished in 1872 as *Living Female Writers of the South*. These volumes, Weaks suggests, indicate that by mid-century white women writers of the South saw themselves as working within a regional tradition that included journal writing, as well as composing novels. Yet as Ellen H. Todras points out, "[i]n the entire 245-year history of slavery in America, only two southern [white] women had the will and the conviction to speak out [publicly] against this most peculiar institution."[8] The separate writings of the sisters Angelina and Sarah Grimké are direct collisions with the ideologies of their native region on the subjects of both race and gender. Born in South Carolina to a slaveholding family, the sisters moved to Philadelphia as young women to assume active roles in the American Anti-Slavery Society. In "An Appeal to the Christian Women of the South" (1836), Angelina not only defies prevailing attitudes of white supremacy, but also provides an early example of resistance of a different sort. She claimed a political voice, affirming certain elements of the "cult of domesticity" and its figuration of woman as society's moral compass, at the same time that she claimed involvement for her gender on a public stage. Her sister's subsequent *Letters on the Equality of the Sexes and the Conditions of Woman* (1838) anticipates the Seneca Falls convention by a decade. Anne Goodwyn Jones, in what remains the most useful treatment of nineteenth-century Southern women's literature, *Tomorrow Is Another Day* (1981), suggests that the pronounced role of white Southern womanhood in Lost Cause rhetoric begins in antebellum stylizations; thus in the women of Kennedy's *Swallow Barn* readers encounter somewhat ironic prototypes of belles and ladies, but in Angelina and Sarah Grimké, their nineteenth-century contemporaries found gendered expectations simultaneously acknowledged and resisted nearly one hundred years before suffrage was achieved.

Despite its regional inflection, the literature of the 1830s South is a national literature, preoccupied with national issues that prominently include westward expansion. The decade may be laced with barely contained racial anxieties and sectionally motivated congressional debates, but even if North and South could not agree on the status of a territory as slave or free, they could agree on an urgent need to eradicate native populations in order to make expansion feasible. Thus the decade actually commences, not with slave revolt, but with the legislative sanction of genocide in the form of the Indian Removal Act, articulated by Andrew Jackson, but inspired by decades of chafing between white and red. As Melanie Benson Taylor points out in *Reconstructing the Native South* (2011), we "have only just begun to reckon candidly with the numerous ways in which the plantation South and its Native neighbors crossed paths, bloodlines, and histories in profoundly altering and continually influential ways."[9] The Indian is there in the literature of the 1830s, but there as a displaced specter, one of many that will haunt the South's self-story as well as the national narrative of progress. Prolific antebellum novelist William Gilmore Simms, for instance, lent a regional perspective to a number of nation-building moments, particularly in his fictional treatments of the Revolutionary War. His most famous novel, however, *The Yemassee* (1835), laments the passing of native culture in conflict with white settlement. Despite the novel's eighteenth-century setting, Simms's elegiac tone more closely matches the tenor of Removal, and the inevitability of the novel's outcome bespeaks the more comprehensive vision of manifest destiny, Southern style. Taylor's point – that native removal from the southeast is only one of several regionally specific Lost Causes – will undoubtedly return scholars to the region-defining moments of the 1830s to discover what the literary margins reveal. In the closing paragraphs of Simms's novel, for instance, various strains of the nineteenth century coalesce. The powerful female figure at the book's center, Matiwan, "was unconscious of all things ... save the Yemassee was no longer the great nation." She speaks metaphorically but also literally. Slaves finish off the clash between settlers and natives; the narrator tells us that "wild almost as the savages ... they hurried over the forests with a step as fleet, and a ferocity as dreadful – sparing none, whether they fought or pleaded, and frequently inflicting the most unnecessary blows, even upon the dying and dead." The threat is displaced, then, from native resistance to slave revolt, but both forces trouble the narrative of white power.

At the same time, a rich literature of settler life emerges during the 1830s and persists until the mid-1860s. Southwestern humor, written by men observing primarily the life of other men on what was then the Southern frontier (Georgia, Alabama, Mississippi, Arkansas, and Louisiana), arguably begins with Augustus Baldwin Longstreet's 1835 collection, *Georgia Scenes*. That frontier humor and Indian removal converge on an antebellum Southern timeline is not coincidental. Evacuating native inhabitants literally clears the space for the characters who surge forward in these raucous tales of life on the border. Kenneth Lynn's long-standing theory of the *cordon sanitaire*, in which the more aristocratic storyteller is separated from his subject material by his use of a frame narrative and the objectifying power of humor, has come under considerable scrutiny of late. Scott Romine frames its most compelling rebuttal in *The Narrative Forms of Southern Community* (1999) by pointing out the reductive pattern into which much of the genre has been fitted: "gentleman narrators against bumbling and sometimes sinister yokels in a relentlessly repetitive and monological justification of class privilege."[10] In fact, Romine maintains, Longstreet grapples in *Georgia Scenes* with a spectrum of social groups the narrator could not successfully ignore, even if he tried to do so. Our contemporary understanding of the function of humor within the tales has expanded as critics confront the characters once considered purely supplemental to the yarn spinner at the story's center, most particularly women and African Americans. The adage of Johnson Jones Hooper's recurrent character, Simon Suggs – "IT IS GOOD TO BE SHIFTY IN A NEW COUNTRY" – cuts multiple ways to emphasize the newness of the West, but also the "new country" resulting from altered balances of power in terms of race and gender. The genre becomes, then, a negotiation among different contingencies for the power to tell stories.

Although the most crucial historical events of the nineteenth century are certainly those which fall between 1861 and 1865, the decade of the 1850s provides an apt stage for discussing regional literary development because so many forces converge during the period, bookended by events signaling the advent of irreconcilable sectional tension: the passage of the Fugitive Slave Law in 1850 and the raid on Harper's Ferry in 1859. Harriet Beecher Stowe's publication of *Uncle Tom's Cabin*, serialized in the antislavery periodical *The Nation* between 1851 and 1852, demonstrates the utility of plantation fiction; the genre could be productively turned against the institution it initially sought to protect, particularly when so heavily influenced by the conventions of the sentimental novel. Beginning with Mr. Shelby's well-manicured plantation and devolving into the degradation of Simon's Legree's, *Uncle Tom's Cabin* exposes slavery's ability to ruin every person and place it touches, a portrait that directly contradicts Kennedy's in *Swallow Barn*. Appealing especially to the assumed experience of motherhood throughout the text, Stowe sought to mobilize a female readership to action by revealing the slave's humanity. In the character of Eliza, for example, Stowe drove home her point: slave women love their children in precisely the same way white women do. She thus underscored domestic space as political space and triggered a series of impassioned rebuttals to her portrait of slavery, many of which adopted martial language that foretold the clash of actual weaponry at the same time that it disallowed her womanhood. Including *Uncle Tom's Cabin*, then, in a discussion of Southern literature necessarily broadens the scope of the field by redefining its very base: Southern literature is not just that produced in the region or authored by a native of it.[11] Rather, "Southern literature" becomes writing that engages with the place and the idea of "the South," regardless of its origin. In the twentieth century, then, Toni Morrison's *Beloved* (1988) becomes as necessary a participant in discussions about the legacy of slavery as Stowe's *Uncle Tom's Cabin* was in conversations about the institution more than a century earlier.

The novel elsewhere participated in the sectionalism of the 1850s by way of the reconciliation romance. As Nina Silber explains in *The Romance of Reunion* (1993), politicians of the 1850s frequently figured the nation as a family, a metaphor to which they would return as Reconstruction neared an end and that both antebellum and postbellum writers seized upon as a means of exploring a healed nation. Reconciliation romances of the 1850s follow a similar formula: one member of the pair is a Northerner, one a Southerner, and the former, after being exposed to the lifestyle of the latter, comes to share his or her point of view. This plot line clearly drives Caroline Hentz's *The Planter's Northern Bride* (1854), for example, which emerges as a prototype of the antebellum genre in its conciliatory stance toward the South. *Uncle Tom's Cabin* borrows from the form as well, so that Miss Ophelia, come to sniff at slavery's morally crippling effect on both black and white, takes on the slave girl Topsy as her personal project, but also as her property, thereby muddling the moral message of Stowe's text. Postbellum work in the genre more frequently situates the Southerner as a woman, thus feminizing the region and reifying the power bestowed by military victory.

At least one post-Reconstruction Southern writer resisted the formula, however. Katherine Sherwood Bonner McDowell (who wrote as "Sherwood Bonner") penned an anti-reconciliation romance called *Like Unto Like* (1878) in which the heroine ultimately throws over her reformist Northern beau in favor of pursuing her own course of independent womanhood.

Antebellum Southern women writers experimented with similar outcomes for female protagonists. The fiercely independent heroines of Augusta Jane Evan Wilson's novels, including the eponymous *Beulah* from 1859, reveal themselves to be remarkably learned, sophisticated, and worldly in their knowledge and interests, yet ultimately willing to sacrifice all to their husbands in marriage. But Wilson's female characters also resist being subsumed into paternalism until the novel's closing pages. They demonstrate a kind of interlocality – that is, the use of seemingly disparate geographical locations as a way of understanding one's own situatedness – that belies the exceptionalist model of Southern identity being simultaneously formulated in the 1850s and 1860s. Edna Earle, the protagonist of Wilson's novel *St. Elmo* (1866), acquiesces to her role as wife and the public silence that will be one of its defining features, but not before she learns Latin and Greek, Hebrew and Chaldee, hears the letters from St. Elmo Murray of his adventures on the Indian Ocean and in Persia, and guards the documents he has entrusted to her care, entombed within the story's physical centerpiece, "a splendid marble miniature, four feet high, of that miracle of Saracenic architecture, the Taj Mahal at Agra." Thus Edna stretches her imagination beyond the confines of prescribed womanhood, linked to the geography of the South, just as its strictures tighten. Recalling an earlier transgression in the wake of Edna's kindness, St. Elmo feels his conscience stir "feebly, startling him with a faint moan, as unexpected as the echo of Morella's tomb, or the resurrection of Ligeia."[12] This echo of Poe's women, scarcely contained by death or the body, subtly suggests Edna's power as well, not to haunt, but to overcome and resist the confining nature of prescribed gender roles in the nineteenth-century South. A later Edna, Edna Pontellier of Kate Chopin's *The Awakening* (1899), will face a similar dilemma on the cusp of the twentieth century.

African-American voices likewise resist silencing efforts during the 1850s. Traditional formulations of the period highlight the steady production of slave narratives in the thirty years preceding the Civil War, but often fail to acknowledge adequately other forms in which African-American creative voices were emerging during the 1850s. Frederick Douglass had already called attention to the ironic juxtaposing of "American" and "slave" in the subtitle to his *Narrative* (1845), but he continued to underscore the shortcomings of the American ideal with the linguistic pairing in the title of his 1851 novel, *The Heroic Slave*, about a mutiny aboard a slave ship. He thus offered an alternative to acquiescent black masculinity as figured by Stowe in the character of Tom, as did Martin Delany in his more militant novel of slave insurrection, *Blake*, serialized in the *Afro-American Magazine* between 1859 and 1860. Certainly African-American writers saw literature outside of the slave narrative as an alternate means of engaging the contemporary political climate. William Wells Brown's 1853 novel, *Clotel; or the President's Daughter*, took aim at the nation's miscegenated roots in focusing on Thomas Jefferson's mixed-race daughter. Frances E. W. Harper began publishing short stories and poems in the 1850s that anticipate her later concerns with the color line. She directly engages, for example, Stowe's portrayal of motherhood as a state transcending racial boundaries in her poem about the heroine of *Uncle Tom's Cabin*, "Eliza Harris" (1853), and in "The Slave Mother" (1854) she emphasizes the slave's body as capitalistic commodity when a child is literally torn away from his mother by "cruel hands." Yet her work is not solely dependent on contemporaneous white writing for its theme or shape; in the story "The Two Offers" (1859), she directly confronts the degrees of power linked to lightness or darkness of skin tone within the African-American community, a theme to which she returns in her 1892 novel *Iola Leroy*. The creative production of other African-American women writers about whom less is known, Harriet Wilson, author of *Our Nig* (1859), and Hannah Crafts, author of *The Bondswoman's Narrative* (written at some point mid-century), suggest that scholarly efforts to raise the volume of repressed voices during the period may be only beginning to shape the narrative arc of African-American writing that depends on the idea and the place of the U.S. South.[13]

By the 1880s, the white South had lost its bid for political independence, but nation-building of a different sort engaged the white regional imagination. As Charles Reagan Wilson explains in *Baptized in Blood* (1980; 2009), "the dream of a separate Southern identity did not die in 1865 ... the dream of a cohesive Southern people with a separate cultural identity replaced the original longing .... It was a Southern civil religion, which tied together Christian churches and Southern culture." This Lost Cause ideology, marked on the landscape through a series of late-century monuments to the Confederate war dead, for instance, steers much white postbellum thinking by Wilson's reckoning, and is reflected in the period's literature as anchored to the body, as well as the mythology, of white women as the "highest symbol of Southern virtue."[14] Thomas Nelson Page's 1887 collection *In Ole Virginia*, for instance, provides a now classic example of a moonlight and magnolia South that harkens back to antebellum plantation fiction in its evocation of a place where slaves and masters remain yoked together out of affection and duty, despite the end of the institution that once compelled one to serve the other. In his later observations about the region, *The Old South* (1892), Page stretches his imagery of the Southern woman into something mythological. The lady he found to be "often delicate and feeble in frame, and of a nervous organization so sensitive as to be a great sufferer; but her force and her character pervaded and directed everything, as unseen yet as unmistakably as the power of gravity controls the particles that constitute the earth." Her companion, the belle, was "a creature of peach-blossom and snow; languid, delicate, saucy; now imperious, now melting, always bewitching" – conclusions that dovetail with Wilbur Fisk Tillet's 1891 summary in "Southern Womanhood as Affected by the War": "No matter what may be one's sympathy with or prejudice against the institution of slavery, there is no denying the fact that American civilization had nowhere produced a purer and loftier type of refined and cultured womanhood than existed in the South before the war."[15] Thus the question of slavery is elided by white anxiety concentrated in the form of an idealized woman who could originate only in the corporate body of the region she embodies.

Page's revitalization of the never fully lapsed plantation tradition encapsulates "the South" then gaining traction in the national imagination – a land populated once again by contented black retainers and mammies, thus assuaging any concerns on the part of "the North" about how recently emancipated slaves were to be woven into national life. They did not have to be; they would live in the South instead. This South is a romantic vision that enjoyed wide circulation in periodical publications of the 1870s and 1880s. For instance, Edward King, in his 1875 travel narrative *The Great South*, taken from his earlier *Scribner's* series of the same name, described Louisiana as "Paradise Lost. In twenty years it may be Paradise Regained .... It is the battle of race with race, of the picturesque and unjust civilization of the past with the prosaic and leveling civilization of the present."[16] "Race with race" only obliquely suggests a black and white struggle, then; it more directly pits an idyllic past against a less satisfying present, and thus sets the stage for many subsequent portrayals of the South by residents and nonresidents, both of whom fell in love with an invention. Even the business community suggested racial issues were not an impediment to the future. In his 1886 address to the New England Society of New York, Atlanta *Constitution* editor Henry W. Grady offered a vision of the South that differed from Page's idyll in its emphasis on a region rebuilt through grit and determination into a place that could prosper according to even the standards of the industrialized North. Grady and Page agree on one central point, however: with the end of Reconstruction, relations between black and white had returned to a recognizable power differential, and the nation could relax back into its earlier reliance on the South to manage itself.

The advent of regional literature was dependent both on local idiosyncrasy and national appeal, as the wide range of writing from different places in the 1870s, 1880s, and 1890s attests. Sarah Orne Jewett's tales of the Maine coastline, Hamlin Garland's accounts of life in the upper Midwest, Bret Harte's stories of California, and Constance Fenimore Woolson's observations of a variety of locales from Michigan to Florida signal a retooled function for literature. Rather than the literary civil war of the 1850s, writers of the 1880s stage a literary reconciliation that calls attention to the details of specific locales as a means of reacquainting the nation's sometimes far-flung, sometimes proximate, but always recently alienated sections. In the period's most successful writing, the emphasis on the local has the effect of helping place materialize in the imagination; in the period's least successful work, detail is primarily recycled from earlier publications, or wholly invented, because the writer hoped to cash in on the public's expansive appetite for writing in the genre. Southern authors produce prodigious amounts of both and reveal a fundamental contradiction at work within them: the heightened particularity of individual place versus a desire for a more unified "Southland" set in opposition to a "Northland." Although too numerous to list exhaustively here, the roster of postbellum Southern regional writers would certainly include Joel Chandler Harris, Thomas Nelson Page, Grace King, Ruth Stuart, Mary Noailles Murfree, John Fox, Jr., Sherwood Bonner, Idora Moore, Mark Twain, George Washington Cable, Charles Chesnutt, Kate Chopin, Alice Dunbar-Nelson, Sarah Barnwell Elliott, M. E. M. Davis, Opie Read, and Will Allen Dromgoole. That list in itself is controversial because it blends what the academy has routinely distinguished as "good" and "bad" practitioners, the former devoted to highlighting universal elements of human kinship that ultimately transcend particularities of experience and the latter focused on the peculiarities of a "way of life" that metastasize into racism, sexism, and xenophobia. This essay makes no counterargument as to the ethical stance of the literature, but it does suggest that the works of writers in the 1880s are seldom simply classified or wholly representative of one impulse or the other. Rather, they reflect a wide range of forces at work in the postbellum South.

Much southern literature produced during the 1880s, for instance, barely conceals the racial anxiety rumbling just beneath its surface. George Washington Cable's *The Grandissimes* (1880) offers a variegated picture of Louisiana life at odds with the manufactured comforts of Lost Cause ideology. His portrait of Creole life in New Orleans, crisscrossed by transgressions across the color line, has embedded at its center the figure of the rebellious slave, Bras-Coupé, still struggling to escape Kennedy's earlier formulation of that character type and to live into the promise Delany's *Blake* believed he contained. George Handley suggests that Bras-Coupé's rebellion and subsequent death echo a regional unrest, most clearly revealed by situating the U.S. South within the broader hemispheric context of slave revolt. If in the end, as Handley maintains, Cable arranges his text in order "to catalyze the white Creole romance," he has first signified his "willingness, so unusual for his time, to come to terms with the consequences of slavery."[17] Cable's companion on the lecture circuit, Mark Twain, seems to vacillate in a similar way a few years later in *Adventures of Huckleberry Finn* (1884–1885), where he first explores the repercussions of Huck and Jim's cross-racial friendship, for which Huck seems willing to risk eternal damnation, before submitting the runaway Jim back into the hands of an illogical slave culture, embodied by Tom Sawyer.

Elsewhere the anxieties of race are more obliquely explored, but resistance to the dominant plantation narrative forms an equally plausible interpretation. Sherwood Bonner's short stories, for instance, many of which are collected in *Dialect Tales* (1883), reveal an unusual blend of Southwestern humor and regional narrative that plainly demonstrates the decade's and the century's generic fluidity. In "The Gentlemen of Sarsar," for example, white frontiersmen in the spirit of Hooper's Simon Suggs are in league with African-American characters who initially appear to be of Page's ilk, to play a trick on a white landowner whose pompous lack of knowledge about them makes him the ideal target of their ruse. Bonner seemingly restores the balance of power at the tale's end, but by naming the duped gentleman Ned Meriwether, Bonner plays against the protagonist of *Swallow Barn*, Frank Meriwether, in a moment of parodic intertextuality that Michael Kreyling in *Inventing Southern Literature* (1999) does not attribute to Southern women writers for another century. Bonner's work, consistently marked as it is by references to far-flung places – Madagascar, Persia, and Europe – suggests the sort of interlocality also evident in antebellum women's writing. Thus, just as Page and others were pinioning white Southern womanhood to the axis of Lost Cause ideology, the imagination of some female writers took flight, seeking frames of reference other than region that were less likely to limit their vision.

Similar pockets of resistance characterize the writing of African-American authors in the 1880s. Although Charles Chesnutt's stories are not collected and published as *The Conjure Woman* until 1899, the first of his Uncle Julius tales, "The Goophered Grapevine," appears in *The Atlantic Monthly* in 1887. Chesnutt adopts the frame narrative popular in regional stories; the African-American narrator, Uncle Julius, recounts tales to the two lately arrived Northern white owners of the plantation he still inhabits, but he does so with a difference from the good old days. Now Uncle Julius shapes the master's narrative with his own storytelling. That his tales of plantation life typically privilege the intelligence of their black characters over the obtuseness of their white owners seems lost on the owners themselves and potentially on the new residents as well, save the careful listening of Miss Annie who alone seems potentially capable of unlocking their subversive register. Thus Chesnutt redirects the genre of plantation fiction from its nostalgic support for Lost Cause narratives into his vision of a differently ordered South.[18]

When, at the end of the nineteenth century, the nation rediscovers a means to unity through the Spanish-American War (1898) and other imperialistic maneuvers that direct its attention toward international, rather than sectional, conflict, "the South" of the American imagination is intact and ready to enter the twentieth century. Yet even seemingly straightforward imagery barely conceals its complex makeup, and the nineteenth century emerges as fertile ground for exploring the elements of regional, national, and hemispheric identity. In revisiting what we thought we already knew, scholars and readers encounter more than source material for later work; we encounter a richly diverse period in U.S. literature and culture that has much to reveal about how Americans made sense of their self-contradictory country at a crucial moment in its development.

NOTES

1 Louis Rubin, *The History of Southern Literature*, ed. Rubin et al. (Baton Rouge: Louisiana State University Press, 1984), p. 1.

2 Jennifer Greeson, *Our South: Geographic Fantasy and the Rise of National Literature* (Cambridge, MA: Harvard University Press, 2010), p. 1.

3 George Handley's literary remapping in *Postslavery Literatures in the Americas* (Charlottesville: University Press of Virginia, 2000) coincides with Matthew Pratt Guterl's later argument about the ways in which U.S. Southern slaveholders conceived of the hemisphere and moved through it. Guterl suggests in *American Mediterranean* (Cambridge, MA: Harvard University Press, 2008) that the Civil War "recast the nineteenth-century U.S. South as a messy, complicated borderland of sorts between North America and the Caribbean, a transitional region of the hemisphere with conflicting and overlapping political, economic, social, and cultural identities" (p. 11).

4 Paul Jones, *Unwelcome Voices: Subversive Fiction in the Antebellum South* (Knoxville: University of Tennessee Press, 2005), p. 124.

5 Investigations of links between Poe's preoccupation with darkness and racial anxiety occur in Louis Rubin's *The Edge of the Swamp* (Baton Rouge: Louisiana State University Press, 1989) and Richard Gray's *Southern Aberrations* (Baton Rouge: Louisiana State University Press, 2000).

6 Patricia Yaeger, *Dirt and Desire* (Chicago: The University of Chicago Press, 2000) p. 20.

7 Yaeger touches glancingly on Poe's novel in her list of works by male writers that treat whiteness as meaningless and blackness as evil, concluding that "images of frozen whiteness speak very differently in fictions by white southern women" (p. 21). I would suggest that Poe's work deserves a second look in this regard – that, in fact, he may be articulating an anxiety in *The Narrative of Arthur Gordon Pym* that is tied to the meaning whiteness takes on when juxtaposed to blackness.

8 Mary Louise Weaks, "Introduction to Part I" and Ellen H. Todras, "The Grimke Sisters," *The History of Southern Women's Literature* (Baton Rouge: Louisiana State University Press, 2002), pp. 15, 70.

9 Melanie Benson Taylor, *Reconstructing the Native South* (Athens: The University of Georgia Press, 2011), p.13.

10 Scott Romine, *The Narrative Forms of Southern Community* (Baton Rouge: Louisiana State University Press, 1999), p. 25. In the anthology *Southern Frontier Humor* (2010), Thomas Inge and Ed Piacentino counter many long-standing assumptions about the roles of female and African-American characters in southwestern humor, and several of the essays in their earlier collection, *The Humor of the Old South* (2001), focus on such figures.

11 Riché Richardson makes a similar point in *Black Masculinity and the U.S. South* (Athens: University of Georgia Press, 2007): "[S]outhern literature might be enriched by breaking its own more traditional rules and expanding its textual repertoires to become more inclusive of works written by authors who were not born in the South and who don't live there but who have things to say about it" (p. 115).

12 Augusta J. Evans [Wilson], *St. Elmo* (New York: G.W. Dillingham Company, 1866), pp. 88, 90.

13 Sherita Johnson in *Black Women in New South Literature and Culture* (New York: Routledge, 2010) takes as her starting point Anna Julia Cooper's *A Voice from the South* (1892) and its acknowledgment of the black woman's double bind, defined by rigid expectations for both race and gender, to argue that "it is impossible to consider what the 'South' and what 'Southernness' mean as cultural references without looking at how black women have contributed to and contested any unified definition of this region" (p. 1).

14 Charles Reagan Wilson, *Baptized in Blood* (Athens: University of Georgia Press, 2009), pp. 1, 46.

15 Thomas Nelson Page, *The Old South: Essays Social and Political* (New York: Chautauqua Press, 1892), pp. 153, 162; Wilbur Fisk Tillet, "Southern Womanhood as Affected by the War," *Century Magazine* (November 1891): 9.

16 Edward King, *The Great South: A Record of Journeys in Louisiana, Texas, The Indian Territory, Missouri, Arkansas, Mississippi, Alabama, Georgia, Florida, South Carolina, North Carolina, Kentucky, Tennessee, Virginia, West Virginia, and Maryland.* 2 vols. (New York: Burt Franklin, 1875), p. 17.

17 Handley, p. 71.

18 Arguably the most popular text of the period, Joel Chandler Harris's *Uncle Remus*, published, like Cable's novel in 1880, likewise takes the plantation as its setting. Critics continue to debate whether Uncle Remus, the African-American storyteller, subverts the patriarchy through his storytelling or does its bidding.

2

JUDIE NEWMAN

Slave Narratives and Neo-Slave Narratives

One of the few new genres that the United States has contributed to the literary canon is the slave narrative, the autobiographical account of a former slave's life once he or she had escaped to freedom. Drawing on the captivity narrative (though in this case the savage captors are American whites, not Native Americans) and the spiritual conversion narrative (though converting to a belief in freedom and selfhood rather than a Christian God), the slave narratives were published in the nineteenth century to aid the cause of abolition, and enjoyed massive sales. Frederick Douglass sold 30,000 copies of his narrative in 5 years, as compared to the 60 copies of *Moby Dick* sold in 10 years. Criticism of the slave narrative tends to focus on a small group of narratives, by Frederick Douglass, Harriet Jacobs, William Wells Brown, Henry Bibb, Otobah Cuguano, Olaudah Equiano, Ignatius Sanchez, and Briton Hammon, but there is a wealth of variety in the thousands of oral histories of former slaves, and hundreds of published slave narratives, the conventions of which were identified persuasively in the 1980s.[1]

While it is often the case that marginalized writers gain access to print by using the familiarity of genre to present an unfamiliar world, demonstrating that they have mastered the norms of the genre and therefore "belong" to the culture, the slave narrative is a particularly sharp example of a minority culture forced to present itself inside a majority straitjacket. Gaining access to the slave's story almost always involves an obstacle course of other materials so that the tale itself is firmly buttressed by such additions as a portrait, a title page (often affirming that the story was "written by himself" as in the case of Douglass), testimonials by white sponsors who guarantee the authenticity of the tale, a poetic epigraph (further evidence of superior literacy, and therefore of full humanity), and, after the tale itself, a series of appendices and documents furnished as proof. Even inside the narrative itself, the reader encounters a whole host of conventional elements, including the struggle for literacy, whippings, cruel masters, despair and a failed escape, conversion or epiphany, a successful escape, renaming, and celebration (qualified or not) of freedom. Broadly speaking, where the male slave tends to follow the pattern of literacy-identity-freedom ("teach'em to read and run"), the woman writer emphasizes family-identity-freedom, placing more emphasis on community than individualist values.

While there are exceptions (James A.U. Gronnisaw, Venture Smith, and Sojourner Truth, for example, who were enslaved in the North), the majority of slave narratives are written about the escape from the South: from Maryland (Douglass, James W.C. Pennington), North Carolina (Jacobs, Moses Roper, Lunsford Lane), Virginia (Elizabeth Keckley, Henry "Box" Brown), and Kentucky (Henry Bibb, William Wells Brown.) Details of specific locations are strategically important to the slave narrator, who needed to prove the authenticity of the story by marshalling every available verifiable fact. Frederick Douglass is typical in beginning his account: "I was born in Tuckahoe, near Hillsborough, and about twelve miles from Easton, in Talbot County, Maryland."[2] Proslavery campaigners routinely questioned the accuracy of slave narratives, hence their resemblance at times to a geography primer. Any provable date or place was ammunition in the hands of the abolitionist. Even in the twentieth century it was only the patient geographical research of Jean Fagan Yellin that established Jacobs's account of her life was an authentic autobiography and not a novel by Lydia Maria Child. Modern editions often contain maps of Edenton, North Carolina, her hometown, to reinforce the point. The autobiographies of some 2,000 former slaves living in the 1930s, interviewed as part of the Federal Writers' Project during the Depression, are almost entirely based on Southern experience.[3]

Strikingly, however, neither the slave narrative nor its descendant, the neo-slave narrative, features on the map of Southern literature. The reader who examines anthologies of, or monographs on, the topic of the slave narrative will find the term "Southern literature" conspicuously absent, in text or index. Why is this? Granted, the slave narrative is not merely Southern. Equiano's account of his trajectory from Africa to Barbados, Virginia, and Britain, or Cuguano's from Africa to Grenada and England, makes of it a transatlantic genre, with Caribbean and British embodiments. And, of course, once a slave was writing a narrative (or dictating it in some cases to a white amanuensis, in the "as told to" model), he or she was no longer likely to be residing in the South. If a slave was not considered to be a human being in the antebellum period, he or she was even less likely to be considered a Southern human being. Yet the blindness persists into the present. The *Oxford Companion to African-American Literature* (1997) moves seamlessly from the film *Sounder* to the poet Ellease Southerland, without any entry on the South, either as concept or literary field. The index to Maryemma Graham's *Cambridge Companion to the African American*

Novel (2004) moves from sorrow songs to spirituals. In Audrey Fisch's edited *Cambridge Companion to the African-American Slave Narrative* (2007), contributors consider its relationship to abolition, political philosophy, Anglo-American literary traditions, revolutionary autobiography, and sentimental novel, inter alia, but the South only features in a subtitle, in John Ernst's discussion of H. Mattison's *Louisa Piquet: the Octoroon: or Inside Views of Southern Domestic Life.*

What is true of the slave narrative is also true of the neo-slave narrative, a term coined by Bernard W. Bell to describe "residually oral, modern narratives of escape from bondage to freedom."[4] Historically it has been seen as a genre with a discontinuous history, disappearing from view for almost a century to resurface in a generic renaissance in the neo-slave narratives of Margaret Walker, Sherley Anne Williams, David Bradley, Ishmael Reed, Paule Marshall, Octavia Butler, Caryl Phillips, Charles Johnson, Toni Morrison, Edward P. Jones, Bernardine Evaristo, and a host of others. While not all these writers are Southern, most are of Southern heritage and all are writing about a fictional South. Critics of the neo-slave narrative, however, tend to replace the South with other master categories, under the general headings of history and memory, gender, and postmodernism. Ashraf Rushdy looks to history and locates the "moment of their formal origins"[5] in relation to the 1960s, firstly as "writing back" against Styron's *The Confessions of Nat Turner* (1967), and secondly in the relation between writers and advocates of a Black Aesthetic, when the rise of the New Left made it clear that history was made not only by the imperial powers of a nation but by those without any discernible power at all. "History from the bottom up" made its appearance, in labor and working-class history, women's and ethnic studies, and a revised respect for oral history and testimony. The nineteenth-century slave narratives were suddenly back in favor, and as a new black political subjectivity emerged, the parallels between the two periods were obvious, with a renewed interest in questions of race and power. Rushdy argues that contemporary novels concentrate particularly on issues of power relations in the field of cultural production – what the forces are behind the creation of a literary tradition, how national narratives emerge, which groups get to tell their story as *the* story, and which stories are "minority" or marginalized, controlled by cultural institutions.

Which stories, then, are Southern? Rushdy locates the neo-slave narratives in relation to the South primarily in his emphasis on them as reactions to William Styron's *The Confessions of Nat Turner*, thus placing a white Southern novelist rather than a nineteenth-century black genre in an important position at the head of the tradition. Styron's novel became a literary *cause célebre* and was challenged by Black Power intellectuals because it represented a slave revolt in non-heroic terms, because it presumed that a white writer could assume the voice of a slave, because it was historically uninformed, and because it offered a conservative, traditional image of slavery. In the novel, Turner's wife is excluded from the action, while the role of Margaret Whitehead, a white woman, is exaggerated; sexual lust becomes the mainspring of revolutionary activity. Turner is forever engaging in erotic fantasies. Unfortunately, as Rushdy unforgettably puts it, he is "not an equal opportunity masturbator" – only white women will do.[6] Styron plays into the stereotype of the black man as would-be rapist. As a result, the novel effectively killed the white-authored novel of slavery stone dead for half a century, the only exceptions being Joan Brady's *Theory of War* (1994), in which the slave is actually white, and Margaret Atwood's *The Handmaid's Tale* (1984), in which the oppression of women is dramatized through the conventions of the slave narrative.

Several critics have considered the neo-slave narrative in terms of gender. For Elizabeth Beaulieu in *Black Women Writers and the American Neo-Slave Narrative: Femininity Unfettered* (1999), neo-slave narratives place the enslaved mother at the heart of the tale, reacting against the overemphasis in the nineteenth century on the male paradigm and the underestimation of the female paradigm. Beaulieu emphasizes the importance of Alex Haley's *Roots* (1976) in relaunching the story of slavery, but points out that Haley's tale is very much a male story; its hero, Kunte Kinte, is a loner, and his daughter Kizzy a stock character of the suffering slave woman. In contrast, the stories of women in the novels of Morrison, Butler, or Williams put gender back on the agenda, and especially validate maternity. In Williams's *Dessa Rose* (1986), Dessa's pregnancy is what saves her life; motherhood is the source of her strength. Motherhood is absolutely central to *Beloved* (1988), in the infanticide plot, the milk-stealing, and the connections between foremothers, mothers, and daughters. Beaulieu's account of *Kindred*, however, may suggest some reservations concerning the issue of empowering women. In *Kindred* (1979), Dana goes back to the past to facilitate the rape of her enslaved great-great-great-grandmother, the acknowledged starting point for her own family line. Dana has to keep Rufus, the white slaveholder's son, alive long enough for procreation to occur. As a result she is in some senses a surrogate mother, birthing her ancestor as well as herself, protecting and nurturing Rufus. It is a completely new take on the "Black Mammy" model of maternalism, with Mammy as the rapist's accomplice. Stephanie Sievers also focuses on women writers, as do Carolyn Rody, who focuses on the reclamation of the mother by the daughter, and Angelyn Mitchell, who reads the novels as analyzing the concept, nature, and problem of freedom, using intertextuality as a method of encoding memory.

Other critics have considered neo-slave narratives in even broader terms, again largely ignoring the South and focusing on time rather than space. Alison Landsberg places neo-slave narratives within a nonracial paradigm as examples of the late-twentieth-century tendency toward "prosthetic memory" produced in response to new electronic and visual media.[7] She is interested in how individuals come to own and inhabit memories of events the experience of which they never lived through, so that memories are rather like artificial limbs, worn by the body, or like clothes that we change at will in order to re-tailor our identities. Landsberg is not interested in authenticity at all, but in the constructedness of memory, and the popular longing to experience history in a personal, even a bodily, way. Other critics who have tended to ignore the South, and to be more interested in problems of time and memory than of spatial representation, include Rushdy, in his second book that focused on "palimpsest narratives" in which different historical periods are marked in the same textual space and plots revolve around discovering family secrets.[8]

More heavily theorized accounts also avoid the South, except as a mythic location. Arlene Keizer argues that black writers are primarily concerned with theorizing black subjectivity, through the depiction of slavery.[9] A. Timothy Spaulding focuses on novels that reject narrative realism and critique the "objectivity" of traditional history, by using the genres of science fiction, Gothic, metafiction, and even vampire stories. Spaulding argues for postmodernism as the major influence on the neo-slave narratives, especially in relation to the instability of the narrative representation of the past.[10] Madhu Dubey also responds to problems of postmodernity, arguing that where neo-slave narratives showcase the South, it is as a reaction to postmodern urban existence. A turn toward Southern regionalism thus functions as a step backward to "organic" rural communities, a return to Southern folk culture, offering the rural South of a bygone era as an imaginary elsewhere to postmodern urban existence. In Morrison's *Song of Solomon* (1977), for example, the hero goes south to a very old place, using magic and folklore on a roots quest.[11] Interestingly, however, the location is explicitly signposted as fictional. The town of Shalimar does not exist on the Texaco map, just as Willow Springs in Naylor's *Mama Day* (1989), located off the coast of Georgia, is also not on the map of the United States. The image of the unmapped location provides a subtextual recognition that these stories are in – but not of – the South.

One recent critical account, however, does connect the neo-slave narratives to the South, and to works by white Southern writers to boot. Tim Ryan challenges the notion of historical discontinuity between slave and neo-slave narratives, pointing to the continuous tradition of novels about slavery through the 1920s, 1930s, and 1940s.[12] While some of these novels are plantation potboilers by Frank Yerby and Kyle Onstott, Ryan draws attention to *The Slave Ship* (1924), by Mary Johnston, a white Virginian writer who started publishing novels in the nineteenth century. In this case the slave is a white Jacobite rebel, shipped to Virginia for permanent servitude, who escapes to become captain of a slave ship, and is recaptured and re-enslaved in America. The novel (reissued in 2011) concentrates on the ways in which the slaveholder mentality functions, its evasions and rationalizations. Other early neo-slave narratives tend to focus on revolt rather than escape, in reaction to the myth of the passive "Uncle Tom" figure and to conceptualizations of African Americans as lacking in agency. Arna Bontemps's *Black Thunder* (1936), about the Gabriel Prosser revolt, is clearly inspired by the radical politics of the 1930s. The revolt involves black and white participants, French revolutionary activists, and reference to the revolution in Haiti. Frances Gaither's *The Red Cock Crows* (1944) is also a dramatization of a slave revolt, albeit from the pen of a white writer. Carefully historicized, Ryan's readings of individual novels highlight the topic of class in the South, and the ways in which it complicates our understanding of race and slavery. In Margaret Walker's *Jubilee* (1966), for example, often described as the first neo-slave narrative, the heroine, Vyry, encounters racism in Reconstruction from poor whites as well as from plantation owners under slavery. Walker's novel has sometimes been read as the black *Gone With the Wind* (1936), but can also be persuasively linked to the radical writers of the 1930s and 1940s, the period in which Walker began to write. In this approach to the genre, one tradition calls out a response from the other in a reciprocal cultural conversation between black and white, master and slave, slave narrative and neo-slave narrative, popular and literary writing. Ryan is unusual, however, in firmly locating the novels in the Southern literary tradition and drawing a very different map of the genre, as porous to Southern and international influences, slipping between different traditions, and perpetually challenging the reader's expectations.

Does the erasure from the map matter? What would reconnecting the narratives to their origins in the South say about them? In the first place it would avoid a literary reproduction in our time of the tactics of slavery. Slaves may have been in the South but many of them hardly knew it. If slaves often did not know who they were, they often also had little understanding of where they were. Without maps or the access to literacy necessary to decode them, escape depended on oral advice. Only the coded directions in the slave songs and spirituals could furnish directions for an escape route, as in "Follow the Drinking Gourd," in which the singer maps the route North by stars and rivers. The literate today may not be as well equipped. Deprived of maps, the students in my seminar on neo-slave narratives were even less able to cross the campus to hypothetical freedom across the river to the North. Following the North Star and checking for moss on the northern side of trees was not something that occurred to them, still less the possibility of wading in the campus lake to throw off the scent of pursuing dogs.

In many novels about slavery, despite careful historical detail and reference to the slave narratives, the sense of being "off the map" is vividly rendered. In *Middle Passage* (1990), when Charles Johnson's hero, Rutherford, sets out across the Atlantic from Africa, he is astonished to find that the whole star system appears to have been switched on him, and the universe has become unreadable. He has absolutely no idea where he is.[13] When in *Kindred* Octavia Butler's time-traveling heroine, Dana, repeatedly travels from twentieth-century America to her slave ancestors in nineteenth-century Maryland, she swiftly realizes the necessity of taking a good map back with her. To her horror, however, Rufus begins to read her book and she realizes that it contains "history that he must not read" because too much of it has not yet happened.[14] At this point in the past Sojourner Truth is still a slave in New York; if she were to be sold south, she could never even become the author of a slave narrative. Frederick Douglass and Harriet Tubman are living a few miles away, and in Virginia Nat Turner has yet to revolt. If history can be changed, Dana's presence in the past may be extremely unproductive, potentially betraying the escapees of the future to the masters in the past. Dana burns the book and its map, comforted by the knowledge that she has memorized the position of the North Star by night and knows to keep the morning sun to her right by day. Having a map on her person would only convince any white man that she planned to escape. Slaves must not have or understand maps.

Kindred offers very precise intertextual links to the earlier slave narratives. It is set in Talbot County, the birthplace of Frederick Douglass, and Dana is modeled on him. She wears pants, is taken to be male, and gains her freedom in a violent fight. Like Douglass's, her story demonstrates how easily slaves are made, although it lacks the regenerative message of Douglass's more affirmative story. *Kindred* is a reverse slave narrative: Dana is born free in the twentieth century and is enslaved in the nineteenth, becoming steadily more and more habituated to slavery and less able to resist. Dana's ancestor, Alice, like Harriet Jacobs, at first is unaware that she is a slave; she is pursued by her master, yields to seduction to avoid worse, and is situated at the center of a supportive communal and familial network that stands in strong contrast to Dana's solitary individualism. While the novel has a didactic quality, rehearsing the important facts of slavery, it remains radically unfamiliar at the same time, as a result of the time-traveling plot.

Without Dana's time travel it would be a realistic historical novel. Slave narratives focused on making the facts of slavery known – rendering it, in the title of Edward P. Jones's novel, *The Known World* (2003). Genre is another word for the familiar – the reassurance of a known form despite the contents of horror or shock. It remains important for each generation to remind readers of the facts of slavery, but as Ryan notes, there is thus a risk of producing automatic responses. The story needs to be told anew to avoid it becoming familiar and our sympathies blunted – that is the risk of the genre. Neo-slave narratives therefore pursue a process of defamiliarization even within the bounds of the familiar form.

One major feature of neo-slave narratives, therefore, no matter how careful they are to reproduce the history of slavery and to maintain a connection to the genre of the slave narrative, is an emphasis on remapping the world, scrambling agreed definitions of place or time, and drawing attention to the limits of conventional conceptions. The reader is forced to experience the kind of disorientation in time and space felt by the slave. Neo-slave narratives not only challenge the established history of the South, and of the United States; they overlay the South of the maps with an alternative geography. In this, Bernadine Evaristo's *Blonde Roots* (2008), by a black British writer of Nigerian and Brazilian heritage, is typical. The novel incorporates almost all the familiar elements of the slave narrative genre: capture, failed escape, Middle Passage, branding, slave auctions, family separation, renaming, whippings, the acquisition of literacy, and a final escape to freedom, to a long-established community of maroons. Along the way the heroine, Doris Scagglethorpe, kidnapped from the Cabbage Coast of Northern England (a replacement for the Gold Coast of Africa), is enslaved in Londolo, a mixture of London and Mombasa, which has recognizable landmarks such as Paddingto and Mayfah but also a tropical climate and crocodiles in the River Temz. Evaristo's imaginative reversals maintain the reader's awareness of the main features of slavery, while compelling a continual translation between racialized spaces and cultures, which effectively transforms black into white and vice versa. The most startlingly original element in the novel is the global reorganization of space. Evaristo makes the Middle Passage a metaphor for both temporal and geographical dislocation by setting events in an unspecified time (both futuristic and historical) and by rearranging the geography of the globe so that Aphrika and the United Kingdom of Great Ambossa, though on the Equator, lie to the north of Europa, whence "whyte" slaves are kidnapped by "blaks" to be exported across the Atlantic to work on the plantations of the West Japanese Islands. By moving everything south, Evaristo effectively transfers Paul Gilroy's "Black Atlantic" from northern to southern hemispheres, correcting Gilroy's Anglophone bias, relegating "Amarika" to the sidelines, and inducing a powerful sense of disorientation in the reader. Although Doris works in the South, the whole concept of "South" has been revised and reconfigured.

In more overtly "Southern" terms, *Dessa Rose* is instructive in the ways in which it reconfigures Southern space. The novel begins almost as an extended dialogue with Styron. The "Author's Note" describes Williams's outrage over Styron's portrayal of Turner, and the first section, "The Darky," is a parody of the interviews Thomas Gray undertook with Nat Turner. Dessa is interrogated in custody by Adam Nehemiah, just as Styron portrays Gray interviewing Turner. Gray was planning to write an account of the rebellion, which would defuse its politics; Nehemiah plans to write a tract advising masters how to prevent slave revolts using Dessa as evidence. As the "object" of his study Nehemiah tries to read Dessa, to interpret her and thus control her. As Rushdy argues, the opening section is largely a battle between literacy (Nehemiah) and orality as Dessa uses voice to play with meanings, outwit Nehemiah, discover information from him, and communicate surreptitiously with escaped slaves. Williams makes Nehemiah not a freelance writer but an author with a commission, writing at the suggestion of his publisher. He has institutional backing; there is a cultural and commercial machine behind him. The novel also begins with an erotic fantasy, a black woman remembering in dream a burning love for her black husband, a love fully requited, again as a riposte to Styron. Williams focuses on the disparity of access to power of those who write master texts as opposed to those who write slave narratives, but nevertheless shows blacks as the agents of their own lives and communities.

What Williams also highlights is the unmapped nature of Southern space. Sievers notes how the descriptions of space in the first part of the novel slowly evolve from Nehemiah's point of view to Dessa's, reflecting her perceptions, not his, and reconfiguring the spaces around her. Nehemiah emphasizes geographical location in his diary, but as he becomes more and more disoriented, the entries become vague and he loses his place. Whereas his first diary entry is boldly headed "The Hughes Farm, Near Linden, Marengo County, Alabama," his last entries are headed "Somewhere South and West of Linden" and "July 4, 1847. Early Morning." By the Fourth of July he no longer knows where he is in the United States. Dessa, however, has already learned to identify the drinking gourd with the North Star in its handle, and when she hears an unidentified voice singing a spiritual, sings out herself, "When my soul be free?" to receive the answering refrain:

> Souls going to ride that heavenly train
> Cause the Lord have called you home.[15]

In a flash she takes her bearings and understands that some fellow slaves have survived the uprising and are about to rescue her. The heavenly train in this context refers to the journey to freedom, drawing on the notion of the Underground Railroad. Once escaped, she finds herself off the map in a positive sense – at Sutton Glen, a house that is invisible from the road, never visited, and appears to have been "swallowed up by the forest" (113), a place akin to Sleeping Beauty's palace. The house is all on one level, as are its occupants, white or black. Unfinished, its elegant staircase leads nowhere. In this nonhierarchical location whites (in the shape of the plantation mistress) and blacks set themselves free from psychological enslavement to stereo-typed conceptual frameworks. Sutton Glen functions as a hall of mirrors, demonstrating how each character fails to see anything but their own pro-jections, unable to see beyond conventional frameworks and stereotypes, whether white or black. Rufel, the mistress, sees the black people around her through images of minstrels or the stock cuts of runaways; Dessa sees Rufel as voraciously sexual. Slowly, however, Sutton Glen evolves from a space of narcissism to a heterotopic location where black and white can unite to a common purpose – escape to the Utopia of the West. The members of the group finance their journey to freedom by repeatedly selling themselves and escaping, assisted by their white mistress. "Slaves" are sold by her in various towns and then escape to be sold again, defusing the horrors of slavery by performing the role over and over again.

Once the group unites, it is striking that they return to a mapped environ-ment and to a specific sense of place, setting off from the unlocated Sutton Glen to Wilkerson on the shores of Lake Lewis Smith, by boat down the Warrior River, to Haley's Landing "just over the line in Tuscaloosa County" (194), then overland through the towns between the Warrior and Sipsey rivers to Tuscaloosa, Pickens, and Green counties, eventually making it to Council Bluffs and a wagon train. The narrative space of the novel reinforces the point that Dessa has made her own place in the world. The final section in first-person narrative establishes Dessa herself as the authority over her own experience and the frames to the story (a dream, reflections on her life) establish the story as hers. She has settled and occupied a free space in the West, and now tells her story repeatedly to her children and grandchildren.

Dessa Rose remains an optimistic novel, with the escape from bondage to freedom offering a happy ending of sorts. More recent novels lack this tele-ology of freedom. In *The Known World*, Edward P. Jones defamiliarizes the story of slavery primarily by concentrating on the story of free blacks who owned slaves, depicting the "peculiar institution" through a multiplicity of different stories as a complex social system, ranging from absolute horror to something approaching benevolence. Black slaveholders did exist. The 1830

U.S. census included 3,775 free blacks who owned 12,740 slaves.[16] Some of these were family members, "owned" in order to protect them and to avoid the threat of family separation on manumission (when the law often insisted that the freed slave leave the state). Others were owned for commercial reasons. In *The Known World*, two forms of map are contrasted, the one demonstrating the invisibility of the slave in the United States, the other restoring the slave to full presence. The first map is a version of the Waldseemuller world map, entitled "The Known World," made in 1507 and celebrated as America's birth certificate, the first document on which the name "America" appears. Sherriff Skiffington's wife banishes the object (it is eight feet by six feet) from her home, and it hangs on the wall of the town jail. The map is highly inaccurate. North America is far too small and the name "America" is attached only to South America. North America is actually nameless. In particular, the map of the South is wrong. (Florida does not exist.) Broussard, a prisoner shortly to be executed, offers to get a better map, but Skiffington is happy with "The Known World" as it is. Slavery is so much the status quo for him that he pays no attention to the action in the background: the sale of Moses away from his fellow slave Bessie, despite all his desperate entreaties.

The ironies of the map cut in several directions. On the one hand it is a Utopian image, an object of some beauty and value. On the other its position on the wall of the jail recalls Hawthorne's opening chapter "The Prison Door" in *The Scarlet Letter* (1850), where the first thing the colonists do on founding their "Utopia of human virtue and happiness" is to build a jail, thus suggesting that the New World is just the same as the old world, the familiar world they knew before, and that it is founded on and underwritten by crime.[17] Only one copy of this map exists today, bought for $10 million in 2003 by the Library of Congress and exhibited that year in the Thomas Jefferson Building in Washington, DC. Readers who know the map, however, may also remember that Waldseemuller had doubts about Amerigo Vespucci, and by 1513, when it was reprinted, had rechristened it "The Unknown World" (Terra Incognita).[18] The map is an object of considerable ideological power, but it is also a fiction, and can be read in different ways. Like Jones's novel, it supposedly depicts a real world, but at the same time renders it strange and deeply disturbing.

Skiffington's map is empty of people (though the reader who cares to look at the original will note that on the African part of the map small naked figures are visible carrying bows). But two other maps populate the image and ultimately fulfill Broussard's offer of a better cartography. When Calvin, a free black, visits Washington on the eve of the Civil War, he is astonished to see two maps on exhibition, both of them made by Alice Night, a slave who has escaped from his sister's plantation, in Manchester County, Virginia. The first is an enormous wall hanging, part tapestry, part painting, part clay structure, "a kind of map of life of the County of Manchester, Virginia. But a "map" is such a poor word for such a wondrous thing."[19] There are no people in the map but it displays an intimate knowledge of the County, its houses, barns, roads, wells, and cemeteries. On the opposite wall is exhibited a second hanging, made in the same way, but depicting in minute detail his sister's plantation, in Calvin's view, just as God would see it: "There is nothing missing, not a cabin, not a barn, not a chicken, not a horse. Not a single person is missing" (385). Slaves and slave owners are standing in front of their homes, their eyes raised as if to look into the eyes of God. Even the dead are present, standing where they once lived, the tiny infants in their mothers' arms. The only missing people are the three slaves, Priscilla, Alice, and Jamie, who, having escaped, are now in Washington. Everything about the image is deeply familiar to Calvin – but the position of the image in the middle of Washington is utterly astonishing to him. Humbled, he sinks to his knees, overcome by fear that people will remember that he had once owned slaves.

Calvin describes this in a letter to his sister dated April 12, 1861, the date of the bombardment of Fort Sumter and thus of the start of the Civil War. Waldseemuller's map was drawn shortly after the beginning of slavery in the Americas; Alice's marks its end. Alice's first map demonstrates her access to full geographical knowledge; on the plantation she was considered mad and thus allowed to wander at will, getting to know every aspect of her location as a result, which facilitated her escape. Her second map restores the memory of slavery to the record, resurrecting the dead and placing their world at the heart of U.S. power, in its capital. Effectively it says "we slaves are all here, right at the centre of America, and we always will be." Jones replaces the exhibition of 2003 with a rival exhibit, a slave-authored remapping of American power, a local image which replaces a global one. The intertextual reference to the slaves' eyes explicitly pays homage to black art. In *Their Eyes Were Watching God* (1937), Zora Neale Hurston also celebrated black community and her title refers to the irrelevance of whites. In a hurricane the blacks sheltering in a cabin realize that the time has passed to ask whites what to look for: "Six eyes were questioning God.... Their eyes were watching God."[20] Maps are fictions; their apparent facts reflect cultural imperatives. As the rival maps demonstrate, we need to redraw our mental maps, reorder the world that we thought we knew, and put slavery firmly on the map. Beginning with the definition of Southern literature.

NOTES

1 See William L. Andrews, *To Tell a Free Story: The First Century of Afro-American Autobiography, 1760–1865* (Urbana: University of Illinois Press, 1986); Charles T. Davis and Henry Louis Gates Jr., eds. *The Slave's Narrative* (Oxford: Oxford University Press, 1985); John Sekora and Darwin T. Turner eds., *The Art of Slave Narrative: Original Essays in Criticism and Theory* (Macomb: Western Illinois University Press, 1982).

2 Frederick Douglass, *Narrative of the Life of Frederick Douglass, An American Slave* (New York: Norton: 1997), p. 12.

3 George P., Rawick, ed., *The American Slave: A Composite Autobiography* (Westport, CT: Greenwood, 1972).

4 Bernard W. Bell, *The Afro-American Novel and its Tradition* (Amherst: University of Massachusetts Press, 1987), p. 289.

5 Ashraf H.A. Rushdy, *Neo-Slave Narratives: Studies in the Social Logic of a Literary Form* (Oxford: Oxford University Press, 1999), p. 95.

6 Rushdy, *Neo-Slave Narratives*, p. 64.

7 Alison Landsberg, *Prosthetic Memory. The Transformation of American Remembrance in the Age of Mass Culture* (New York: Columbia University Press, 2004).

8 Ashraf H.A. Rushdy, *Remembering Generations: Race and Family in Contemporary African American Fiction* (Chapel Hill: University of North Carolina Press, 2001).

9 Arlene B. Keizer, *Black Subjects: Identity Formation in the Contemporary Narrative of Slavery* (Ithaca, NY: Cornell University Press, 2004).

10 Timothy Spaulding, *Re-Forming the Past: History, the Fantastic, and the Postmodern Slave Narrative* (Columbus: Ohio State University Press, 2005), p. 14.

11 Madhu Dubey, *Signs and Cities: Black Literary Postmodernism* (Chicago: University of Chicago Press, 2003).

12 Tim A. Ryan, *Calls and Responses: The American Novel of Slavery since Gone with the Wind* (Baton Rouge: Louisiana State University Press, 2008).

13 Charles Johnson, *The Middle Passage* (New York: Plume, 1991), p. 158.

14 Octavia A. Butler, *Kindred* (London: Women's Press, 1988), p. 140.

15 Sherley Anne Williams, *Dessa Rose* (Virago, 1998), p. 64. Page numbers follow subsequent quotations in parentheses.

16 Katherine Bassard, "Imagining Other Worlds: Race, Gender, and the 'Power Line' in Edward P. Jones's *The Known World*," *Fall African American Review* 42 (2008), pp. 407–419. See also Richard H. King, "Review of The Known World," *Rethinking History* 9 (2005), pp. 355–380.

17 Nathaniel Hawthorne, *The Scarlet Letter* (Oxford University Press, 1990), p. 47.

18 John R. Hébert, "The Map That Named America," http://www.loc.gov/loc/lcib/0309/maps.html Accessed 13/12/2011

19 Edward P. Jones, *The Known World* (New York: Amistad 2003), p. 384. Page numbers follow subsequent quotations in parentheses.

20 Zora Neale Hurston, *Their Eyes Were Watching God* (London: Virago, 1986), pp. 235–236.

3

WILL KAUFMAN

Literature and the Civil War

"Southerners are very strange about that war," the Mississippi novelist and historian Shelby Foote memorably observed.[1] The South's body of Civil War literature, both wartime and postbellum, can indeed appear at times as a repository of strangeness, given that it has emerged from the unique combination of American schism, American defeat, and the enforced reincorporation of a huge population into a re-United States. Much of the strangeness reflected in Southern writing about the war is based on a perception of Southern otherness, imposed, it should be noted, not only by Northern and foreign writers observing the South, but also by Southern writers themselves. A bold and direct line can be traced, for example, from the mid-eighteenth-century portraits fabricated by Virginia planters (the aristocratic or yeoman Southern farmer or "husbandman" versus the money-grubbing Yankee industrialist) to the anti-industrial characterizations of the "Nashville Agrarians" of the 1930s. Thomas Jefferson, writing in his *Notes on the State of Virginia* (1785), argued: "Those who labor in the earth are the chosen people of God, if ever he had a chosen people, whose breasts he has made his peculiar deposit for substantial and genuine virtue"; these "chosen" are contrasted with the godforsaken inhabitants of the urban wasteland, both Northern and European: "'The mobs of great cities add just so much to the support of pure government, as sores do to the strength of the human body. It is the manners and spirit of a people which preserve a republic in vigor. A degeneracy in these is a canker which soon eats to the heart of its laws and constitution."[2] By 1930, the Nashville Agrarian Frank Owsley could look back on the Civil War and conclude: "This struggle between an agrarian and an industrial civilization ... was the irrepressible conflict, the house divided against itself, which must become according to the doctrine of the industrial section all the one or all the other. It was the doctrine of intolerance, crusading, standardizing alike in industry and in life. The South had to be crushed out; it was in the way; it impeded the progress of the machine."[3]

Such a view of the Civil War, of course, removes slavery from its central position as the war's primary cause – a denial still perpetuated by a host of neo-Confederate apologists, not least the Daughters of the Confederacy, who declare as one of their creeds "to study and teach the truths of history (one of the most important of which is, that the War Between the States was not a rebellion, nor was its underlying cause to sustain slavery)."[4] Such denial flies in the face of the explicit declaration made by the Confederacy's first vice-president, Alexander Stephens, who in 1861 not only cited slavery as the war's "immediate cause," but also argued that the Confederacy's "foundations are laid, its corner-stone rests, upon the great truth that the negro is not equal to the white man; that slavery, subordination to the superior race, is his natural and moral condition.... This, our new Government, is the first, in the history of the world, based upon this great physical, philosophical, and moral truth."[5]

By the time Stephens made that statement, the war was an accomplished military fact; but it was by then a literary fact as well. A war of words had long been building on a parallel track with the growing political schism, its shots being fired across the Mason-Dixon line with increasing ferocity since the 1830s, when the Northern abolition movement produced its first antislavery novel, Richard Hildreth's *The Slave: Or, Memoirs of Archy Moore* (1836), which extolled the virtues of Northern free enterprise as much as it excoriated the brutality of the Southern plantation system. The reinforcement of Southern American difference was inscribed throughout the reflections of the escaped mixed-race narrator, culminating in the damning declaration: "There are slaves in many other countries; but no where else is oppression so heartless and unrelenting. No where else, has tyranny ever assumed a shape so fiendish. No where else is it of all the world beside, the open aim of the laws, and the professed purpose of the masters, to blot out the intellects of half the population, and to extinguish at once and forever, both the capacity and the hope of freedom."[6]

Such ferocious indictments increasingly drowned out the bland assurances of a benign slave system promulgated by Southern novelists writing within the Walter Scott-influenced "plantation cult," such as William Alexander Caruthers's *The Cavaliers of Virginia* (1835) or Nathaniel Beverley Tucker's *The Partisan Leader* (1836). It was Hildreth's *The Slave*, along with such slave narratives as *The Life of Josiah Henson, Formerly a Slave* (1849), that ultimately won the attention of Harriet Beecher Stowe, who, aroused by hatred of the 1850 Fugitive Slave Act enforcing the return of escaped slaves from the North to the South, penned her own battle cry in the form of *Uncle Tom's Cabin* (1852). Thrown on the defensive by the whirlwind of Stowe's immediate global popularity, Southern apologists responded in a rash of embittered parodies or "Anti-Tom" novels. Mary Henderson Eastman's *Aunt Phillis's Cabin* (1852) laments the "degraded condition" of free blacks in the North, with "no one to care for them when they are sick or in trouble," where, "since the Abolitionists have intermeddled there, the free blacks have become intolerable; they live from day to day in discomfort and idleness."[7] Likewise, John W. Page's *Uncle Robin, in His Cabin in Virginia, and Tom Without One in Boston* (1853) condemns Stowe in particular and, in general, the "officious meddling with Southern rights, miscalled philanthropy."[8] Thus, when Abraham Lincoln (perhaps apocryphally) called Stowe "the little woman who made this great war," he was on fairly secure ground when it came to the literary civil war, if not the military one.[9]

The war years themselves (1861–1865) produced surprisingly little published literature that would today be recognized as anything other than ephemera. This was inevitable, given that the exigencies of martial activity – and martial law – held publishing in a stranglehold. This was as true of the South as it was of the North. Much has been written about the Lincoln administration's iron grip on civil liberties during the war, such as the suspension of habeas corpus and the summary imprisonment of newspapers editors deemed seditious. Less is conventionally known about the muzzles imposed in the Confederate states, where one Richmond, Virginia, newspaper editor noted that he and his Southern colleagues had "a fear of having their offices closed, if they dare[d] to speak the sentiments struggling for utterance"; it was "indeed, a reign of terror."[10] In any event, as the South Carolina poet and novelist William Gilmore Simms lamented, Southerners were, for the most part, reading "none but military books now."[11] Partisan poetry flourished in such organs as the *Southern Literary Messenger*, *DeBow's Review*, the *Magnolia Weekly*, and *Russell's Magazine*. Countless municipal and regional newspapers offered verse fillers such as Albert Pike's reworking of the minstrel song, "Dixie" (1861), which sounded the alarm to the readers of the Natchez, *Mississippi Courier*: "Northern flags in South winds flutter."[12] Similarly, South Carolina's Henry Timrod, the "Poet Laureate of the Confederacy," matched his pastoral ode to the plantation life, "The Cotton Boll," with his "Call to Arms" (1861), which enjoined readers to resist the invading "despot" by watering the South's "sacred dust / With floods of crimson rain."[13]

At the same time, the slave narrative was calling for attention in the earliest years of the war. While the slave narrative (like the bulk of Civil War literature) would see its greatest flowering in the postbellum years, one of its most significant titles appeared in 1861, Harriet Jacobs's *Incidents in the Life of a Slave Girl*. Jacobs, a North Carolinian writing under the pseudonym of Linda Brent, set out to place before a Northern readership a frank description of the exploitation, sexual as well as civil, endured by female slaves in the South. Such writings would help elevate the conception of the war from a mere struggle for political union to a struggle for emancipation and the affirmation of human rights. For Jacobs, as for Stowe before her, the key lay in capturing the sympathies of "the women of the North" who, presumably, would exert influence on their husbands in the corridors of power, much as Stowe depicted in *Uncle Tom's Cabin*, wherein an influential senator is convinced by his wife to vote against the Fugitive Slave Act. Jacobs, for her part, strove to place the Northern wife, ever so briefly, into the shoes of the slave woman: "O, ye happy women, whose purity has been sheltered from childhood, who have been free to choose the objects of your affection, whose homes are protected by law, do not judge the poor desolate slave girl too severely! If slavery had been abolished, I, also, could have married the man of my choice; I could have had a home shielded by the laws; and I should have been spared the painful task of confessing what I am now about to relate."[14] Such an appeal to sentiment is one of the major characteristics of Civil War literature, both Southern and Northern, and from the pens of both black and white authors.

It is thus perhaps unsurprising that the great mass of postbellum writing should be freighted with sentiment, in the form of what Nina Silber has termed the "romance of reunion," which relied on a depiction of secession and independence as a noble "lost cause" and which provided the white South "with an emotional vehicle that had profound religious, psychological, and social functions – functions that were especially suited for a society that suffered from defeat, humiliation, and internal dissension."[15] This was a depiction that many white Northern writers were only too happy to endorse, given that it effected a sense of racial solidarity across the Mason-Dixon Line at the expense of the new black citizens for whom the short ten years of Reconstruction would mark the briefest of hopeful periods (even as white Southerners limned the same period as the South's darkest hour, as Scott Romine's essay discusses). From within the heart of a region reeling in defeat, its earth scorched – so its apologists claimed – under the heels of a new invading army of carpetbaggers as heartless as the Federal troops who had preceded them, poets like Abram Joseph Ryan, "the Poet of the Lost Cause," painted a constituency "Defeated yet without a stain."[16] Assiduously sidestepping any admission of Southern culpability, William Gilmore Simms collected a host of ephemeral texts into his *War Poetry of the South* (1866), equating its contents with the captured ordnance of the Confederate army, now "the property of the whole" – the re-United States. Simms implied that Southern expression was balanced, at least morally, with any Northern wartime expression; both bodies of verse were to be treated equally and with as much evenhanded objectivity as "the rival ballads of the cavaliers and roundheads" during the English civil war.[17] Not all Southern writers followed this line, however; Sidney Lanier's novel *Tiger-Lilies* (1867) set out to excoriate the South for inviting calamity upon its own head: none "between Maryland and Mexico" were guiltless for the war that had brought the South to its knees.[18]

Black Southern writers would, of course, agree – not that their voices were all that audible amid the mass of proliferating "Lost Cause" apologia. In 1867, the Kentuckian William Wells Brown redrafted his 1853 novel *Clotel; or, the President's Daughter*, about a fictional mixed-race daughter of Thomas Jefferson, to foreground the war's military dimension in an effort to secure a twinning in the reader's mind between the South's defeat and its attempted preservation of slavery. In similar fashion, Frances E. W. Harper offered in *Minnie's Sacrifice* (1869), a morality tale in which its mixed-race protagonists, who could easily pass as white, choose to identify with the side of right, the African Americans who had ennobled what would otherwise have been a shabby war for power and territory. But black writers like Wells and Harper found themselves ranged against an army of white writers who shamelessly depicted the former slave population as overwhelmingly loyal, content, docile, and – cut adrift into the rough seas of freedom offered by Reconstruction – pining for the security of the old plantation: hence the enormous popularity of Joel Chandler Harris's "Uncle Remus" tales (1881), in which the aged black storyteller, as Harris himself admits, "has nothing but pleasant memories of the discipline of slavery" and who always speaks "from the standpoint of a Southerner."[19] In one astounding tale, "A Story of the War," Uncle Remus recounts how he had shot a Union soldier who had drawn a beam on his beloved "Mars Jeems." An incredulous visitor, Miss Theodosia, asks him, "Do you mean to say ... that you shot the Union soldier, when you knew he was fighting for your freedom?" to which Uncle Remus proudly replies, "Co'se, I know all about dat ... but w'en I see dat man take aim ... I jes disremembered all 'bout freedom en lammed aloose."[20]

By the turn of the century, the "romance of reunion" was in full swing, with former Confederate soldiers such as Alexander Harper seeking to balance the experiences of the wartime adversaries in a fraternal equation. Placing his fictional characters in a journalistic and carefully researched context, Harper took extraordinary pains to explain that his terminology, and his title, *Johnny Reb and Billy Yank* (1905), were "used without offense meant to either side"; his "earnest endeavor" had been "to present a faithful and non-partisan statement" based on "that profound respect for a brave foe which every veteran cherishes for another."[21] There had been no bitterness in defeat, Harper argued: "As for myself, though I was conquered, I felt no shame in having been vanquished by such a vast multitude of warriors who 'Followed their flag / To the tap of the drum'." Given that "the soldiers in the field did their part" and "the women at home did theirs," there were only two parties left to claim culpability: the Confederate government, which had "failed lamentably," and, crucial to the project of white reunion, "the negro," who had been "a burden and a curse to the South before the conflict." (And yet, Harper was at least astute enough to acknowledge: "It was the negro who tilled the crops and fed the armies. It was the negro that cared for the women and children and managed the farms; and there was no time during the contest that they could not have ended the war within a week.")²²

In 1905, the same year that Harper published *Johnny Reb and Billy Yank*, the insane accusation of black culpability for the war reached its most hysterical pitch with the appearance of Thomas Dixon's *The Clansman: An Historical Romance of the Ku Klux Klan*, the second title in a "Reconstruction Trilogy" that also included *The Leopard's Spots: A Romance of the White Man's Burden, 1865–1900* (1902) and *The Traitor: A Story of the Fall of the Invisible Empire* (1907). Dixon's agenda was clear and shameless. As he recalled, he wrote the trilogy with one object in mind: "to teach the North ... what it has never known – the awful suffering of the white man during the dreadful Reconstruction period ... [and] to demonstrate to the world that the white man must and shall be supreme."²³ In *The Leopard's Spots*, a black takeover of Southern legislatures had resulted in chaos and depredation, a "drunken revel" that had brought the South to ruin, a slander promulgated by the Southern Democratic party, of which the North Carolinian Dixon was a staunch member.²⁴ In point of fact, there had never been any black domination of Southern legislatures; for Dixon, however, black voters and politicians were the tools of the Northern carpetbaggers and their Radical Republican masters. "Congress," he proclaimed in *The Leopard's Spots*, "became to the desolate South what Attila, the 'Scourge of God,' was to civilized Europe."²⁵ In *The Clansman*, Dixon lent credence to the black activist William Monroe Trotter's charge of his being an "unasylumed maniac" by claiming in the preface that the Ku Klux Klan – "the reincarnated souls of the Clansmen of Old Scotland" – had arisen "against overwhelming odds, daring exile, imprisonment, and a felon's death, and saved the life of a people" (namely "the Aryan race").²⁶

Dixon's sensational glorifications of the plantation culture and the South's "Lost Cause" have overshadowed the more carefully analytical novels of fellow Southerners such as the Virginian Ellen Glasgow's *The Battle-Ground* (1902), which set the war in the larger exploration of the waning of the plantation aristocracy and the rising of a powerful middle class. In *The Battle-Ground*, the protagonist, Dan Montjoy, scion of a landowning family, befriends a poor white Virginian and serves with him in the Confederate army. Developing a sympathetic class consciousness through his battlefield bonding with the mountaineer "Pinetop," Montjoy eventually surveys the changed landscape in the immediate wake of Appomattox and concludes: "Despite the grim struggle and the wasted strength, despite the impoverished land and the nameless graves that filled it, despite even his own wrecked youth and the hard-fought fields where he had laid it down – despite all these a shadow was lifted from his people and it was worth the price."[27] Such sentiments, so far from the inherent denial of Lost Cause apologists such as Dixon and his later protégés (notably Margaret Mitchell), indicate a budding hope for the birth of an economically vital New South emerging from the wreckage of war and Reconstruction. Glasgow's forward vision set her in the avant-garde in relation to other Southern novelists who, even though writing a decade after the appearance of *The Battle-Ground*, preferred to invoke the martyrdom of Stonewall Jackson, such as Mary Johnston in *The Long Roll* (1911), or raise the specters of Antietam, Chancellorsville, and the brutality of Federal prison camps, as in James Boyd's *Marching On* (1927).

The Wall Street Crash and the onset of the Great Depression in 1929 inaugurated a reassessment of the meanings of regionalism and poverty in the South. The South Carolinian novelist and playwright DuBose Heyward, known primarily as the author of the novel and play *Porgy* (out of which came the Gershwins' classic opera, *Porgy and Bess*), published *Peter Ashley* (1932), a novel so scathing in its interrogation of the antebellum class system that Heyward found himself openly charged as "a defector to New South thinking."[28] In the novel, the protagonist, a young writer watching the South careening helplessly toward disastrous secession and war, deludes himself with visions of making Charleston "the intellectual capital of the Confederacy," where all the literati would gather "when the fever of war had burned itself out of their brains."[29] This ironic commentary on H. L. Mencken's excoriation of the postbellum South as the "Sahara of the Bozart" (i.e., "beaux arts"), which still rankled Southerners since its publication in 1920, put Heyward on a collision course with the most prominent collective voice of Southern writing in the 1930s, the Nashville Agrarians of *I'll Take My Stand* (1930) who included Owsley, John Crowe Ransom, Donald Davidson, Robert Penn Warren, Stark Young, and Allen Tate, among others. As far as the Agrarians were concerned, the "New South" was an entity complicit with the violently industrializing project of the victorious North. Thus, a line of dialogue in Young's plantation-set novel, *So Red the Rose* (1934), implicitly links the regional solidarity of the Agrarians, once again taking their stand, with the antebellum resistance to northern domination: "Northern threats have made and are making the South a unit."[30]

Two years on the heels of Young's fictional critique, Margaret Mitchell weighed in with her own assessment of what had brought the South to its present pass. First there had been "the scourge of war ... followed by the worse scourge of Reconstruction." Mitchell's heroine, Scarlett O'Hara, dwells bitterly upon "the Scallawags – Southerners who had turned Republican very profitably – and the Carpetbaggers, those Yankees who came South like buzzards after the surrender with all their worldly possessions in one carpetbag." She recalls her "unpleasant experience with the Freedmen's Bureau" and the "free negroes" now "getting quite insolent." This seems the strangest of all to her, for – until the plantation system had come crashing down – "she had never seen an insolent negro in her life."[31] Scarlett's nostalgia for that system, now "gone with the wind," adds a significant, if ironic, layer of meaning to Rhett Butler's departing reflection, uttered just prior to his famous refusal to "give a damn" about her any longer: "What is broken is broken – and I'd rather remember it as it was at its best than mend it and see the broken places as long as I lived."[32]

It was inconceivable that Mitchell, or any other Lost Cause apologist, would heed the advice embedded – again, ironically – in the title of Caroline Gordon's 1937 retrospective fiction, *None Shall Look Back*. Indeed, some might never have heard of Gordon's novel at all, practically buried as it was beneath the fanfare surrounding *Gone With the Wind*, and as Gordon herself ruefully complained, "Margaret Mitchell has got all the trade, damn her. They say it took her ten years to write that novel. Why couldn't it have taken her twelve?"[33] Gordon's novel, with a subplot celebrating the heroism of the Confederate general Nathan Bedford Forrest (the first Grand Wizard of the Ku Klux Klan and presiding officer at the Fort Pillow massacre of 1864), focuses on the supposedly tragic fate of the Allard family plantation as war comes and its slaves flee. *None Shall Look Back* explicitly recycles the main tenet of Lost Cause orthodoxy: "No, it was not a question of slavery"; it came down to the fact that the South had been "invaded – it did not much matter on what grounds the invaders had come."[34] The Kentuckian Gordon, for a time married to Allen Tate, championed and was intimately associated with the Nashville Agrarian project, which had hysterically set out to equate the brutality of Northern industrialism with that of "the Communist menace." (As Tate had written in the introduction to the Agrarian manifesto: "It is simply according to the blind drift of our industrial development to expect in America at last much the same economic system as that imposed by violence upon Russia in 1917".)[35] Implicitly, the preservation of the Allard plantation, or the system that supported it, would have prevented such a catastrophe from befalling America.

In *Gone with the Wind*, Melanie Wilkes at one point scoffs at the prospect of any organized African-American resistance to the plantation system. "And as for all this talk about the militia staying here to keep the darkies from rising," she exclaims, "why, it's the silliest thing I ever heard of. Why should our people rise?"[36] Such bewilderment at black Americans' failure to share the Southern whites' fondness for the old plantation is a trope that runs through much of the Lost Cause fiction (just as, in the early 1930s, Caroline Gordon expressed bewilderment at the quitting of her black housekeeper: "I am still puzzling over her sudden defection. Niggers are unfathomable").[37] If David Blight is correct in observing that "the image of the loyal slave may be one of the most hackneyed clichés in American history,"[38] the same could be said for Lost Cause fiction. But more problematically, it also shows itself in a Southern work that, in Craig A. Warren's estimation, otherwise sets out "to challenge the most basic tenets of the Lost Cause."[39] William Faulkner's *The Unvanquished* (1938) refocuses attention away from the heroics of the Confederate army and on the development and maturity of a white son of the Old South, Bayard Sartoris. Bayard's closest friend, Ringo, a family slave, is no less loyal than Huck Finn's Jim. Consequently, in a historically impossible instance of deracination, Bayard is able to view Ringo and himself as transcending the very circumstances that enabled the "foundations" (to revisit Alexander Stephens) of the Confederacy to be laid: "Ringo and I had been born in the same month and had both fed at the same breast and had slept together and eaten together for so long that Ringo called Granny 'Granny' just like I did, until maybe he wasn't a nigger anymore or maybe I wasn't a white boy anymore, the two of us neither, not even people any longer: the two supreme undefeated like two moths, two feathers riding above a hurricane."[40] A similar wish-fulfillment infects Faulkner's later novel, *Intruder in the Dust* (1948), in which the dubious claim is made that: "For every Southern boy fourteen years old, not once but whenever he wants it, there is the instant when it's still not yet two oclock on that July afternoon in 1863"[41] – that is to say, "the instant" before the Confederacy's doom was sealed at Gettysburg with the disaster of Pickett's charge. The implication is that Ringo or any other black Southern boy would feel the same remorse at the defeat of the Confederacy; yet as Leon Litwack observes, "In much that is written and filmed about the South, the perverse assumption persists that southerners are necessarily white.... If 'southerners' is defined to include blacks as well as whites, it becomes highly debatable how many southerners actually supported the Confederacy."[42]

This very debate became the focus of one Mississippian who declared himself fed to the teeth with the legend of the Lost Cause. In 1942, James Street published his novel *Tap Roots*, based on the Jones County rebellion of 1863–1864, when a group of Confederate deserters under the command of Captain Newton Knight fought a guerrilla war against Southern forces in the swamps and pine woods of Mississippi and, according to a controversial legend, actually declared the "Free State of Jones" in the midst of the Confederacy. As Street wrote in his Foreword, "It may surprise some of you to read that the South had many Unionists, Abolitionists and slavery haters. As a matter of fact, few Southerners owned slaves, and the South had its share of appeasers, copperheads and draft-dodgers. The idea that the South rose to a man to defend Dixie is a stirring legend … and nothing more." And, in a final stab at all the defenders of the Lost Cause project, Street concluded: "If, in this story, you miss the oft-told tale of the Civil War of Gettysburg and Lee, then I am glad."[43] The publication of the novel, and the film adaptation that George Marshall directed in 1948, sparked a wave of denial from Confederate apologists, not least the white descendants of Newton Knight who were distressed by the fact of the interracial community inaugurated through their ancestor's sexual liaison with a slave woman. One of these outraged descendants, Ethel Knight, published a biography of Knight, *The Echo of the Black Horn*, in 1951, which, as historian Victoria Bynum notes, was, "a thinly disguised effort to discredit the anti-Confederate uprising and to rid the white branches of the Knight family of the taint of miscegenation."[44] Ethel Knight herself declared that her aim was simply to counter Street and like-minded "fiction writers with itching palm, which has too often been greased."[45]

While Knight sat working on her exculpatory biography, her fellow Mississippian, Shelby Foote, was spending his evenings on the battlefield of Shiloh in Tennessee, where his great-grandfather had fought, musing on what James Panabaker has called "the central tension between 'objective' and subjective viewpoints" concerning "the first modern battle" (as Foote later described Shiloh in his epic narrative history *The Civil War*), redolent with signifiers of unimaginable bloodletting: the Peach Orchard, the Sunken Road, and the Hornet's Nest, where the casualties dwarfed the number of those in all previous American wars combined.[46] In his novel, *Shiloh* (1952), Foote framed the battlefield events through the contrasting viewpoints of eighteen Confederate and Union participants, each aiming to reflect what they "saw in our own little corner."[47] In some respects, *Shiloh* was a masterwork of combined engagement and evasion, for the tension between the objective and subjective remained stridently apolitical. As C. Stuart Chapman notes: "In future decades this ability to combine facts and experience would

... make [Foote] the symbol of a late-twentieth-century understanding of the Civil War in nonpolitical terms"; *Shiloh* had turned the war from an event rooted in political and historical causes into "an arena for individual bravery, devoid of political considerations" and, when flagging up politics, doing so only "for the sake of exorcising them."[48] In some respects, Foote was revisiting the territory already scouted by Herman Melville in the poem "Shiloh – A Requiem (April 1862)" which, as Randall Fuller argues, is Melville's comment on "the damage caused by individuals certain about their reading of divine intention," as so many politicians and battlefield generals demonstrably were.[49] Yet, while implicitly holding such individuals to account, Melville at the same time forestalled any political discussion of the carnage:

> Foemen at morn, but friends at eve –
> Fame or country least their care:
> (What like a bullet can undeceive!)[50]

Unlike Melville, however, Foote set out to negotiate, among other things, "a culture rooted in slavery," a connection that, as Chapman observes, "threatened to doom his sympathetic treatment of the Southern soldiers."[51] Hence Foote's decision to highlight the military brilliance of Nathan Bedford Forrest, whom he would later call, along with Lincoln, one of the war's "two authentic geniuses" in spite of his connections with Fort Pillow and the Ku Klux Klan.[52] In *Shiloh* one can see the groundwork being laid for such future "nonpolitical" understandings of the war as Daniel Woodrell's *Woe to Live On* (1987), the basis for Ang Lee's 1999 film, *Ride with the Devil*, and Charles Frazier's *Cold Mountain* (1997), both of which foreground the individual's struggle against hostile forces that could be replicated outside of a Civil War canvass.

The year after *Shiloh*'s publication, a Northern writer, Ward Moore, inaugurated one of the strangest practices to emerge in Civil War fiction: the imagining of an America in which the South had won the war. Moore's *Bring the Jubilee* (1952) is a science-fiction tale and an early classic of alternative history told by a young historian (tellingly named Hodge Backmaker) born in the twentieth century in a great agricultural nation underpinned by black slavery: the Confederate States of America. With the aid of a time machine, Backmaker travels back to the Battle of Gettysburg and is inadvertently instrumental in securing a Northern victory, erasing not only his own future but that of the Confederate nation into which he was born. Two literary tracks subsequently emerged from the milestone of *Bring the Jubilee*. One was the science-fiction/fantasy track that, arguably, culminated in Harry Turtledove's bizarre *The Guns of the South* (1992), in which a band of white supremacists from South Africa travel from the year 2014 back to Gettysburg with a supply of AK-47s to ensure a Confederate victory and give birth to a powerful ally that could, a century later, block the rise of Nelson Mandela (they are ultimately thwarted by the Confederate president, Robert E. Lee, who deems them too extreme in their racism). The other literary track led to the speculative history of MacKinlay Kantor's extended essay, *If the South Had Won the Civil War* (1960), which initially appeared in *Look* magazine's Civil War centenary issue. Along this track, it is once again the fate of particular individuals, rather than collective political or social movements, that determines the course of history. It is this choice that bears out David Blight's perception of a schism in public memory "between the war's results and the American tradition of civil rights reform," at least before Martin Luther King Jr. explicitly yoked them together in his "I Have a Dream" speech of 1963; as Blight argues, "In the period of the Centennial, from the 1950s to the mid-1960s, the two phenomena were too often like planets in separate orbits around different suns."[53] James Baldwin sensed the same thing in the midst of the centennial celebrations, as he wrote in an open letter to his nephew, published in the December 1962 issue of *The Progressive*: "You know, and I know, that the country is celebrating one hundred years of freedom one hundred years too soon."[54] Thus in Kantor's centennial essay – written even amid the unfolding of the integrationist sit-ins of Greensboro, North Carolina, and the birth of the Student Non-Violent Coordinating Committee – the historical tide is turned not by the accumulated energy of millions of activists on the battlefield, in the legislatures, and on the oratorical circuit, but rather by the death of one man: Ulysses Grant. In similar fashion, subsequent novels such as Benjamin King's *A Bullet for Stonewall* (1990) and Douglas Lee Gibboney's *Stonewall Jackson at Gettysburg* (1997) place the fate of an alternative America solely in the hands of the Confederacy's great martyr.

Edmund Wilson, writing from an avowedly Northern perspective in the midst of what he called "this absurd centennial" ("a day of mourning would be more appropriate"), argued: "We have tried to forget the Civil War, but we have had the defeated enemy on the premises, and he will not allow us to forget it."[55] If the Civil War has indeed continued to infect the literary mind and voice of the South, the output of two particular Southern authors may perhaps be seen as a metafictional commentary on that infection. Mississippi's Barry Hannah allowed the Civil War to intrude on his reflections of Vietnam in his short-story collection *Airships* (1978) and his novel *Ray* (1980), in which the Confederate general J.E.B. Stuart is a hallucinatory presence. The North Carolinian Allan Gurganus, in his epic novel *Oldest Living Confederate Widow Tells All* (1989), makes a similar historical connection through the eyes of his narrator, Lucy Marsden, widow of the last surviving Confederate veteran. At one point Lucy observes: "'The Rebs and the South Asian vets, they both lost. Makes your being home-and-hurting mean something different. You win, you're forgiven more. Lose, means you've lost, both in your own head and in others'."[56] For Lucy, the only way to soothe her husband's troubled memory is to whisper into his ear the mantra of the South's defeat: "Appomattox, Appomattox, Appomattox, baby."[57] Yet while that freighted word may have signalled the end of the Confederacy itself, it hardly serves as a descriptor for the war's end in the South's literary practice, for that end is not yet in sight.

NOTES

1 Shelby Foote in Ken Burns, *The Civil War* (Florentine Films, 1994), Episode 7.

2 Thomas Jefferson, *Notes on the State of Virginia* (Philadelphia: Pritchard and Hall, 1783), p. 175.

3 "Twelve Southerners," *I'll Take My Stand: The South and the Agrarian Tradition* (Baton Rouge: Louisiana State University Press, 1977), p. 91.

4 United Daughters of the Confederacy, *Creed of the Children of the Confederacy*: http://www.hqudc.org/CofC/index.html (accessed January 10, 2012).

5 Alexander Stephens in Henry Cleveland, ed., *Alexander H. Stephens in Public and Private: With Letters and Speeches Before, During, and Since the War* (Philadelphia: National Publishing Co., 1866), p. 721.

6 Richard Hildreth, *The Slave: Or, Memoirs of Archy Moore*, 2 vols. (Boston: John H. Eastburn, 1836), Vol. 2, p. 161.

7 Mary Henderson Eastman, *Aunt Phillis's Cabin; or, Southern Life As It Is* (Philadelphia: Lippincott, Grambo and Co., 1852), p. 260.

8 John W. Page, *Uncle Robin, in His Cabin in Virginia, and Tom Without One in Boston* (Richmond: J. W. Randolph, 1853), p. 265.

9 Lincoln quoted in Annie A. Fields, ed., *Life and Letters of Harriet Beecher Stowe* (Whitefish, MT: Kessinger Publishing, 2004 [1897]), p. 269.

10 Unidentified Richmond editor quoted in James M. McPherson, *Battle Cry of Freedom: The Civil War Era* (New York: Oxford University Press, 1988), p. 434.

11 William Gilmore Simms quoted in Alice Fahs, *The Imagined Civil War: Popular Literature of the North and South, 1861–1865* (Chapel Hill: University of North Carolina Press, 2001), p. 20.

12 Albert Pike, "Dixie," in Walter C. Bronson, ed. *American Poems, 1625–1892* (Chicago: University of Chicago Press, 1912), p. 498.

13 Henry Timrod, *The Poems of Henry Timrod, Ed., with a Sketch of the Poet's Life by Paul H. Hayne* (Ann Arbor: University of Michigan Scholarly Publishing Office, 2006 [1872]), pp. 83–84.

14 Harriet Jacobs, *Incidents in the Life of a Slave Girl*, ed. L. Maria Child (Boston: Published for the Author, 1861), p. 83. Electronic text at http://docsouth.unc.edu/southlit/harris/harris.html (accessed January 10, 2012).

15 Nina Silber, *The Romance of Reunion: Northerners and the South, 1865–1900* (Chapel Hill: University of North Carolina Press, 1993), p. 5.

16 Abram Joseph Ryan, "The Sword of Robert E. Lee," in *Father Ryan's Poems* (Mobile: Rapier and Co., 1879), pp. 18–19. Electronic text at http://docsouth. unc.edu/southlit/ryan/ryan.html (accessed January 10, 2012).

17 William Gilmore Simms, Preface, *War Poetry of the South* (Whitefish, MT: Kessinger Publishing, 2004 [1866]), p. 9.

18 Sidney Lanier, *Tiger-Lilies. A Novel* (New York: Hurd and Houghton, 1867), p. 120.

19 Joel Chandler Harris, *Uncle Remus, His Songs and Sayings* (New York: D. Appleton and Co., 1881), pp. 12, 179.

20 Harris, pp. 184–185.

21 Alexander Harper, *Johnny Reb and Billy Yank* (New York: Neale Publishing Co., 1905), p. 13.

22 Harper, pp. 712, 715.

23 Thomas Dixon quoted in Leon Litwack, "*The Birth of a Nation*," in Mark C. Carnes et al., eds., *Past Imperfect: History According to the Movies* (New York: Henry Holt and Co., 1995), pp. 136–141 (p. 138).

24 Thomas Dixon, *The Leopard's Spots: A Romance of the White Man's Burden, 1865–1900* (New York: Doubleday, Page and Co., 1902), p. 117.

25 Dixon, p. 101.

26 Thomas Dixon, *The Clansman: An Historical Romance of the Ku Klux Klan* (New York: Doubleday, Page and Co., 1905), p. 2. William Monroe Trotter quoted in Robert Lang, "*The Birth of A Nation*: History, Ideology, Narrative Form," in Robert Lang, ed., *The Birth of a Nation* (New Brunswick, NJ: Rutgers University Press, 1994), pp. 3–24 (p. 9).

27 Ellen Glasgow, *The Battle-Ground* (New York: Doubleday, Page and Co., 1902), p. 485.

28 James Hutchisson, Introduction to DuBose Heyward, *Peter Ashley* (Charleston, SC: History Press, 2004), p. 17.

29 Heyward, *Peter Ashley*, p. 364.

30 Stark Young, *So Red the Rose* (Nashville, TN: J. S. Sanders and Co., 1992), p. 44.

31 Margaret Mitchell, *Gone with the Wind* (New York: Warner Books, 1993), p. 511.

32 Mitchell, p. 1022.

33 Gordon in Sally Wood, ed., *The Southern Mandarins: Letters of Caroline Gordon to Sally Wood, 1924–1937* (Baton Rouge: Louisiana State University Press, 1984), p. 202.

34 Caroline Gordon, *None Shall Look Back* (Nashville, TN: J. S. Sanders, 1992 [1937]), p. 25.

35 "Twelve Southerners," *I'll Take My Stand*, p. xlii.

36 Mitchell, p. 177.

37 Gordon quoted in Nghana Tamu Lewis, *Entitled to the Pedestal: Place, Race, and Progress in White Southern Women's Writing, 1920–1945* (Iowa City: University of Iowa Press, 2007), p. 114.

38 David Blight, *Race and Reunion: The Civil War in American Memory* (Cambridge, MA: Harvard University Press, 2001), p. 284.

39 Craig A. Warren, *Scars to Prove It: The Civil War Soldier and American Fiction* (Kent, OH: Kent State University Press, 2009), p. 106.

40 William Faulkner, *The Unvanquished* (New York: Random House, 1938), pp. 7–8.

41 William Faulkner, *Intruder in the Dust* (London: Vintage, 1996), p. 194.

42 Leon F. Litwack, "Telling the Story: The Historian, the Filmmaker, and the Civil War," in Robert Brent Toplin, ed., *Ken Burns's* The Civil War: *Historians Respond* (New York: Oxford University Press, 1996): 119–140 (p. 133).

43 James Street, *Tap Roots* (New York: Book League of America, 1942), pp. 9, 11.

44 Victoria E. Bynum, *The Free State of Jones: Mississippi's Longest Civil War* (Chapel Hill: University of North Carolina Press, 2002), p. 3.

45 Ethel Knight quoted in Bynum, p. 3.

46 James Panabaker, *Shelby Foote and the Art of History: Two Gates to the City* (Knoxville: University of Tennessee Press, 2004), p. 168; Shelby Foote, *The Civil War*, 3 vols. (London: Pimlico, 1992 [1958]), Vol. 1, p. 354.

47 Shelby Foote, *Shiloh* (New York: Dial, 1952), p. 164.

48 C. Stuart Chapman, *Shelby Foote: A Writer's Life* (Jackson: University Press of Mississippi 2006), p. 108.

49 Randall Fuller, *From Battlefields Rising: How the Civil War Transformed American Literature* (New York: Oxford University Press, 2011), p. 68.

50 Herman Melville, "Shiloh – A Requiem (April 1862)," *Battle-Pieces and Aspects of the War: Civil War Poems* (Amherst: Prometheus Books, 2001), p. 63.

51 Chapman, p. 108.

52 Foote in Ken Burns, *The Civil War*, Episode 7.

53 David Blight, *American Oracle: The Civil War in the Civil Rights Era* (Cambridge, MA: Belknap/Harvard University Press, 2011), p. 2.

54 James Baldwin, "My Dungeon Shook: Letter to My Nephew on the One Hundredth Anniversary of the Emancipation" (1962), reprinted in Baldwin, *The Fire Next Time* (Harmondsworth: Penguin, 1964), p. 18.

55 Edmund Wilson, *Patriotic Gore: Studies in the Literature of the American Civil War* (New York: Oxford University Press, 1966 [1962]), p. xxxi.

56 Allan Gurganus, *Oldest Living Confederate Widow Tells All* (London: Faber, 1990), p. 207.

57 Gurganus, p. 6.

4

SCOTT ROMINE

Literature and Reconstruction

In "The Propaganda of History," the final chapter of his monumental *Black Reconstruction in America* (1935), W. E. B. Du Bois cast a withering glare at the historiography of Reconstruction. Noting that there is "scarce a child in the street that cannot tell you that the whole effort was a hideous mistake and an unfortunate incident, based on ignorance, revenge and the perverse determination to attempt the impossible," Du Bois attributed this childish knowledge to a propagandistic effort "to use history for our pleasure and amusement [and] for inflating our national ego." This usage, he argued, meant sacrificing the "scientific" nature of history and leaving "no room for the real plot of the story."[1] In inflecting the loss as both scientific *and* narrative – a loss of "accuracy and faithfulness of detail" on the one hand and of the *authentic plot* on the other – Du Bois gestures toward what his study, grounded in Marxist economics, tends elsewhere to elide: the deep connection between Reconstruction and the representational forms in which it was encoded. Despite its often tenuous connections to on-the-ground realities, the plot of Reconstruction's story – its distinctively *literary* dimension – had moved counter to the tale Du Bois wished to tell in 1935. There were counternarratives, to be sure, but the masterplot of Reconstruction, as both history and literature, evolved forcefully toward the account known to his child in the street.

When the *Atlantic Monthly* closed a year-long series of articles on Reconstruction in 1901, it noted that "[t]he final stage of the long reconstruction controversy seems to close, singularly enough, in the reversal of the very process which marked its inception. Reconstruction began with enfranchisement; it is ending with disfranchisement."[2] Dominated by the historian William A. Dunning and his professional cohort (interrupted notably by Du Bois in an article on the Freedman's Bureau), the series foregrounded the failed policies of national reunion as they were based in utopian notions of racial equality. As Dunning explained in the final article, the "Undoing of Reconstruction" naturally followed as the "abolitionist fervor" abated following the Civil War. History had shown, he wrote, that place of slavery "must be taken by some set of conditions which, if more humane and beneficent in accidents, must in essence express the same fact of racial inequality." Reconstruction was therefore doomed as an attempt to manage on an egalitarian basis the "coexistence in one society of two races so distinct in character as to render coalescence impossible."³ Perceptions of the "inevitability" of Reconstruction's failure were not new to Dunning. In an 1889 speech delivered in Boston's Faneuil Hall, the Southern journalist and New South propagandist Henry Grady described the futility of the South being asked to "reverse, under the very worst conditions, the universal verdict of racial history" – specifically, that "no two races, however similar, have lived anywhere at any time on the same soil with equal rights in peace!"⁴

Although Dunning and Grady appeal to racial truths they call *historical*, the print record of Reconstruction shows that race relations were quite often and explicitly understood as having literary influences. In a 1902 review of Thomas Dixon's *The Leopard's Spots*, the *New York Times* wrote that "[i]t took the good people of the North some time to discover that the negro is not as Mrs. Stowe imagined him, an Anglo-Saxon bound in black, and not a little sentimental gush characterized the early efforts for his improvement."⁵ However unjust, the claim accurately depicts a swerve away from the influence of Stowe toward less sympathetic literary representations of African Americans, and toward understandings of Reconstruction as an effort underwritten by "sentimental gush." As Jennifer Rae Greeson remarks of Reconstruction's "failure," it is "startling, indeed, to recognize how early the judgment on the project of Reconstruction was rendered in U.S. letters."⁶ References to Stowe in particular were ubiquitous in the postbellum period, not infrequently by African-American writers who, observing how the literary tide had turned since her day, urged an increased attention to literary efforts. As William Wells Brown wrote in *My Southern Home* (1880), "Feeling that the literature of our age is the reflection of the existing manners and modes of thought ... we should give our principal encouragement to literature," both as a means of developing "inward culture" and as a vehicle for, as Pauline Hopkins would later put it, "*Agitation and eternal vigilance in the formation of public opinion.*"⁷ As suggested by the title of Brown's work, which stakes a distinctively *African-American* claim to the South, the meaning of the South in Reconstruction writing emerged as a central concern. Here, too, however, the tide was against the efforts of Brown and his cohort as the South was transformed from a national antagonist, a military enemy defined by the institution of slavery, to a section whose reintegration – both political and literary – reproduced a racial hierarchy understood to be national in scope.

Literary efforts to facilitate the reconstruction of the nation followed soon after the war. John William De Forest's *Miss Ravenel's Conversion from Secession to Loyalty* (1867) follows the title character, a young Southern woman "strictly local, narrowly geographical in her feelings and opinions," as she abjures her treasonous and "barbarous" affiliations with the South to "make confession of her conversion" to national feeling and Unionist sentiment. In charting Miss Ravenel's marriage to two Union officers, the novel is unremittingly hostile to the South, a "compendium of injustice and wickedness."[8] By the time of *The Bloody Chasm* (1881), however, De Forest had muted his sectional critique. Although early in the work, a Bostonian finds the "flame-blackened desolation" of postwar Charleston to be "very comforting and exhilarating," the main thrust of the novel works to "clasp hands across the bloody chasm," as Horace Greeley had phrased his celebrated plea. The process of reconciliation is dramatized through a bizarre courtship plot between a Union veteran, Henry Underwood, and Virginia Beaufort, the sole descendant of a prosperous planter family devastated by the war. In order that Virginia receive an inheritance that will save her household, the couple marry (literally) in the dark and as total strangers before separating. Later, however, Henry courts Virginia in Paris posing as a Virginian. He wins her hand by producing, in response to her desire for "a great poet of the Southland – to mourn for our overthrow," a heroic poem celebrating the soldierly valor of Pickett's Charge. The none-too-subtle allegorical implications of the marriage – like the nation, Virginia and Henry are formally joined, but must learn to love "heart and soul" for the union to be meaningful – are happily resolved when Virginia, learning at last that the man she loves is actually her husband, swoons into his arms "as southern in her love as she had been in her hate."[9] Unlike the politicized courtship plot of *Miss Ravenel's Conversion*, which requires the ideological conversion of the Southern bride, here the Northern groom must learn to empathize with Southern suffering in order for sectional difference to be surmounted.

The shift from *Miss Ravenel's Conversion* to *The Bloody Chasm* marks in two particulars the changing literary and cultural climate between the onset of Reconstruction and its immediate aftermath. First, as Nina Silber shows in *The Romance of Reunion* (1993), the courtship plot had evolved to produce endless variations of the "symbolic marital alliance which became the principal representation of sectional reunion."[10] In addition, soldierly valor had emerged as a cultural fetish largely severed from the politics of the war. The Union soldiers of De Forest's earlier novel fight for a cause, whereas *The Bloody Chasm* explains that soldiers "may fight under hostile flags, but still they are comrades."[11] Both trends appear in works as dissimilar as Thomas Nelson Page's "Meh Lady: A Story of the War" and Henry James's

The Bostonians, both published in 1886. Page's story, which appeared in *Harper's Monthly*, is a standard allegory of sectional reconciliation realized through the title character's courtship with a Union soldier. Her own brother having fallen in a heroic cavalry charge, Meh Lady initially refuses the attentions of her "Virginia' enemy," a distant cousin whom she nurses after he is wounded in a charge nearly identical to her brother's. As a result of his gallant behavior, she eventually relents, and the marriage signals the resolution of what proves to have been, all along, a family affair. Written in an entirely different literary key, James's novel was serialized in *The Century Magazine* alongside a series of Civil War remembrances by Union and Confederate soldiers. The novel follows Confederate veteran Basil Ransom as he courts a Boston feminist, eventually persuading her to renounce her public activism to inhabit the private space of his household. The turning point of the courtship comes at Harvard's Memorial Hall when Basil, confronting the memorialization of the Union dead, forgets "the whole question of sides and parties" and experiences the monument as "arch[ing] over friends as well as enemies, the victims of defeat as well as the sons of triumph."[12] The sentiment permeates more politicized works. One of the conventions of anti-Reconstruction novels is that veterans north and south are willing to let bygones be bygones, while the vicious carpetbaggers and scalawags inevitably come from the ranks of the draft-dodgers and profiteers.

As Reconstruction emerged as a literary subject, the depoliticized memorialization of the War signaled neither a renunciation of politics nor the triumph of Southern ideology over a beguiled, if victorious, North. The oft-repeated formula that the North won the war but the South won the peace neglects that the North hardly lost the peace, remaining the locus of national economic and political power throughout the late nineteenth century. Moreover, Northern demand for Southern accounts of Reconstruction, both literary and journalistic, signaled an active desire for the ideological work such texts performed. Albion Tourgée only slightly overstated the case in his 1888 essay "South as a Field for Fiction" when he wrote that "[o]ur literature has become not only Southern in type, but distinctly Confederate in sympathy."[13] Certainly this was true of periodical literature, as Tourgée noted in observing that popular monthlies and newspapers were dominated by Southern stories and sketches. Although Tourgée saw potential in this trend, no one in American letters had done more to check its more pernicious ideological effects, and no writer had been more acute in critiquing Reconstruction's shifting position in the national consciousness.

In *A Fool's Errand* (1879), the first major novel of Reconstruction, Tourgée had taken dead aim at the nation's peculiar hostility toward the aims and agents of Reconstruction policy. Of the "carpet-bagger" (the most "perfect and complete ... epithet" in "all history"), he writes that "there is no other instance in history in which the conquering power has discredited its own agents, denounced those of its own blood and faith, espoused the prejudices of its conquered foes, and poured the vials of its wrath and contempt upon the only class in the conquered territory who defended its acts, supported its policy, promoted its aim, or desired its preservation and continuance." A carpetbagger himself, Tourgée based *A Fool's Errand* on his postwar experiences in Greensboro, North Carolina. As its title suggests, the novel's protagonist, Comfort Servosse, is positioned in a quixotic effort quickly abandoned by Reconstruction's "managers" in the nation's capital. Conceding late in the novel that Reconstruction was a "magnificent failure" as a "logical sequence of the war," as "it attempted to unify the nation" and sought "to fix and secure the position and rights of the colored race," Servosse nonetheless affirms that "Reconstruction was a great step in advance" because "[i]t recognized and formulated the universality of manhood in governmental power, and, in one phase or another of its development, compelled the formal assent of all sections and parties." Precisely because he refuses one ending – the Civil War as the end of slavery, which he claims continues in fact if not in law – he can refuse another: the real history of Reconstruction has not ended because "the struggle between North and South" has "just begun!"; the "irrepressible conflict" yet confronts the nation.[14]

In characterizing Reconstruction as an open-ended process best understood as a sectional conflict, Tourgée sharply contested an alternative account that saw Reconstruction as a closed chapter doomed by racial difference. In his sustained critique of the Northern press – he writes, for example, of how the term "carpetbagger" "Instantly ... spread through the press of the South; and, with its usual subserviency, that of the North followed in its lead, and re-echoed its maledictions" – Tourgée identified a likely antagonist.[15] A Reconstruction advocate writing anonymously in 1874 imagined the white South, stymied in its military and political efforts to deny "the negro ... all the rights of a free citizen," formulating a new strategy: "Let us carry the war into a department into which [the negro] cannot follow us; let us bring the press to bear against him, that we may make him odious, after which we may somehow get rid of him." The effort, the writer conceded, had shown marked success; from Southern newspapers to the Northern media flowed unimpeded allegations of "the most terrible charges against those 'negro governments'" and depictions of a "scene of horror and ruin all over that 'sunny land' that only the hardest-hearted could fail to pity."[16] Although exaggerated, the claim was hardly inaccurate.

As this account suggests, the selection bias at work often turned on representations of "negro rule." In an 1868 article entitled "Negro Rule at the

South," the Northern journalist Edward Kingsbury reported, following a visit to South Carolina, that he "could no longer be blind to the fact that soon *all* the offices would be held, and the laws made, by the colored men." Their manifest "lack of capacity to govern or well-provide for themselves" led Kingsbury to empathize with the "humiliating and deplorable" position of white South Carolinians.[17] In *The Southern States since the War, 1870–1871*, the British writer Robert Somers similarly lamented that "the negro has, up to this period of 'reconstruction,' enjoyed a monopoly of representation, and has had all legislative and executive power moulded to his will .... For five years past, the negroes have been King, Lords, and Commons, and something more, in the Southern States."[18] Edward King's massive *Great South* project – serialized in *Scribner's* in 1873–1874 and published in book form in 1875 – repeatedly characterizes Reconstruction governments as corrupt, often attributing the corruption to racial characteristics. In Louisiana, the Reconstruction government, "composed of ignorant and immoral negroes," is said to have held the state "completely in its power, and gross frauds were perpetrated." From Charleston, King reports that "[t]he Negro is impressed with the idea that South Carolina should be in some measure a black man's government.... The black man lets the African in him run riot for the time being ... [and finds] fascination in the use of political machinery for purposes of oppression and spoliation."[19] Modern historians have amply demonstrated that Reconstruction governments were neither as corrupt nor dominated by African Americans as the contemporaneous picture usually suggested, which raises the question of why this iconography was so pervasive. Clearly, the specter of negro rule delimited the terms in which sovereignty was conceivable to a nation increasingly committed to the project of modernity; typically, the freedman appears in Reconstruction writing as an embodiment of backwardness and barbarism, a subject lacking in self-government and thus unable to function as a citizen of the modern nation-state.

Perhaps no work better captures the nation's changing attitudes toward Reconstruction than Stephen T. Robinson's *The Shadow of the War: A Story of the South in Reconstruction Times* (1884). Although the novel includes a standard romance of reunion, the more important conversion occurs in the Northern bride's father, who comes south to invest in cotton manufacturing. Basil Gildersleeve is a Republican and an Abolitionist, and the narrative initially displays a deep antipathy toward Southern efforts to reverse "what her sword could not prevent" through Black Codes and Kukluxism – efforts that "degrade her civilization before the world." Initially outraged that the freedman, "now an American citizen, entitled to all the rights, privileges, and protection which that citizenship confers," is denied those rights by "despicable methods," Gildersleeve comes to view negro rule as an even greater assault on the American nation, concluding that while Reconstruction was a well-intentioned effort to render the Union's victory permanent, "if the authors of that measure could have foreseen the horrors and crimes which the establishment of Radical government entailed ... they would surely have shrunk from its contemplation." As it arcs toward a deep antipathy to negro rule – a reality represented as unknown in the North, where the press continues to recycle old mythologies of racial oppression – *The Shadow of the War* involves a reconfiguration of locality that would deeply influence the literary landscape of the late nineteenth century. Although Gildersleeve initially imagines that he is moving to a place "in many respects very provincial" – a backwater in dire need of economic and cultural development – his experience shows that local arrangements in the South have pedagogical implications of national import.[20]

In representing a local polity under racial siege, Robinson prefigures many later writers, several of whom made their literary reputations in the genre of local color or regionalism. Joel Chandler Harris, the creator of Uncle Remus, begins *Gabriel Tolliver: A Story of Reconstruction* (1902) in "the serene repose of Shady Dale," which "no doubt stood for dulness and lack of progress in that day and time."[21] Although the novel begins in the standard locale of literary regionalism – to borrow Richard Brodhead's formulation, in a palpably fictitious "representation of vernacular cultures as enclaves of tradition insulated from larger cultural contact" – it ends with the insulation gone and the community fully wired to the nation-state.[22] This transition involves a compromising logic that disavows revenge as a response to Reconstruction outrages. Despite the injuries he has suffered at the hands of marauding carpetbaggers, Gabriel Tolliver gives a climactic speech in which he whips the crowd into a Unionist frenzy by denouncing redeemer politicians who "turn us against a Government under which we are compelled to live." In the interim, however, the novel develops an antagonism between locality and nation that accumulates with great force around the trope of negro rule.

As *Gabriel Tolliver* shifts from a local color mode that dominates its early chapters to its story of Reconstruction, the narrative becomes, for a time, quite hysterical. Despite assuming a distant, retrospective posture in assuring readers that "matters have changed greatly since those days," the narrative also affirms that it is "[i]mpossible for any impartial person" to ignore that the "prime movers of the Reconstruction scheme" were intent on deliberately "placing the Governments of the Southern States in the hands of ignorant negroes" and "on stirring up a new revolution in the hope of that the negroes might be prevailed upon to sack cities and towns, and destroy the white population." Against such a threat, the community of "repose and serenity" is forced to mobilize through the Knights of the White Camellia, a Klan-like organization whose racial terrorism receives full narrative sanction.[23]

If, as Amy Kaplan argues, regionalist writing sought the "primal origins of American nationality in prenational communities and clans," the ascendant narrative of Reconstruction configured such communities as *proto*-national, as latent sites of nationalist feeling awakened to history – often forcefully and against their will – and, in turn, awakening the nation to its authentic (racial) origins and sense of mission.[24] Drawing as well on the power of sympathy underlying the sentimental tradition, such narratives embed melodramas of besieged locality whose racial premises would prove desirable in an age of empire requiring new structures of national feeling. Like *Gabriel Tolliver*, Thomas Nelson's Page's *Red Rock: A Chronicle of Reconstruction* (1898) begins in a provincial "Old Country" "*far from the centers of modern progress*" and ends with the province integrated into a nation whose authority is validated once the carpetbagger "harpies" are "put to flight." Page's novel is even starker than Harris's in depicting how the inhabitants of Red Rock "*were subjected to the greatest humiliation of modern times: their slaves were put over them – they reconquered their section and preserved the civilization of the Anglo-Saxon.*" Ironically, Reconstruction is, for most of the Northern characters, a principled assault on economic disorder, racial tyranny, and cultural backwardness. Good intentions up north, however, do not export well to Dixie, as becomes evident to Mrs. Welch, a Yankee matron duped by the carpetbagger journalism into supporting what she believes to be a philanthropic project of moral and cultural uplift. Upon arriving in Red Rock, however, she overhears a speech by a freedman politician that concludes with the same sentiment that so struck Edward King in Charleston: "the bottom rail is on top, and we mean to keep it so till the fence rots down, by – -!" Soon, her letter homes suggest to her Northern friends that she "was already succumbing to the very influence she repudiated"; as one puts it, "I never knew anyone go down there who did not … fall a victim to the influences of those people."[25]

Mrs. Welch's mission, to found a school for the newly freed slaves, was a common subject in Reconstruction writing. As Peter Schmidt shows in *Sitting in Darkness: New South Fiction, Education, and Rise of Jim Crow Colonialism, 1865–1920* (2008), black education emerged as a central scene of evaluating, promoting, or denigrating the freedman's capacity to acquire the mental and cultural habits understood as prerequisites of citizenship. Among the most powerful efforts to document the cultural meaning of education for the African-American community was Tourgée's *Bricks Without*

Straw (1880). Two scenes in that novel, however, suggest the limits of education as a vehicle of racial ascent. When, early in the novel, the black community desires to use the local schoolhouse as a polling place, the Northern
schoolmistress opposes the plan, believing that the overt exercise of political
rights there would "excite unnecessary antipathy" in the white community
and thus threaten what she perceives as "the most important element of
the colored man's development, the opportunity for education."[26] Whatever
Tourgée's intentions, the schoolmistress's accommodation characterizes
an increasing gap between educational attainment and political agency.
Although Northern support of black education far outlived its support of
Radical Reconstruction, it was increasingly dissociated from the political
aims of that project, culminating in the support of such politically neutered
institutions as Booker T. Washington's Tuskegee Institute. Evolving from
earlier tendencies in abolitionist discourse, the discourse of racial uplift
through education positioned the freedman as an object of white benevolence in a way that proved curiously consonant with the idiom of Southern
paternalism. Even African Americans were not immune from the trend.
The black historian George Washington Williams wrote in 1883 that the
"unceremonious" removal of the Negro from Southern politics was regrettable, but also inevitable. "The government," Williams explained, "placed
him in the Legislature when he ought to have been in the school-house."
Calling on the black community to "rejoice that they are out of politics,"
Williams looked forward to a future time when an educated people would
return to politics "equal to all the exigencies of American citizenship."[27]

In a later scene from *Bricks without Straw*, Eliab Hill, the spiritual and
intellectual leader of the black community, explains to the schoolmistress
that he is functionally illiterate, able to read "words" but not the meanings
they carry. Although he characterizes this dysfunction as cultural – a matter
of lacking the "part of knowledge that can't be put in books" – alternative
readings of low educational attainment proceeded along predictable racial-
ist lines.[28] Constance Fenimore Woolson's "King David," a sketch originally
published in *Scribner's* in 1878, shows an ineffectual Northern schoolmas-
ter, David King, buffeted on the shoals of African-American ignorance. Full
of fervor, he moves south to do "work fitted for his hand" despite the skepticism of New Hampshire neighbors who affirm that "[w]e've paid dear
enough to set 'em free, goodness knows, and now they ought to look out for
themselves." Practical education, however, proves impossible as the black
community of Jubilee lapses into drunkenness, riot, and indolence. Despite
his antipathy toward personal contact with the freedmen, King persists in
his quixotic hope that success "would come in time." The Southern patrician
to whom he voices this opinion, however, responds that "[t]he Negro with

power in his hand, which you have given him, with a little smattering of knowledge in his shallow, crafty brain – a knowledge which you and your kind are now striving to give him – will become an element of more danger in this land than it has ever known before." Getting much the better of the exchange, the Southerner is further authorized by two ironies: first, that the "smattering of knowledge" he fears amounts to hardly that among a cohort struggling to spell "cat" after half a year's effort; and second, that he receives from his servant, a man described as having "scarcely more intelligence than the dog that followed him," an affection that King realizes is altogether absent in his relationship with his students. Although Woolson halfheartedly attempts to introduce a measure of pathos into King's quixotic mission, the dominant note of the sketch is one of contempt for the freedman; the last word goes to the New Englander who, chortling over King's return to teach at the local (white) school, observes that he "[d]idn't find the blacks what he expected, I guess."[29]

It is difficult to overstate how widely that sentiment – frustration that "the Negro" was not "as expected" – was expressed in national print culture, even among writers supportive of African-American civil rights. A Union soldier in De Forest's *Miss Ravenel's Conversion* reports that, "hav[ing] freed … as many of these lazy bumpkins as I have," he feels at liberty to report that "I am as much an abolitionist as ever, but not so much of a 'nigger-worshipper.'" A character in Frances E. W. Harper's *Iola Leroy, or Shadows Uplifted* (1892) similarly recognizes Northern prejudice, observing that "some of these northern soldiers do two things – hate slavery and hate niggers."[30] George Washington Cable's *The Grandissimes* (1880), set in New Orleans around the time of the Louisiana Purchase but obviously intended as a commentary on Reconstruction, presents black characters who are dominated by a desire for revenge (Palmyre Philosophe) or, worse, apathy. In a dispiriting preview of Du Bois's theory of double-consciousness, the free man of color Honoré Grandissime is described as "[w]ithered … not in the shadow of the Ethiopian, but in the glare of the white man." Honoré refuses the encouragement of his Northern interlocutor to work collectively to gain "public education for the rights of all." Prodded that, "[a]s your class stands before the world today – free in form but slaves in spirit – you are … a warning to philanthropy," Honoré responds, plaintively, "Ah cannod be one Toussaint l'Ouverture."[31] An active engagement with a shifting social and political environment is reserved for his white half-brother, also named Honoré Grandissime, who escapes the bind of his family's tribal code of honor and adapts to the new American government. Moreover, the white Honoré scandalizes his family by entering into a business partnership with his half-brother.

Despite the novel's powerful rendering of racial trauma and its sincere effort to steer a middle course between radicalism and reactionary traditionalism, it fails to imagine a place for the free man of color in the Louisiana of the early nineteenth century or its encoded postbellum counterpart. As in "The Freedman's Case in Equity," Cable's celebrated 1885 essay that argued for political but not social equality for African Americans, *The Grandissimes* denies its black characters access to the novel's social and erotic economies. Romance is strictly limited to intraracial encounters despite desires that transgress a murky color line. As John Morán González observes, while the dual courtship plots among whites signal, respectively, the Old South's accession to commercial modernity and the "new national unity achieved through such modernization," the novel "offers no such happy union for the freedman."[32] Near the conclusion of the novel, Honoré f.m.c. commits suicide.

When, in his 1894 *John March, Southerner*, Cable turned to Reconstruction as an explicit subject, he produced a work more oriented toward the perspective of the black community. Although the novel avoids the taboo subject of social equality, it offers in Cornelius Leggett one of the most compelling black characters in Reconstruction writing. Personally objectionable – he is a philanderer, child-beater, and political scoundrel – Leggett also genuinely works for the welfare of his people and articulates the core ideals of Cable's post-Reconstruction South. His assertion that "niggers steals with they claws, white men with they laws" is borne out when a Confederate war hero defrauds the public by profiteering from a plan to develop land in a way that will benefit the entire community. In a more positive vein, Leggett suggests that the South needs to become not a "white man's country, naw a black man's country, naw yit mix the races an' make it a yaller man's country," but a "po' man's country" – that is, "a country what's good for a po' man."[33] Reflecting the logic of the Fusionist movement of 1890s, Leggett privileges social class over race, emphasizing the need for a public education system that would benefit all.

African-American writers of the 1890s similarly emphasized the importance of education. The title character of Harper's *Iola Leroy* works for a time in Reconstruction schools attempting to build "more stately temples of thought and action" by which "the true reconstruction of the country" might be accomplished.[34] Iola, raised as a white girl before her racial identity is revealed by a malicious relative, refuses (as her mother had not) the respectable intentions of a white man who seeks to marry her. Although Harper documents the economy of rape that would reduce Iola to a sexual object of white desire, her staging of interracial domesticity – achieved by Iola's father and sought by Dr. Gresham, the principled Northerner who wishes to marry Iola – constitutes a more nuanced intervention in the discourses of Reconstruction sexuality. Even for white liberals such as Cable, the private space of the home remained marked by the color line as impassable, while the romance of reunion inevitably assumed racial homogeneity. For Page in *Red Rock*, sectional reconciliation through marriage is possible because (white) "[g]entlemen" – and gentlewomen – are "the same the world over," a formulation that privileges genteel protocols of social recognition.[35] In the character of Iola, Harper constructs a paragon of genteel virtue – chaste, beautiful, culturally accomplished – but one who remains committed to racial solidarity. Harper stages her novel as a family reunion, as Iola reconstitutes a family geographically fractured by slavery and Reconstruction and ends by marrying a black physician who will join her in the project of racial uplift to make their lives "a blessing to others."[36]

In conceding the need for uplift, however, Harper, like most black writers of the decade, moved on a literary terrain sloped against African-American interests. Interrogating the "mighty working of cause and effect" in race relations, Pauline Hopkins followed Harper in adapting the sentimental novel and its dependence on genteel conventions. In *Contending Forces* (1900) and other novels, Hopkins offers a range of characters whose mixed-race backgrounds unsettle the certainties of white supremacy, but often by reproducing the causal assumptions behind those certainties. In one of the novel's frequent discursive asides, the narrator of *Contending Forces* adopts the language of social Darwinism to opine that "the Negro race must be productive of some valuable specimens, if only from the infusion which amalgamation with a superior race must eventually bring." *Contending Forces* includes a not unsympathetic portrait of a black leader (clearly modeled on Booker T. Washington) who declares that "politics is the bane of the Negro's existence," abjures any "wish to rule," and defers to "the superiority of brain and intellect which hundreds of years have developed" in the white man. By no means, however, does he have the last word; two later speakers rhetorically obliterate his speech by recounting the abuses of slavery and demanding a commitment to civil rights in a postwar nation to eager to "sacrifice any race, any principle" to bring an end to sectional division.

The delicate balancing act on display in what Hopkins characterizes as a project of "[a]gitation and eternal vigilance in the formation of public opinion" – the only weapons that will combat "the systematic destruction of the Negro by every device which the fury of enlightened malevolence can invent" – is also evident in Sutton E. Griggs's *Imperium in Imperio* (1899). The novel involves a revolutionary plot by the Imperium, a secret African-American organization that (repeating an earlier moment of U.S. expansionism) plans to annex Texas as an African-American nation.

Provoked by two events – the nation's entrance into the Spanish-American
War and a historically based lynching of a black postmaster – the Imperium
is on the verge of declaring that "the hour for wreaking vengeance for
our multiplied wrongs has come" when it is interrupted by the novel's
hero, Belton Piedmont, who denounces the plan as treasonous. Although
Piedmont excoriates mob law, the corruption of the courts, and the "stolen
ballot box," he also reiterates key features of white discourses surrounding
Reconstruction, suggesting that freedmen had misused the ballot, that "our
race has furnished some brutes lower than the beasts of the field," and,
most crucially, that Anglo-Saxon civilization had awakened the "the negro
… asleep in the jungles of Africa" and provided him with education, a conception of freedom, and Christianity.[37]

Belton Piedmont ends his speech with an appeal to the pen, a weapon he
calls mightier than the sword or the ballot. As the United States entered a
new age of imperialism, however, the weaponized pen was wielded more
violently, and more successfully, by Griggs's literary antagonists, foremost among them Thomas Dixon, Jr., whose Reconstruction trilogy – *The
Leopard's Spots* (1902), *The Clansman* (1905), and *The Traitor* (1907) –
intervened with malignant genius in the discursive field of Reconstruction.
Where Griggs, Hopkins, and Harper were forced to contend with representations of Reconstruction that diminished the cultural and political capacities
of African Americans, Dixon extended the narrative in the opposite direction,
telling Reconstruction as a story of Negro barbarism threatening a besieged
and imperiled white nation. Although the historical Klan had been met by
genuine alarm in the national press and occasioned in some states force-
ful federal intervention, Dixon reconfigured the Klan as culture heroes of
an Anglo-Saxon nation. *The Clansman*, which would serve as the basis for
D. W. Griffith's monumental film *Birth of a Nation* (1915), revises many of
the conventions and themes of the evolving Reconstruction narrative, always
by emphatically linking them to white supremacy. The courtship plot, which
had, in the work of Page and others, embedded a conception of gentility
available to the likes of Harper and Hopkins, becomes, in Dixon's work,
an explicitly racial matter. Where Dunning school historiography had presented Reconstruction as a doomed and misguided effort, Dixon describes an
intentionally malicious plan to "Africanize ten great states of the American
union." The political ascent of African Americans appears not merely as corrupt "negro rule," but an inevitable precursor to the sexual assault of white
women. Masterminded by Austin Stoneman, a lightly fictionalized version
of the Radical Republican Thaddeus Stevens, Reconstruction is intended as
a plot not to rebuild the nation, but to destroy it. When Lincoln describes
his plan to reconstruct an "indissoluble Union," Stoneman counters that

the "so-called [southern] states" are but "conquered provinces," "waste territories ... unfit to associate with civilized communities."[38]

As this passage suggests, the idiom of empire pervades Dixon's fiction, most prominently in *The Leopard's Spots*. Subtitled "A Romance of the White Man's Burden, 1865–1900" (an allusion to the Kipling poem occasioned by U.S. intervention in the Philippines), *The Leopard's Spots* devotes only its first third to the Reconstruction era and the triumph of the Klan. After the Klan "saves civilization," one of its leaders announces that the "redeemed" white state can survive only "so as long as the white people are a unit." As the novel shifts to its climactic encounter in the late 1890s, white unity is under siege from a Fusionist coalition of white Republicans and African Americans, thereby unsettling what Dixon imagines as the key question confronting the nation: "*Shall the future American be an Anglo-Saxon or a Mulatto?*" The U.S. entrance into the Spanish-American War clarifies the issue, causing the "Anglo-Saxon race" to become "united into one homogeneous mass" and banishing the "the Negro" from his position as "ward of the nation." In a climactic speech, the novel's protagonist, Charles Gaston, offers the lesson of Reconstruction to an imperial nation. With reference to the Philippines, Gaston observes that "our flag has been raised over ten millions of semi-barbaric black men in the foulest slave pen of the Orient. Shall we repeat the farce of '67, reverse the order of nature, and make these black people our rulers?"[39] Although Dixon's racism was extreme even by the standards of his time, his linkage of white supremacy and the ideological demands of imperialism was not unusual; appeals to a sense of Anglo-Saxon mission in an age of empire were common in the flood of Reconstruction novels published in the decade after 1898.

The previously cited *Times* review of *The Leopard's Spots* goes on to claim that "[t]he author does not overstate the evils resulting to both races from the bestowal of the ballot upon the negro, nor the carnival of insolent misrule attending negro domination." In comparing Dixon's novel with the "self-evident" historical realities of the period it represents, the reviewer reiterates Dixon's own insistence that he was writing history, taking only the liberty "to tone down the [historical] facts to make them credible in fiction."[40] Altogether lacking on the reviewer's part (but probably not on Dixon's) is an awareness of how fiction had *shaped* history, or what passed for it. Reconstruction narratives of Southern communities under racial siege found an eager national audience, at once permitting the "race problem" to be banished to an imagined geography south of Mason-Dixon *and* underwriting the prerogatives of whiteness – the *imperatives* of whiteness – for an expansionist nation at the edge of empire. From this vantage, Reconstruction appeared increasingly as a deviation from national ideals, and the communities who suffered its assault as the sources of an American identity fitted for an imperialist age.

When, in *Black Reconstruction*, Du Bois set about undoing what the *Atlantic* had called the "undoing of Reconstruction," he did so as a historian, and it must be said that professional historiography, in the figures of C. Vann Woodward, Kenneth Stampp, Eric Foner, and others, has done more to combat the mythologies of the period than has modern fiction. Margaret Mitchell's *Gone with the Wind* (1936) reproduces the standard account of an era of riot and misrule dominated by carpetbaggers, as does, in a different key, William Faulkner's *Go Down, Moses* (1942), which characterizes a "dark and bloody time" shaped by freedmen "upon whom freedom and equality had been dumped overnight and without warning or preparation or any training in how to employ it" and by carpetbaggers driven by "a single fierce will for rapine and pillage."[41] The socialist writer Howard Fast countered this version in *Freedom Road* (1944), a historical novel whose debt to Du Bois is evident throughout, most conspicuously in borrowing Du Bois's concept of the "psychological wage" of whiteness; the novel's villains enact revenge by playing "a symphony on that white skin [and making] it a badge of honor." *Freedom Road* traces the postwar development of the interracial community of Carwell, which operates successfully until the Klan destroys it following the withdrawal of federal troops. In an afterword, Fast observes that the memory of this "eight year period of Negro and white cooperation" had been "expunged" from national memory; "powerful forces" had conspired to prevent the American people from knowing that the "experiment had worked."[42]

For modern African-American writers, Reconstruction has most frequently appeared as a dispiriting era of unfulfilled promise, although one often juxtaposed against the promises of the present. The narrator of Ralph Ellison's *Invisible Man* (1952) is haunted by the deathbed advice of his grandfather (a self-described "spy in the enemy's country ever since I give up my gun back in the Reconstruction") to "agree 'em to death and destruction" – words the narrator finally understands as a call to "affirm the principle on which the country was built, and not the men, or at least not the men who did the violence."[43] Margaret Walker's *Jubilee* (1966) powerfully describes the deteriorating political landscape for African Americans in Alabama and especially Georgia, where a former suitor of the author's great-grandmother is driven from his land by a reactionary white politician. The subtitle of the "Reconstruction" section of Ernest Gaines's *Autobiography of Miss Jane Pittman* (1971), "A Flicker of Light; and Again Darkness," indicates the transition from hope to despair experienced by that novel's characters, who move essentially from one form of slavery to another. Later, however, from the vantage of the civil rights movement, the title character describes Reconstruction as a crucial scene of black persistence and desire for cultural heroes: "People's always looking for somebody to come lead them.... They did it in slavery; after the war they did it; they did it in the hard times that people want call Reconstruction; they did it in the Depression – another hard times; and they doing it now."[44] The hopefulness of Gaines's novel is intensified in Alice Randall's *The Wind Done Gone* (2001), which describes the end of Reconstruction's "short night" as "our Götterdämmerung."[45] The twilight of the African-American gods is only momentary, however, as the narrative soon shifts to a present landscape of black political and cultural ascent.

Despite the existence of these works (many of which treat the period only briefly), it must be observed that Reconstruction has never proven to be the fertile literary ground of the historical periods – antebellum slavery and the Civil War – to which is it most closely connected. When Woodward called attention to the parallels between Reconstruction and the civil rights movement, he did so hopefully – by noting crucial differences that pointed to "the triumph of the Second Reconstruction – *in the long run*."[46] The failures of the First have perhaps rendered it resistant to subsequent use, even in art.

NOTES

1 W. E. B Du Bois, *Black Reconstruction in America: An Essay toward a History of the Part Which Black Folk Played in the Attempt to Reconstruct Democracy in America, 1860–1880* (Oxford: Oxford University Press, 2007), pp. 587, 584, 585.

2 "Reconstruction and Disenfranchisement," *Atlantic Monthly* 88 (1901), p. 343.

3 William A. Dunning, "The Undoing of Reconstruction," *Atlantic Monthly* 88 (1901), p. 449.

4 Henry Grady, "The Race Problem in the South," *The New South: Writings and Speeches of Henry Grady* (Savannah, GA: Beehive Press, 1971), pp. 92, 91.

5 "Mr. Dixon's 'The Leopard's Spots,'" *New York Times* (April 5, 1902), p. BR10.

6 Jennifer Rae Greeson, *Our South: Geographic Fantasy and the Rise of National Literature* (Cambridge, MA: Harvard University Press, 2010), p. 254.

7 William Wells Brown, *My Southern Home: Or, The South and Its People* (Boston: A. G. Brown and Company, 1880), pp. 242, 241; Pauline Hopkins, *Contending Forces: A Romance Illustrative of Negro Life North and South* (New York: Oxford University Press, 1988), p. 245.

8 J. W. De Forest, *Miss Ravenel's Conversion from Secession to Loyalty* (New York: Harper and Brothers, 1867), pp. 17, 463, 206.

9 J. W. De Forest, *The Bloody Chasm* (New York: D. Appleton and Company, 1881), pp. 21, 232, 298.

10 Nina Silber, *The Romance of Reunion: Northerners and the South, 1865–1900* (Chapel Hill: University of North Carolina Press, 1993) p. 6.

11 De Forest, *The Bloody Chasm*, 24.

12 Thomas Nelson Page, "Meh Lady: A Story of the War," in *In Ole Virginia* (New York: Charles Scribner's Sons, 1887), p. 102; Henry James, *The Bostonians* (New York: Modern Library, 2003), p. 235.

13 Albion W. Tourgée, "The South as a Field for Fiction," *The Forum* 6 (1888), p. 405.

14 Tourgée, *A Fool's Errand* (Cambridge, MA: Belknap Press, 1961) pp. 168, 338, 338, 340.

15 Tourgée, *A Fool's Errand*, p. 158.

16 "What Shall Be Done with the Freedman?," *Christian Advocate* 49 (August 27, 1874), p. 276.

17 E. Kingsbury, "Negro Rule at the South," *New York Evangelist* 39 (May 1868), p. 2.

18 Robert Somers, *The Southern States since the War, 1870–1871* (London: Macmillan, 1871), p. 129.

19 Edward King, *The Great South* (Hartford, CT: American Publishing Company, 1875), pp. 91, 452–453.

20 Stephen T. Robinson, *The Shadow of the War: A Story of the South in Reconstruction Times* (Chicago: Jansen, McClurg, and Company, 1884), pp. 6, 34, 185, 7–8.

21 Joel Chandler Harris, *Gabriel Tolliver: A Story of Reconstruction* (New York: McClure, Phillips, and Company, 1902), p. 18.

22 Richard Brodhead, *Cultures of Letters: Scenes of Reading and Writing in Nineteenth-Century America* (Chicago: University of Chicago Press, 1993), p. 121.

23 Harris, *Gabriel Tolliver*, pp. 441, 242, 243, 242.

24 Amy Kaplan, "Nation, Region, Empire" in *The Columbia History of the American Novel: New Views*, ed. Emory Elliott (New York: Columbia University Press, 1991), p. 223.

25 Thomas Nelson Page, *Red Rock: A Chronicle of Reconstruction* (New York: Charles Scribner's Sons, 1898), pp. vii, 580, viii, 321, 333.

26 Albion W. Tourgée, *Bricks without Straw* (New York: Fords, Howard, and Hulbert, 1880), p. 145.

27 George Washington Williams, *History of the Negro of the Negro Race in American from 1619 to 1880: Negroes as Slaves, As Soldiers, and as Citizens: Volume II* (New York: G. P. Putnam's Sons, 1883), pp. 527, 528.

28 Tourgée, *Bricks without Straw*, p. 169.

29 Constance Fenimore Woolson, "King David" in *Rodman the Keeper: Southern Sketches* (New York: Harper and Brothers, 1886), pp. 255, 262, 262–263, 263, 275.

30 De Forest, *Miss Ravenel's Conversion*, 240; Frances E. W. Harper, *Iola Leroy Or, Shadows Uplifted* (Philadelphia: Garrigues Brothers, 1893), p. 49.

31 George W. Cable, *The Grandissimes: A Story of Creole Life* (New York: Charles Scribner's Sons, 1880), pp. 197, 255, 256.

32 John Morán González, *The Troubled Union: Expansionist Imperatives in Post-Reconstruction American Novels* (Columbus: The Ohio State University Press, 2010), p. 14.

33 George W. Cable, *John March, Southerner* (New York: Charles Scribner's Sons, 1894), pp. 95, 121–122.

34 Harper, *Iola Leroy*, p. 236.

35 Page, *Red Rock*, p. 419.

36 Harper, *Iola Leroy*, p. 281.

37 Hopkins, *Contending Forces*, pp. 87, 232, 243, 245, 244; Sutton E. Griggs, *Imperium in Imperio* (Cincinnati, OH: Editor Publishing Company, 1899), pp. 226, 237, 231.

38 Thomas Dixon Jr., *The Clansman: An Historical Romance of the Ku Klux Klan* (New York: Doubleday, Page, and Company, 1905), pp. n.p., 44, 43.

39 Thomas Dixon Jr., *The Leopard's Spots: A Romance of the White Man's Burden, 1865–1900* (New York: Doubleday, Page, and Company, 1902), pp. 169, 159, 435.

40 "Mr. Dixon's 'The Leopard's Spots,'" BR10; Dixon, *The Leopard's Spots*, n.p.

41 William Faulkner, *Go Down, Moses* (New York: Vintage, 1990), pp. 276–277.

42 Howard Fast, *Freedom Road* (New York: Duell, Sloan, and Pearce, 1944), pp. 92, 263.

43 Ralph Ellison, *Invisible Man* (New York: Vintage, 1995), pp. 16, 574.

44 Ernest J. Gaines, *The Autobiography of Miss Jane Pittman* (New York: Dial Press, 2009), pp. 67, 209.

45 Alice Randall, *The Wind Done Gone* (Boston: Houghton Mifflin, 2001), p. 202.

46 C. Vann Woodward, *The Strange Career of Jim Crow* (New York: Oxford University Press, 1957), pp. 178–179.

5

ERNEST SUAREZ

Southern Verse in Poetry and Song

In 1903, W. C. Handy "discovered" the blues while waiting for a train in Tutwiler, Mississippi, and John Crowe Ransom entered Vanderbilt University as a precocious fifteen-year-old freshman. Both men would help lay the foundations for dramatic changes in Southern verse. Handy played an important role composing and promoting the blues, a form that changed musical verse composition and influenced poetry. Ransom, with his students Allen Tate and Robert Penn Warren, set the course for two distinct types of verse that dominated Southern poetry for much of the twentieth century. Alongside the lyric and narrative branches of poetry that Ransom, Tate, and Warren cultivated, Sterling Brown, Margaret Walker, and others nurtured a poetry closely tied to the blues. Late in the century these trends gradually merged, resulting in new styles of verse, including hybrid forms of poetry and song.

The South's two most prominent nineteenth-century poets – Edgar Allan Poe (1809–1849) and Sidney Lanier (1842–1881) – believed poetry and music were closely associated, but an almost mechanical use of meter plagued their verse. Poe's poetry influenced the French Symbolists and through them Tate, who claimed that Poe's portraits of "dehumanized" characters who are "machines of sensation and will" anticipated later writers.[1] But even Poe's best poems – "Israfel," "The City in the Sea," "The Sleeper," "The Raven," "Ulalume," "Annabel Lee" – tend to be mood pieces with overwrought dramatic affects encased in monotonous cadences. Lanier, of Macon, Georgia, was a Confederate war veteran whose health was severely impaired as a Union prisoner in Maryland. He lived most of his adult life in Baltimore, where he taught at Johns Hopkins University, served as first flutist for the Peabody Orchestra, and wrote *The Science of English Verse* (1880), a study of the relationship between poetry and music. However, like Poe, Lanier filled his verse with heightened emotions and stilted metrical effects. In many poems – including "Corn," "The Symphony," and "The Waving of the Corn" – he depicts life as a battle between "Trade," or materialism, which he equates with the North, and "Chivalry," or honor, which he associates with the South.

During the nineteenth century, African Americans created and advanced musical forms that would later influence poetry. Around 1900, jazz and blues developed out of slave spirituals, jump-ups, field hollers, and work songs. New Orleans and the Mississippi Delta played particularly important roles. In New Orleans, downtown Creoles – primarily lighter-skinned mulattos – were trained according to European traditions at the city's famed French Opera House. But uptown black musicians – primarily darker-skinned people who migrated from the country – seldom received any formal training. Early ragtime, blues, and jazz musicians picked up on speech patterns and other sounds they heard around them and incorporated them into their music. New Orleans horn players and Delta guitarists played and sang what they heard, and created music that had little to do with European scales and meters.[2]

Blues musicians anticipated poets' turn toward free verse and pseudo-confessional narration by several decades. The call-and-response structure of the spiritual and field holler tended to consist of a dialogue between two individuals or groups. Blues songs isolated the dynamic, turning it into an internalized, contemplative mode of self-questioning and confession. Blues songs follow a variety of patterns, but the dominant configuration consists of sets of identical or near-identical lines followed by a line that offers a comment or response, resulting in reflective meditations. In the groundbreaking history, *American Literature: The Makers and the Making* (1973), Robert Penn Warren noted this quality, asserting the blues "represent a body of poetic art unique and powerful" and that "much of the poetry recognized as 'literature,' white or black, seems tepid beside it."[3]

In "Empty Bed Blues" (1928), Bessie Smith sings of loneliness and sexual frustration:

> When my bed gets empty, makes me feel awful mean and blue
> When my bed gets empty, makes me feel awful mean and blue
> 'Cause my springs getting rusty, sleeping single the way I do

In "Love in Vain" (1937), Robert Johnson uses train lights as imagery to convey pain and fury for a departing lover:

> When the train it left the station, with two lights on behind
> When the train it left the station, with two lights on behind
> Well, the blue light was my blues and the red light was my mind

Two anthologies – one dedicated to poetry; the other to music – published in the 1920s played important roles in drawing attention to blues verse composition. James Weldon Johnson (1871–1938) – a poet, songwriter, dramatist,

U.S. diplomat, and professor – edited *The Book of Negro Poetry* (1922). In the preface, Johnson, who was born into a middle-class African-American family in Jacksonville, Florida, cited the power of blues that originated in "Memphis, and the towns along the Mississippi." He felt that blues lyrics tended to be "crude, but they contain something of real poetry," and that blues might inspire poetry "expressing the imagery, the idioms, the peculiar turns of thought, and the distinctive humor and pathos, too, of the Negro, but which will also be capable of voicing the deepest and highest emotions and aspirations, and allow of the widest range of subjects and the widest scope of treatment."[4] Although most of Johnson's own poetry was written in traditional European forms, his verse in dialect tends to draw on folk tales, spirituals, and black hillbilly songs. For instance, "July in Georgy" (1917) is narrated from the perspective of a rural black and points to his easy assimi- lation of pleasure and spirituality: "But evehbody is a-restin', fu' de craps is all laid by, / An' time fu' de camp-meetin' is a drawin' purty nigh."

In 1926, Handy (1873–1958) and Abbe Niles published *Blues: An Anthology*, which contains detailed sections on "The Blues as Folk Verse," "The Folk Blues as Music," "The Modern Blues," and the "Adoption and Influence of the Blues." Niles draws parallels between the verse of Handy and Langston Hughes, a Midwesterner whose first book of poetry, *The Weary Blues*, also was released in 1926 and who would become one of the United States' most accomplished poets. Johnson, Edmund Wilson, Carl Van Vechten, and other notable critics lavished the anthology with praise. By the time of its publication, Handy, who was born in a log cabin in Florence, Alabama, was perhaps the best-known blues musician in the world, and the association between blues and poetry had been established.

Three books – Jean Toomer's *Cane* (1923), Sterling Brown's *Southern Road* (1932), and Margaret Walker's *For My People* (1942) – contain accomplished and relatively early examples of verse that draws on African- American music. Like Johnson, these younger writers knew European verse traditions and were well positioned to incorporate rural music into their verse. Toomer (1894–1967) was raised in a well-to-do family in Washington, DC, and studied at the University of Wisconsin and the University of Chicago. He embraced his multiethnic identity and expressed "no desire" to "subdue one" part of his racial lineage "to the other," but a trip to Georgia, during which he "heard folk-songs come from the lips of Negro peasants," "stimulated and fertilized" his "creative talent."[5] *Cane*, a remarkable collage of prose sketches and verse, blends imagist techniques with folk music and spirituals, a quality that led his poetry to be published in the *Double Dealer*, a New Orleans journal dedicated to the modernist movement, where it gar- nered the admiration of a young Allen Tate.

Brown (1901–1989), also of Washington, DC, studied at Williams College and Harvard University and taught at Howard University from 1929 to the end of his career. *Southern Road* (1932) contains sonnets and poems that draw on spirituals and folk songs, but its use of blues makes it a landmark in Southern poetry. In his "Introduction" to the book, Johnson noted Brown had "taken this raw material and worked it into original and authentic poetry," a phase that recalls his hope that blues would stimulate rich forms of poetry.[6] In "Southern Road," "Riverbank Blues," "Tin Roof Blues," and other poems Brown creates the types of accessible internal dialogues that anticipate poetry's shift away from modernism and formalism after World War II. Part Two of the volume, "On Restless River," features poems invoking the Mississippi. The title of "New St. Louis Blues" recalls Handy's famous "St. Louis Blues" (1914), which Bessie Smith and Louis Armstrong popularized in 1925. The poem is divided into three sections – "Market Street Woman," "Tornado Blues," and "Low Down" – consisting of five stanzas cast as three-line blues. In "Low Down," the second stanza's first two lines present the speaker's battered state through images of bodily decay and psychological aggravation, and the third line conveys the cause – relentless work – and potential consequence – "Death" – of his misery: "Bone's gittin' brittle, an' my brain won't low no rest, / Bone's gittin' brittle, an' my brain won't let me rest, / Death drivin' rivets overtime in my scooped out chest." Brown, a prolific scholar of Southern culture and literature, did not publish another book of verse until *The Last Ride of Wild Bill and Eleven Narrative Poems* in 1975.

For My People (1942) won the Yale Younger Poets prize, but like Brown, Margaret Walker (1915–1998) would not publish another book of verse for decades. Her volume contains poems cast in variety of forms, particularly the sonnet, but Part Two draws on African-American folk songs and legends to create ten character portraits. In the foreword, Stephen Vincent Benét points out these poems "are set for voice and the blues," and "could be sung as easily as spoken."[7] Seven of the portraits are based on original characters and set in quatrains with a variety of rhyme schemes. Three poems – "Molly Means," "Bad-Man Stagolee," and "Big John Henry" – draw on folk legends and are cast in irregular, swinging couplets. The legend of Stagolee, a notorious pimp and murderer, had already been popularized in recordings by Ma Rainey, Furry Lewis, Mississippi John Hurt, and Woody Guthrie. Walker describes him as fearless trickster who killed a policeman and evaded punishment, an act that would probably elicit sympathy from an oppressed population: "But the funniest thing about that job / Was he never got caught by no mob / And he missed the lynching meant for his hide / 'Cause nobody know how Stagolee died."

Like blues artists and the African-American poets mentioned earlier in the chapter, John Crowe Ransom (1888–1974) of Pulaski, Tennessee, often used local settings. As a freshman at Vanderbilt University, Warren read Ransom's *Poems About God* (1919) and realized the "world that I knew around me to be the stuff of poetry."[8] However, in contrast to his African-American counterparts, Ransom strictly adhered to traditional European verse practices, a characteristic that would influence Warren and alienate Tate. Warren would become the South's finest poet and one of the United States' most celebrated literary figures, but before World War II, Ransom and Tate were considered the superior poets.

The poetry Ransom composed in the 1920s proved extremely influential, fostering a line of formally oriented Southern lyric poets that extends into the twenty-first century. The son of a Methodist minister, Ransom studied at Vanderbilt and Christ College at Oxford University, where he came to believe aesthetic forms were cultural rituals that could bridge a chasm between rationality and sensibility, which had fractured people's relationship to nature and the metaphysical. *Chills and Fevers* (1924) and *Two Gentlemen in Bonds* (1927) feature subtly crafted poems that reflect his distrust of modernity and devotion to traditional values. "Captain Carpenter" consists of sixteen quatrains in iambic pentameter and presents a tongue-in-cheek account of a Quixote-like figure who valiantly battles for virtue but is gradually dismembered, suggesting how modernity has sundered humans' sense of unity with the past and their surroundings. Many of Ransom's best-known poems – including "Necrological," "Man without Sense of Direction," "Morning," "Vision by Sweetwater," "The Equilibrists," and "Painted Head" – concern people's dualistic natures. But whether addressing tensions between body and spirit, reason and imagination, or past and present, Ransom consistently privileges aesthetic experience, and science often serves as his nemesis. "Persistent Explorer" (1927) concerns whether to value science or the imagination. The poem's narrator hikes to a waterfall and wonders if he should regard "tumbling water" as an "insipid chemical" or as a god's "loud / Words." The explorer decides to remain open to "many ways of living" and to "seek another country," the province of the imagination, rather than experience the world as scientific abstraction.

John Orley Allen Tate (1899–1979) of Winchester, Kentucky, shared Ransom's skepticism of materialism and science, but whereas Ransom thought traditional forms supplied ritualistic elements the modern world lacked, Tate believed that modern poets' tendency to experiment could be likened to modern painters' rejecting the "tyranny of representation" in order to remake the "constituted material world" in a manner that expresses the artist's interior reality.[9] Tate's fervor for Modernism led him to rebuff

Ransom's literary practices. In a 1959 issue of *The Sewanee Review*, Ransom recalled that in contrast to Tate's "fellow students, and to my faculty associates and myself ... Allen in his student days was reading Baudelaire and Mallarmé"[10] Like T. S. Eliot, Tate had made a connection between French symbolism and Elizabethan and Jacobean poetry, and had become enamored of Baudelaire's Theory of Correspondences.

Tate and Ransom's differences were aesthetic, not sociopolitical. Tate's distrust of cultural relativism led him, like Eliot and Ransom, to admire classicism, especially Greco-Roman culture, a characteristic evident in "Aeneas at Washington," "The Mediterranean," "To the Lacedemonians," and other poems. Like Eliot, Tate often couples a deep awareness of tradition with a modernist emphasis on subjectivity and fragmentation. His best-known poem, "Ode to the Confederate Dead," employs the irregular rhymes of Milton's "Lycidas" and uses imagistic stanzas that suspend the narrative. However, his emphasis on subjectivity sometimes resulted in allusive poetry laden with idiosyncratic metaphors that resist comprehension. In much of his best verse – including "Mother and Son," "The Oath," and "The Swimmers" – he simplifies his language and presents relatively straightforward narratives. "The Swimmers" (1960), perhaps Tate's best poem, involves a childhood recollection of a lynched black man. The poem details a boy's shock at encountering evil for the first time, and affirms the community's responsibility: "This private thing was owned by all the town, / Though never claimed by us within my hearing."

The relationship between black and white Southern poets reflected the South's toxic and complex racial climate. In 1932, Tate protested a gathering in honor of Johnson and Hughes. In an open letter he claimed both were "very interesting writers and as such I would like to meet them," and that such an event "would be possible in New York, London, or Paris," but not in segregated Nashville, where "there should be no social intercourse between the races unless we are willing for that to lead to marriage." A year later he explained his position on race in a letter to Lincoln Kirsten, claiming the "psychology of sex says that a man is not altered in his being by sexual intercourse, but that the body of a woman is powerfully affected by pregnancy"; he posited that "miscegenation due to a white woman and negro" endangered families because a "white woman pregnant with a negro child becomes a counter symbol, one of evil and pollution."[11] Yet as the African-American writer Arna Bontemps points out, Tate's verse of the period sometimes reflected shame at his treatment of blacks.[12] In the 1950s Tate converted to Roman Catholicism and began to reverse his positions. In 1953, he surprised the literary world by writing the introduction to Melvin Tolson's *Libretto for the Republic of Liberia*, and in 1959, he spoke at a conference in support of Martin Luther King and the civil rights movement. In 1966, Bontemps and Hughes included Tate's poetry as a "tributary" in a new edition of their anthology *Poetry of the Negro*.

Shifts in Robert Penn Warren's political convictions and racial assumptions contributed to changes in his poetry. Like Ransom and Tate, Warren (1905–1989), born in Guthrie, Kentucky, was wary of romantic idealism, but his attraction to naturalism, particularly the work of Thomas Hardy and Theodore Dreiser, was in sharp contrast to their stress on social and religious traditions. While in England as a Rhodes Scholar, Warren contributed "The Briar Patch" to *I'll Take My Stand: The South and the Agrarian Tradition* (1930), a collection of essays edited by Ransom, Tate and Donald Davidson, which envisioned pastoral life as a panacea to communism and corporate capitalism. In his essay Warren, then in his early twenties, stressed Booker T. Washington's support of vocational education and how agrarianism offered blacks and whites alike a better quality of life. He noted the deficiencies of the separate-but-equal system, but asserted the "negro" should "sit beneath his own vine and fig tree."[13] However, when he returned to the South in 1931 amid the Great Depression, he began to realize the "personal, psychological, and spiritual degradation" segregation caused, which he claimed he had been "too young" and "too stupid to be aware of" previously.[14]

Warren's early verse, collected in *Selected Poems, 1923–1943* (1944), is heavily indebted to Ransom's stress on local settings and metrical regularity and to T. S. Eliot's use of imagery and diction. Decades later in one of his most important poems, "Old Nigger on One-Mule Car Encountered Late at Night When Driving Home from Party in the Back Country," Warren linked his poetic practices of the period to his racial assumptions, viewing both as a restrictive and damaging acquiescence to convention. "The Ballad of Billie Potts," from *Selected Poems*, reflects his restlessness with his verse in the 1940s. The poem breaks away from his previous practices in ballad-like sections laced with sing-song rhythms – "A clabber-headed bastard with snot in his nose / And big red wrists hanging out of his clothes" – but displays his continued debt to Eliot in philosophically oriented passages: "But after, after the irrefutable modes and marches, / After waters that never quench the thirst in the throat that parches." In the years following the publication of *Selected Poems*, Warren wrote novels, criticism, and the verse play *Brother to Dragons* (1953); however, "The Ballad of Billie Potts" was the last new poem he would complete until the mid-1950s. In a 1957 *Paris Review* interview with Ralph Ellison, Warren articulated the dissatisfaction he experienced in that period, declaring that he "quit writing poems for several years; that is, I'd start them, get a lot down, then feel that I wasn't connecting somehow ... they felt false."[15]

Warren's frustration with modernist and formalist verse techniques reflected many American poets' mindset after World War II, but with the exception of Bob Kaufman, Southern poets did not participate in the major contemporary movements – Beat, Confessional, Black Mountain, Deep Image, New York School – that arose after World War II. Instead, Southern poetry split along distinct lines. Ransom's emphasis on aesthetics and the lyric became increasingly influential, especially as university creative writing programs expanded. Tate's influence diminished as a younger generation turned away from modernist poetics, and Randall Jarrell and Warren created a new narrative poetry that examined the self within competing social and philosophical contexts. Blues poetry, the most indigenous line of Southern verse, served as a catalyst for integrating poetry and music throughout the United States and Europe.

Randall Jarrell (1914–1965) studied with Warren and Ransom at Vanderbilt University in his native Nashville, and was one of the first American poets to move towards conversational, neoromantic verse that explores the nature of identity. His psychologically oriented narratives influenced Warren, James Dickey, Eleanor Ross Taylor, and other Southern poets for decades to come. Jarrell's first book, *Blood for a Stranger* (1942), displays his characteristic desire to risk seeming "limp and prosaic" instead of "false and rhetorical ... I want to be rather like speech."[16] A sense of romantic alienation pervades Jarrell's portraits of men and women's lives at various stages. "90 North," one of his best early poems, prefigures his interests in childhood, dreams, and the sense of loss created by the conflict between one's interior landscape and worldly realities.

In *Little Friend, Little Friend* (1945) and *Losses* (1948), Jarrell, who served as a radar instructor in the U.S. Army, focuses on the psychology, speech, and actions of military personnel. "Eighth Air Force," "The Dead Wingman," "Siegfried," "Losses," and other poems explore the mentally and morally tenuous position of young adults whose sense of self is threatened by the role in which the military places them. His subsequent collections, *The Seven-League Crutches* (1951), *The Woman at the Washington Zoo: Poems and Translations* (1960), and *The Lost World* (1965), reflect psychology's increasing influence on his verse. "The Night Before the Night Before Christmas" presents a precocious fourteen-year-old girl grappling with anxieties involving death, aging, politics, religion, and identity. Like many of Jarrell's poems, "Seele im Raum" makes use of fantasy. A woman's persistent vision of an eland at her dinner table acts as a response to the neglect she suffers from her husband and children. In "Jerome," a psychoanalyst's dreams mingle with his patients' as he dreams of being analyzed by a supernatural creature. "The Lost World," a sequence based on Jarrell's memories of an extended stay with his grandparents in Los Angeles, is often considered his most significant poem.

In 1954, Warren resumed publishing poetry, leading to the autobiographically oriented *Promises* (1957), which won the Pulitzer Prize and the National Book Award. *Promises* opens with the five-poem sequence, "To a Little Girl, One year Old, in a Ruined Fortress," dedicated to Warren's daughter, Rosanna. The remainder of the book consists of the nineteen-poem sequence, "Promises," dedicated to his son, Gabriel. Some poems are cast in irregular meters and others feature irregular-rhyming free verse. The trend toward openly autobiographical verse would continue throughout his career, but Warren would never become a confessional poet in the style of Robert Lowell, W. D. Snodgrass, Sylvia Plath, or Anne Sexton. Like most confessional poetry, Warren's verse often introduces seemingly intimate details without the apparent intervention of a persona; however, Warren's later poetry tends to ensconce the personal within large philosophical frameworks that dominate the narrative.

In the 1960s, American Pragmatism, especially the thought of William James and Sidney Hook, began to vigorously mediate Warren's interrogations of the tensions between determinism and idealism. Harold Bloom has asserted that from 1966 to 1986, "between ages sixty-one and eighty-one," Warren entered a "poetic renaissance fully comparable to the great final phases of Thomas Hardy, William Butler Yeats, and Wallace Stevens."[17] The first section of *Selected Poems, Tale of Time: Poems 1960–1966* displays a strong autobiographical impulse and an increasingly fluid and accessible style. The title poem is based on the death of the poet's mother, an event he uses to explore characteristic themes, including people's relationship to time and time's relationship to identity. The narrator's "solution" to comprehending a person's past – "You / Must eat the dead. / You must eat them completely, bone, blood, flesh, gristle, even / Such hair as can be forced," – suggests Warren's practice of confronting recalcitrant philosophical dilemmas from multiple perspectives and rejecting any single answer.

Audubon: A Vision (1969) is often regarded as Warren's most important poem. The poem uses the famous naturalist's life to explore the relationship between fate and identity. Written in free verse that wends between the philosophical and vernacular, *Audubon* depicts existence as a negotiation between idealism, human imperfections, and deterministic circumstances. *Or Else: Poem/Poems 1968–1974* (1974) is an intricately sculpted sequence of poems linked by interjections. The collection contains some of Warren's finest poems, including "The Nature of a Mirror," the surrealistic "I Am Dreaming of a White Christmas: The Natural History of a Vision," "Homage to Theodore Dreiser," and "Rattlesnake Country." *Now and Then: Poems 1976–1978*

(1978) earned him his second Pulitzer Prize for poetry. The book is divided into two sections, "Nostalgic" and "Speculative," and most of the poems examine the relationship between present and past. The verse is conversational, mixing rhymed and unrhymed stanzas without metrical regularity.

In the 1960s and 1970s, Bob Kaufman (1925–1986) of New Orleans, Sonia Sanchez (1934–) of Birmingham, Alabama, and other African-American poets wrote verse based on the blues and jazz, but blues' influence on verse composition became an international phenomenon as recordings on Sun and Chess record labels gained wider circulation. Muddy Waters, Howlin' Wolf, B. B. King, and others began reaching white audiences, and blues soon infused rock music with many of the qualities – an emphasis on a conversational style, on the personal, the local, and the fantastic – that characterized the major contemporary movements in poetry. Kaufman joined the Beats in New York City and San Francisco, where he was a well-known street poet whose book *Golden Sardine* (1967) became a classic of that movement. Sanchez moved to New York City at age seven, and in the 1960s was part of the Harlem-based Black Arts Movement, which included Amiri Baraka and Nikki Giovanni, two Northerners whose verse was influenced by blues and jazz.[18]

James Dickey and Donald Justice's verse suggests the predominance of narrative and lyric branches of Southern poetry during the later twentieth century. Dickey (1923–1997) extended Warren and Jarrell's tendency to explore the paradoxical nature of identity through narrative verse. Dickey, who was born into an affluent Atlanta family, served as a navigator in the U.S. Air Corps during World War II, an experience that formed the basis for much of his work. After the war he enrolled at Vanderbilt University, where he studied with Davidson, the only remaining faculty member who had been associated with *The Fugitive*.[19] However, he quickly realized Jarrell was the Southern poet who "appealed to me most" and focused on writing accessible narratives. During his career Dickey blurred the boundaries between poet and poem, hailing the "creative possibility of the lie" as a poetic technique and freely manipulating his own biography for effect."[20]

Most of Dickey's strongest poetry is collected in *Poems, 1957–1967* (1968), verse that led Peter Davison to assert in *The Atlantic Monthly* that Dickey and Lowell were the only major American poets of their generation. In his poetry Dickey, like Warren, often examined the dynamic between romanticism and naturalism. But unlike Warren, whose poetry became increasingly autobiographical, Dickey, influenced by French existentialism, used a wide array of characters to explore how attempts to connect the self with elemental forces and situations can be an essential, but possibly destructive, stimulus for bestowing existence with meaning.

Dickey's early verse – including "The Performance," "Between Two Prisoners," Cherry Log Road," and "Drinking from a Helmet" – featured heavily cadenced poems composed in dactyls, anapests, and trochees. "The Heaven of Animals," a near-perfect lyric, depicts a mythical cycle of predators and prey fulfilling their fates, suggesting the close link between creation and destruction. In the mid-1960s, Dickey began to use longer lines and display greater metrical variety, including experiments with "split lines" of sonic and imagistic clusters in "The Fire Bombing," "Slave Quarters," and "The Shark's Parlor." In these poems Dickey creates a poetic stream-of-consciousness to regain ground he felt verse had surrendered to prose. "The Firebombing" presents the perspective of a former U.S. pilot confronting his "guilt at the inability to feel guilt" at having bombed Japanese civilians during World War II. In order to induce guilt, the traumatized narrator imagines his own American suburb being firebombed, but the poem ends with the declaration that he still cannot imagine anything that is not as "American as I am, and proud of it" – a moment that stresses the horror of committing state-sponsored acts of violence in a war worth fighting. "May Day Sermon to the Women of Gilmer County, Georgia, by a Woman Preacher Leaving the Baptist Church" and "The Sheep Child" are experiments with what Dickey called "country surrealism." "Falling" is based on a *New York Times* report of a stewardess who plummeted to her death when an airplane's emergency door opened in mid-flight. Dickey used the account as a metaphor for a person's journey through life, in which every second brings one closer to death. During her descent the stewardess engages in creative lying, taking on sundry roles and hoping for survival. Her last words, "AH, GOD," are richly ambiguous, at once expressing hope for immortality and its uncertainty. Dickey's most compelling later poetry includes *Puella* (1982), a series of sonically complex verses written from the perspective of a young girl coming into womanhood, and *The Eagle's Mile* (1990).

Unlike Dickey's use of narrative dramatics to pursue large philosophical issues, Miami native Donald Justice embraced Ransom's fondness for lyric restraint and his propensity to highlight technique. As an undergraduate at the University of Miami, Justice studied classical music and considered pursuing a career as a composer. In 1947, he earned an MA at University of North Carolina with a thesis titled "The Fugitive-Agrarian 'Myth,'" and in 1954 he earned a PhD from the University of Iowa. Three years later he joined the Iowa faculty and went on to become one the nation's most influential teachers of creative writing.

Justice was the first significant white Southern poet since balladeer Donald Davidson to consistently use music as a poetic source. But unlike black Southern poets, Justice insisted that in "poetry the word *music* is pretty much a figure, not a fact – a metaphor at best," a distinction that reflects his emphasis on European verse techniques, which have little to do with Western harmonics, and African Americans' embrace of blues and jazz, which are based on the human voice.[21] *The Summer Anniversaries* (1960) contains sonnets in the style of Fredrick Goddard Tuckerman, as well as variations of traditional forms, particularly the sestina. Justice's next collection, *Night Light* (1967), displays even greater formal dexterity, including prose poems and experiments with free verse. The title of *Departures* (1973) suggests its differences from Justice's previous verse and his tendency to use others' work for inspiration. "Sonatina in Green" and "Sonatina in Yellow" draw on a musical form that employs two parts, with one part repeating the other in a different key. In "Sonatina in Green" the two parts concern two poets, "One spits on the sublime. / One lies in bed alone, reading." "Sonatina in Yellow" shuffles between past and present tenses to summon memories inspired by old photographs of Justice's father.

New work in Pulitzer Prize–winning *Selected Poems* (1979) includes two poems based on blues lyrics, "The Sometime Dancer Blues" and "Angel Death Blues." A series of lyrics, "Memories of the Depression," concerns places his family lived and spent summers, and points to the increasingly autobiographical bent of his later work. His most powerful book, *The Sunset Maker* (1987), compiles interrelated poems, stories, and memoirs that reflect his passion for music and painting. A suite of playful poems is presented as "Tremayne," a character who serves as Justice's alter ego. The new poems in *New and Selected Poems* (1995) and *Collected Poems* (2004) continue his characteristic concern with music, painting, and the South of his youth. "The Miami of Other Days" portrays a time when people danced on the beach to the "new white jazz / of a Victrola on its towel in the sand" and "crackers down from Georgia (my own people) / Foregathered on the old post office steps."

The final third of the century witnessed what Charles Wright called a "flowering" of Southern poetry.[22] Dave Smith, David Bottoms, Fred Chappell, Andrew Hudgins, Betty Adcock, Rodney Jones, Kate Daniels, and others continued Warren, Jarrell, and Dickey's emphasis on narrative verse. Smith (1942–) uses a method he calls "orchestration" – the "exfoliation of imagistic constructs which reinforce each other in such a way that the reader is led to perception by repeating signals" – to create multi-textured narratives with contradictory layers of meaning.[23] Many poems in Smith's early books, including *The Fisherman's Whore* (1974) and *Cumberland Station* (1976), take place in his native Virginia Tidewater, and are plotted in the style of Dickey's longer poems. In the early 1980s, Smith shifted away from an emphasis on action and toward reflective narratives à la Warren. *The Wick of Memory: New and Selected Poems 1970–2006* (2000) collects verse from seventeen previous books, including a series of near-sonnets from *Fate's Kite* (1996). Smith's later work includes *Little Boats, Unsalvaged* (2006) and *Hawks on Wires* (2011).

Miller Williams and Justice's students, Charles Wright and Ellen Bryant Voigt, are among the Southern poets who extended Ransom and Justice's lyric practices. Wright (1935–), born in Pickwick Dam, Tennessee, takes his predecessors' emphasis on the aesthetic over the social in a different direction. Whereas they tended to work in traditional forms, Wright composes in unaccentual syllabics, and the subject/object split consistently informs his verse, creating a fluid dynamic between his narrator's perceptions and the world outside the self. His first trilogy, National Book Award winner *Country Music* (1982), was conceived as a "small time *inferno, purgatorio,* and *paradiso.*"[24] Wright's interest in Eastern thought infuses his second trilogy, *The World of the Ten Thousand Things* (1990). The title alludes to Lao Tzu's phrase concerning the universe's diversity, a concept on which Wright draws to explore the relationship between the landscape, perception, and language. Wright conceived of his final trilogy, *Negative Blue* (2000), as an "Appalachian Book of the Dead" that focuses on the metaphysical possibility of "trying to bring what's not there into terms of what is visible in the visible world." In his subsequent books, including *Buffalo Yoga* (2004), *Scar Tissue* (2006), *Littlefoot* (2007), and *Sestets* (2009), Wright continues to explore the relationship between his totem subjects, "landscape, language and the idea of God."[25]

The achievement of Southern women – including Voigt, Adcock, Sanchez, C. D. Wright, Brenda Marie Osbey, Kate Daniels, Claudia Emerson, and Natasha Trethewey – in the late twentieth and early twenty-first centuries brought renewed attention to Eleanor Ross Taylor (1920–2011) of rural North Carolina. Jarrell helped edit – and secure a publisher for – her first book, *Wilderness of Ladies* (1960), but Taylor's poetry garnered scant attention until the twentieth century drew to a close and other Southern women emerged as notable poets. Adcock calls Taylor the "mother" of subsequent Southern female poets, and Voigt claims that it is "no surprise to find so many pioneers" in her verse "since she herself is one."[26] Like Jarrell, Taylor often writes monologues and uses female *personae*. But unlike Jarrell or other previous Southern poets, Taylor emphasizes rural, Southern white women's experiences. Many of the poems in Taylor's collections, *Days Going/Days Coming Back* (1991) and *Captive Voices: New and Selected Poems, 1960–2008* (2009), address her upbringing on a farm that lacked plumbing or electricity but was filled with religion and an emphasis on education.

Yusef Komunyakaa and T. R. Hummer's work are compelling examples of how the narrative, lyric, and blues branches of Southern poetry merged in the late twentieth and early twenty-first centuries. Komunyakaa (1947–), born in Bogalusa, Louisiana, studied at the University of California-Riverside with Wright, and was "drawn to" his "patterns of images." He was also influenced by Dickey's "attention to detail ... the precise naming of things. I knew those names, the nuances of language." However, he notes that, as an African American, he had a different relationship to those materials than his white counterparts. Komunyakaa's awareness that what "one person may see ... as blasphemous" another may see "as sacred or a song of praise" led to his use of blues and jazz rhythms. Many of the poems collected in Pulitzer Prize–winning *Neon Vernacular: New and Selected Poems* (1993) reflect blues songs' tendency to "talk around a subject or situation." Hughes, Brown, and Kaufman influenced the musical qualities of Komunyakaa's verse, including his tendency to write "tonal narratives" in which a series of compressed images unfold into a "sped-up meditation."[27]

T. R. Hummer and Billy Cioffi's *Highminded* (2010) joins Hughes and Charles Mingus' recording of *The Weary Blues* (1958) as the most successful integration of contemporary music and poetry to date. Hummer (1950–), who studied with Dave Smith at the University of Utah, claims that reading Warren's essay "Pure and Impure Poetry" provided him with a strategy for blending his interests in music, literature, criticism, philosophy, history, and myth.[28] Most of Hummer's early poetry involves life in his native Mississippi and the Deep South, but much of his later work moves away from an ostensibly autobiographical focus toward examining American national identity. *Highminded* continues Hummer's exploration of Americana by mining the intersections between poetry and music, particularly blues-based rock. The recording consists of interrelated songs and poetic vignettes that form an homage to poets and musicians, including Walt Whitman, Emily Dickinson, T. S. Eliot, Elvis Presley, Robert Johnson, Chuck Berry, Richard Hugo, Bob Dylan, and Gram Parsons.

Like the South itself, Southern verse represents a host of diverse traditions that often have resisted one another, but steadily moved toward integration, resulting in new possibilities. Natasha Trethewey (1966–), a Gulf Port, Mississippi native who received the Pulitzer Prize for *Native Guard* (2006), suggests the uneasy convergence of various traditions in "Southern Pastoral," a poem in which Trethewey, the child of an interracial marriage, describes a dream of being photographed with the "Fugitive Poets." The narrator convivially accepts a glass of bourbon she is offered, but when the photographer tells the subjects to say "*race*" – in lieu of "smile" – she senses she is in "blackface again when the flash freezes us." Afterwards, she explains "*My father is white*," emphasizing the inadequacy of stereotypical thinking. Like the poem's narrator, who has been shaped by a range of circumstances, Southern verse continues to be molded and revitalized by an amalgam of forces, a dynamic reflected by the development and confluence of southern lyric, narrative and blues-based verse.

NOTES

1 Allen Tate, "Our Cousin, Mr. Poe," *Essays of Four Decades* (Chicago: Swallow Press, 1968), p. 395.

2 Like many musicologists, Robert Palmer traces the "deep blues" of the Mississippi Delta to various African traditions, particularly Senegambia "drumming, hand clapping, and group singing in call and response form," *Deep Blues* (New York: Penguin, 1981), p. 27.

3 Cleanth Brooks, R. W. B. Lewis, and Robert Penn Warren, *American Literature: The Makers and the Making, Volume II* (New York: St. Martin's Press, 1973), p. 2759.

4 James Weldon Johnson, *The Book of Negro Poetry* (New York: Harcourt, Brace and Co, 1922), pp. xii–xiii, xli.

5 Jean Toomer, *Cane* (New York: Liveright, 1975), p. xvi.

6 James Weldon Johnson, "Introduction to First Edition," in Sterling A. Brown, *The Collected Poems of Sterling Brown*, ed. Michael S. Harper (Chicago: TriQuarterly Press, 1989), p. 17.

7 Stephen Vincent Benét, "Foreword" to Margaret Walker, *For My People* (New Haven, CT: Yale University Press, 1942), p. 6.

8 Warren quoted in Joseph Blotner, *Robert Penn Warren: A Biography* (New York: Random House, 1997), p. 33.

9 Tate "Whose Ox?" *The Fugitive* (December 1922), pp. 99–100.

10 John Crowe Ransom, "In Amicitia," *The Sewanee Review* 76: 4 (Autumn 1959), p. 531.

11 Thomas A. Underwood, *Allen Tate: Orphan of the South* (Princeton, NJ: Princeton University Press, 2000), p. 291.

12 Charles Nichols, ed. *Arna Bontemps-Langston Hughes Letters, 1925–1967* (New York: Dodd Mead, 1980), p. 477.

13 Robert Penn Warren, "The Briar Patch" in *I'll Take My Stand: The South and the Agrarian Tradition* (Baton Rouge: Louisiana State University Press, 1977), p. 264.

14 Floyd C. Watkins and John T. Hiers, *Robert Penn Warren Talking: Interviews, 1950–1978* (New York: Random House, 1980), p. 159.

15 Robert Penn Warren, "The Art of Fiction No 18," interview conducted with Ralph Ellison and Eugene Walter, *Paris Review* 16 (Spring/Summer 1957), collected in *Talking with Robert Penn Warren*, eds. Floyd C. Watkins, et al. (Athens: University of Georgia Press, 1990), p. 34.

16 Quoted in William Pritchard, *Randall Jarrell: A Literary Life* (New York: Farrar, Strauss and Giroux, 1990), p. 62.

17 Harold Bloom, "Introduction," *The Collected Poems of Robert Penn Warren*, ed. John Burt (Baton Rouge: Louisiana State University Press, 1998), p. xxiii.

18 Who is or is not a Southern poet sometimes presents no easy answer. A case could be made that Giovanni, who was born in Ohio and lived outside Cincinnati, but spent time in Nashville at her grandmother's and most of her adult life in Virginia, is Southern. A. R. Ammons, who lived in North Carolina until his late teens, is one of the twentieth-century's most accomplished poets, but he spent almost his entire adult life outside the South, and his verse displays strong similarities to the New England transcendentalists. Similarly, Adrianne Rich of Maryland, a border state, is usually associated with poets from the northeast.

19 *The Fugitive* – a little magazine organized by Ransom, Tate, Warren, and other members of the Vanderbilt University and Nashville community – was published from 1922 to 1925.

20 James Dickey, *Self-Interviews* (New York: Doubleday and Company, 1970), p. 34.

21 Donald Justice in B. Renner, *elimae*, http://elimae.com/interviews/justice.html (accessed 1997).

22 Charles Wright in Ernest Suarez, *Southbound: Interviews with Southern Poets* (Columbia: University of Missouri Press, 1999), p. 49.

23 Dave Smith, *Southbound*, p. 23.

24 Charles Wright, *Southbound*, p. 56.

25 Charles Wright, *Quarter Notes: Improvisations and Interviews* (Ann Arbor: University of Michigan Press, 1988), p. 123.

26 Betty Adcock, unpublished taped panel discussion with Ernest Suarez, *Millennial Gathering of Southern Writers*, Vanderbilt University, April 7, 1999. Ellen Bryant Voigt, "Foreword" to Eleanor Ross Taylor, *Captive Voices: New and Selected Poems, 1960–2008* (Baton Rouge: Louisiana State University Press, 2008), p. xiii.

27 Yusef Komunyakaa, *Southbound*, pp. 141, 138, 133.

28 T. R. Hummer, *Southbound*, p. 105.

6

DAVID A. DAVIS

Southern Modernists and Modernity

In William Faulkner's *As I Lay Dying* (1930), Darl Bundren describes the coffin containing his mother's decomposing, waterlogged, mutilated corpse as "a cubistic bug."[1] Many of the anomalies of Southern modernism coalesce in this unexpected reference to avant-garde visual art in Faulkner's unconventional novel about a family of poor white cotton farmers. The novel is notoriously bizarre both for the grotesque story about transporting Addie Bundren's body from the family's isolated farm to Jefferson to be buried and for the fragmented narrative structure in which each member of the family tells versions of the story in their own idiosyncratic voice. Because of the book's experimental structure, it is often considered an illustration of modernist literary technique, but it deviates from the typical subject matter of most modernist novels because its setting is rural and because its characters are insular, poor white Southerners. *As I Lay Dying* illustrates the inherent contradiction of Southern modernism – the tension between literary experimentation and lagging social provincialism. Most works of literary modernism take place amid the hubbub of cosmopolitan cities and grapple with issues of spiritual alienation and psychological distress, so works of Southern modernism that depict life in a rural, agricultural, and traditional region antagonize the modernist mainstream. In Southern modernism, cubism and cotton coexist uneasily.

Toward the end of the nineteenth century, the nature of everyday life began to change in the United States. Growing networks of railroads, highways, and steamships made long distances seem shorter, industrial factories produced raw materials on a massive scale, newly invented electric machines and mechanical devices saved tedious labor, and expanding cities transformed the agrarian, frontier-focused nation into a capitalist, urban dynamo. But the United States modernized unevenly, and cities, factories, and innovations were clustered primarily in the Northeast. By 1920, the majority of Americans lived in urban areas, mostly in the Midwest and along the East Coast. Only one of the nation's twenty largest cities was in the South, New

Orleans, and the majority of Southerners were still rural. Manufacturing drove the U.S. economy, but the Southern economy continued to depend on production of cotton. While other agricultural regions, such as the Midwest and the Great Plains, implemented tractors, combines, and other agricultural machines to increase yields and decrease labor, Southerners continued to cultivate cotton manually, mostly with mules and sharecroppers. Workers in Northern factories organized into unions, and the progressive political movement yielded significant reforms to benefit poor families living in northeastern cities, but the South clung to its traditional racist, paternalist social hierarchy. As the United States modernized, the South remained economically and socially stagnant.

The term "modernity" refers to the processes of social and economic development that changed daily life in the United States and elsewhere, and these massive changes inspired the movement known as "modernism," a set of intellectual and artistic responses that replaced established Victorian-era tenets of faith and paradigms of taste with new systems of belief and innovative aesthetic experimentation. Modern science challenged religious dogma for cultural primacy by the beginning of the twentieth century, and many modernist writers, artists, and musicians explored nihilism, scientific rationalism, and psychology to offer radical new depictions of modern life. In Europe, Stravinsky and Diaghilev provoked riots with their astonishing departures from classical ballet; Paul Cezanne, Pablo Picasso, and Marcel Duchamp overturned the notion that art should accurately depict reality; and Thomas Mann, Gertrude Stein, James Joyce, and Ezra Pound declared traditional literary forms obsolete. The avant-garde element of modernism developed in cosmopolitan European cities at the end of the nineteenth century, reflecting the sense of a new age emerging with the turning of the new century. Modernity came to a crisis with World War I, where the innovations in science and technology that promised to improve human life proved capable of destroying it efficiently, and the modern art produced during and after the war tends to project an attitude of weariness and wariness. Modernism originated in Europe, but Americans followed suit, and many writers, such as T. S. Eliot, Ernest Hemingway, and Richard Wright, relocated to Europe, at least temporarily, while other writers, such as William Carlos Williams, Wallace Stevens, and John Dos Passos, imported modernist ideas and adapted them to life in the United States.

The South modernized slowly, but some Southern writers incorporated elements of modernism into their portrayals of the region, leading to the tension between artistic experimentation and social provincialism demonstrated in *As I Lay Dying*. Critics have struggled for decades to understand and to explain the emergence of Southern modernism in the relative absence of modernity. Allen Tate, a key figure in Southern modernism, looked back on Southern writing at the middle of the twentieth century, labeled it "the southern literary renascence," and declared that it was already over.[2] Eight years later, Louis Rubin and Robert Jacobs used Tate's phrase as the title of their field-defining collection of essays on modern Southern literature, *The Southern Renascence* (1953), and a generation of critics conceptualized Southern modernism as a self-generating, self-obsessed phenomenon distinct from broader currents of literary and social development. Richard Gray explores in *The Literature of Memory* (1977) how the writers of the Southern Renaissance were obsessed with the past, especially as modernity threatened the traditional ways of living, and Richard King shows in *A Southern Renaissance* (1980) that white, male writers of the 1930s and 1940s were coming to terms with Southern tradition and developing a historical consciousness, so they were more concerned about the past than the present or future.[3] In *After Southern Modernism* (2000), Matthew Guinn describes modernist Southern writers' deliberate fixation on the region's past as a process of redemptive myth-making, the quest for "a usable past."[4]

In *Inventing Southern Literature* (1998), Michael Kreyling points out that the deliberate construction of modern Southern literature as a cultural artifact based on the theories of Allen Tate and his mentor John Crowe Ransom detached the works from the actual circumstances of their time and place, diminished the contributions of women and African Americans to Southern writing, and separated Southern literature from global trends in literature. Although the discourse on Southern literature has been robust for many decades, it has been largely on the margins of U.S. literary scholarship, and many writers labeled Southern have been treated as mere regionalists. At the same time, the canon of Southern writing was an exclusionary collection of primarily conservative white male writers all of whom valorized Southern history, community, storytelling, and connection to the land. Southern literary scholarship in recent decades, however, has engaged in an ongoing recovery project to incorporate women, African Americans, nonnative Southerners, and nonnative Americans into the body of Southern literature and to reposition Southern literature within the broader contexts of U.S. and global culture. For example, Patricia Yeager claims to "dynamite the rails" on which the official white-centered, backward-looking narrative of Southern literature is constructed by analyzing the bonds between black and white women's writing in *Dirt and Desire* (2000), and Houston Baker makes a claim for modernism in the black South in *Turning South Again* (2001). Clearly, the edifice of the Southern renascence is unstable and due for renovation – or demolition.

The result of this complicated critical maneuvering is that the term "Southern modernism" is a recent innovation, displacing the phrase "Southern renascence." Because much criticism has focused on the South as a distinctive region, the actual relationship between Southern modernism as a distinctive form of writing and modernity as a global process of social development has still not been thoroughly examined, and many writers who wrote about the modern South have been pushed to the periphery of both Southern literary criticism and U.S. literary criticism, particularly those writers who focused on poverty and social problems. Yet the emergence of modernity in the United States intensified the perception of the South as a site of tremendous social and economic problems, and the literature of Southern modernism depicts the region as self-conscious about its discontinuity with the development of modernity. Faulkner's experiments in literary form notwithstanding, Southern responses to modernity tended to be conservative, far from the avant-garde forms associated with high modernism. Southern writers portraying the impact of modernity on the region typically used traditionally linear narrative forms that are consistent with the region's comparatively primitive culture. The defining characteristic of Southern modernism is not aesthetic innovation but the inherent tension between modernity and Southern provincialism, a tension that has inherent consequences on aesthetic presentation. Scott Romine argues in *The Real South* (2008) that "the South's economic and cultural backwardness' relative to the U.S. nation has, ironically enough, placed it in the avant-garde of contemporary cultural poetics," which suggests that the term "Southern" labels a critique of modernity.[5]

One of the most enduring problems with the criticism of Southern modernism stems, at least in part, from another assertion Allen Tate made. He dismissed the "sociologists of fiction" who portrayed the South as "backward and illiberal," as a region facing serious social problems that required intervention or deserved moral consideration, and he praised the "traditionalists" who believed in the abstract verities of "honor, truth, imagination," that, in his opinion, redeemed the South's past.[6] He enumerated a small group of writers who embodied these traits, including Stark Young, Elizabeth Madox Roberts, Katherine Anne Porter, Robert Penn Warren, Caroline Gordon, Ellen Glasgow, and William Faulkner. These writers (with the exception of Caroline Gordon, Tate's wife) were the focus of much of Southern literary criticism for more than a generation, which has had three deleterious effects on the field. First, criticism has been focused on abstractions and has privileged a small group of writers, especially Faulkner, who incorporated modernist aesthetics into their works. Second, criticism has been detached from a broader spectrum of writers who focused on the social consequences of modernization in the South. Third, criticism has used a contrived false dichotomy to foreclose considerations of regional sociology – depictions of the way Southerners lived – in literary interpretation. Influential Southern critics Allen Tate, John Crowe Ransom, and Cleanth Brooks established the methods of New Criticism, a form of literary criticism that examines texts as closed systems removed from their historical context, which became the dominant methodology used in the United States after World War II until other methods displaced it toward the end of the twentieth century. But at the same time that the New Critics were developing their methodology, Howard Odum, Arthur Raper, Rupert Vance, and other social scientists, ironically, were examining the causes and consequences of the region's myriad social problems and exposing the realities of how Southerners lived. Reading the literature of Southern modernism both for its aesthetic qualities and its sociological commentaries yields a more comprehensive and productive understanding of modernity in the South.

At the end of the nineteenth century, the South was ideologically ill-prepared for modernity. After the end of Reconstruction, Southern civilization reverted to a state that virtually reconstituted antebellum culture. The Supreme Court's decision in the 1896 case of *Plessy v. Ferguson* upheld black codes that institutionalized racial segregation, legalized racial controls, and enforced white political supremacy. The 1898 race riot in Wilmington, North Carolina, in which Democratic white supremacists violently overthrew the elected party of black Republicans, marked the end of African-American political representation in the South for more than fifty years. The riot inspired Charles Chesnutt's novel *The Marrow of Tradition* (1901), a bleak story about the futility of black self-determination in the racist South. By the beginning of the twentieth century, sharecropping, crop lien, and debt peonage evolved as effective methods to control the agricultural labor necessary to cultivate cash crops, which continued to be the region's primary economic product. And the cult of the "Lost Cause" venerated the Confederacy as a morally superior culture that succumbed to the North primarily because of the latter's advantages in manufacturing and manpower – a view that effectively vilified modernity. In the first decade of the twentieth century, the most popular Southern novels were Thomas Dixon's Reconstruction trilogy, *The Leopard's Spots* (1902), *The Clansman* (1905), and *The Traitor*, (1907). The books dehumanized African Americans, revised the history of the Civil War, and praised lynching as a necessary purgative to maintain white superiority. The novels inspired D. W. Griffith's film *The Birth of a Nation* (1915), the first blockbuster movie, which fused modern entertainment media and technological innovation with a retrograde Southern narrative. As the United States modernized, the dominant images of the South were racism, white supremacy, and fields of cotton.

The images were not far removed from reality. Cotton, in particular, continued to define the southern way of life. Before the Civil War, cotton was one of the most important commodities in the global marketplace, and the South produced more than 75 percent of the world's cotton. After the war, the South's share of the market declined, but cotton continued to be the region's primary economic product, and the fluctuations of the international commodities market dictated the region's solvency. Accordingly, many Southern writers placed cotton at the center of their texts, often as the focus of a quest for self determination. Jack Bethea's *Cotton* (1928) and Harry Kroll's *The Cabin in the Cotton* (1931) both portray sharecroppers' sons who, by dint of hard work and ingenuity, manage to overcome poverty and to manipulate the system of cotton production in their favor, one to become a landowner himself and one to bring down a corrupt landowner. W. E. B. Du Bois's first novel, *The Quest of the Silver Fleece* (1911), uses cotton production as the backdrop for a story about northern philanthropy and African-American education, and the quasi-magical cotton paradoxically symbolizes both the source of racial oppression and the possibility of racial liberation. The South's predominant system of monocrop agricapitalism functions as more than a symbol, however. It defines an elaborate system of race and class stratification that enforces the maintenance of a vast labor pool, and the fact that these novels about cotton all concern the near-impossible struggle for class mobility signals the pervasiveness of this system.

The South's singular production of labor-intensive agricultural commodities delayed the region's urbanization. Until the latter half of the twentieth century, Southern cities tended to be comparatively small and distant from each other, and they also tended to be agricultural hubs where farmers conducted their banking, sold their crops, and bought their goods. So they did not develop diverse, manufacturing economies or progressive, liberal populations on the same scale as their Northern counterparts. Consequently, Southern culture was pervasively rural, agricultural, and conservative, and the majority of Southern literature is set in rural areas and small towns. But the essential ruralism of Southern texts is not necessarily a contrast to modernity; rather, Southern modernity was fundamentally rural – it involved automobiles and tractors more than skyscrapers and factories – and Southern writers portrayed the peculiar and specific material conditions of their time and place. Jefferson, Mississippi, the imaginative landscape of most of Faulkner's great novels, therefore, is every bit as representative of Southern modernity as Joyce's Dublin, Baudelaire's Paris, or Fitzgerald's New York are of cosmopolitan, urban modernity. The notion of modernism as a unified literary movement has, like the notion of the Southern renascence, been largely debunked. Southern modernism is one of several disparate strands of modern literature, one that portrays the impact of a segregated, agricultural society slowly encountering modernity.

The primary system of labor in the rural South, sharecropping, evolved out of the ruins of slavery. In a typical sharecropping contract, a family worked a plot of land for a landowner, cultivating cotton or other staple crops from planting through harvesting over the course of a year, and they divided profits after the crop was sold. The arrangement favored land-owners, who could charge usurious interest on food, fertilizer, and goods advanced to workers and who could manipulate contracts and laws to coerce families into debt. Families who lost money in a year became peons, working without pay until their debt was retired; many families reverted to bound servitude. Sharecropping, unlike slavery, however, extended to white families in addition to black families, and by 1930 white sharecroppers out-numbered black sharecroppers in many parts of the South. Although share-cropping was primarily an economic arrangement, it significantly influenced the South's rigid system of social stratification, its one-party political system, and its culture. The plight of sharecroppers in the modern South particu-larly appealed to writers who identified with communism, which in itself indicates the social marginalization sharecroppers suffered. James Agee and Walker Evans's genre-bending documentary *Let Us Now Praise Famous Men* (1941), for example, catalogs the lives of three white sharecropping families in Alabama, and Grace Lumpkin's novel *A Sign for Cain* (1935) portrays an African-American sharecropper who attempts to organize workers against the landowners for whom they work.

The system that trapped sharecroppers into labor exploitation also fixed other segments of the social structure into inflexible categories. Large land-owners, who were presumably the beneficiaries of economic and political regimes, were themselves subject to precarious cotton markets, fierce com-petition, and the responsibilities of paternalism. William Alexander Percy inherited his family's plantations and political clout, but in his autobiogra-phy *Lanterns on the Levee* (1941) he describes the confinement of Southern society, which forced him to sublimate his homosexuality. And in *Dollar Cotton* (1942), John Faulkner, William Faulkner's brother, caricatures the rise and inevitable fall of a Tennessee backwoodsman who accumulates a vast Mississippi Delta plantation but inevitably loses it through personal excess and falling commodity prices. At the opposite end of the white class structure, poor whites struggled against economic and social debasement in ways that undercut the notion of white privilege, and they captivated American readers. Erskine Caldwell's grossly exaggerated depictions of poor whites in *Tobacco Road* (1932) and *God's Little Acre* (1933) were the best-selling books of their time and both became successful stage plays and films. William Faulkner employed similar caricatures in *As I Lay Dying*, but not all portrayals of poor whites were grotesque. Elizabeth Madox Robert's *The Time of Man* (1935) and George Sessions Perry's *Hold Autumn in Your Hand* (1941) are highly sympathetic, romanticized novels about the dignity and fortitude of poor white families diligently laboring as tenant farmers against forces beyond their control, an idea taken up in another essay in this volume.

Southern social stratification entrapped poor whites, but it was intended more overtly to maintain racial separation and white domination over blacks, and African Americans were systematically demeaned, disfranchised, and dehumanized in the South. Black Southern modernism, however, challenged social hierarchy by juxtaposing African-American folk culture with subversion. Sterling Brown's poetry collection *Southern Road* (1932) and Jean Toomer's collection of poems and sketches *Cane* (1923) use African-American vernacular and scenes from rural life to convey the difficult and sometimes beautiful experience of African-American life in the South. George Wylie Henderson's novel *Ollie Miss* (1935) and Zora Neale Hurston's novels *Their Eyes Were Watching God* (1937) and *Jonah's Gourd Vine* (1934) depict African-American communities in the South as detached from whites, reflecting the extent of segregation that racially bisected the region. Richard Wright's short story collection *Uncle Tom's Children* (1938) confronts the racial inequalities in the rural South. The collection's title alludes to Harriet Beecher Stowe's abolitionist novel *Uncle Tom's Cabin* (1853), but Wright's collection indicates that the decades after Emancipation failed to result in freedom.

Regardless of their race or class, Southern women faced serious challenges that limited their personal agency and social mobility. Southern families were patriarchal, investing most authority in men, and even as modernity led to greater opportunities for women elsewhere, Southern women remained in circumscribed roles, sometimes of their own volition. While the suffrage movement gained traction in the Northeast, for example, many Southern women argued against votes for women, preferring to maintain traditional roles. Women writers represented a broad range of experiences that oscillated from Dorothy Scarborough's novels about women struggling against poverty and weather on Texas cotton farms in *In the Land of Cotton* (1923) and *Can't Get a Redbird* (1929) to Ellen Glasgow's novels about upper-class women in Virginia taking on masculine responsibility while maintaining feminine roles in *Virginia* (1913) and *Barren Ground* (1925). Edith Kelley's *Weeds* (1923), meanwhile, tells an achingly beautiful story of a Kentucky tobacco farmer's wife discovering her sexuality, suffering the challenges of motherhood and domesticity, and inevitably resigning herself to the forces that constrict her life. These writers paved the way for the next generation of Southern women writers, including Eudora Welty, Flannery O'Connor, Carson McCullers, and Alice Walker, who challenged conceptions of femininity and family in the second half of the twentieth century.

Although Southern society was unprepared for modernity at the beginning of the twentieth century, processes emanating from outside the region impacted the South, challenging and changing the social structure, forcing some aspects of modernity on the region, and influencing the region's literature. Some of these processes were natural, such as the march of the boll weevil across the South or frequent cycles of drought and flood, and they ruined crops and damaged the region's agricultural economy and forced entire communities into financial ruin. Other changes were social, and they had even more detrimental consequences for the region. The development of industrialization that shifted the base of the U.S. economy toward manufacturing and that shifted the majority of the U.S. population into cities threatened the agricultural, rural, socially stratified Southern culture more than natural disasters. Although largely ignored at the time of its publication, the collection *I'll Take My Stand* (1930) articulated the worries of a group of conservative Southern writers, including John Crowe Ransom, Allen Tate, and Robert Penn Warren, about the deleterious effects of industrialization on traditional Southern culture, and the collection became more significant as its contributors generated influential theories about literary criticism. The result of worries such as these is that Southern modernist literature typically has a tone of defeatism and defensiveness, and this tone complements and eventually replaces the tone of defiance that defined the culture of the Lost Cause at the end of the nineteenth century.

More than any other event, World War I forced the South into modernity. During the war, the nation galvanized against a common foreign enemy and the war brought Southerners and Northerners into contact on a massive scale. Most U.S. soldiers, including thousands of Northerners, trained at camps hastily constructed in the South, and thousands of Southerners fighting in the war visited Northern cities and Europe, which broadened their provincial perspectives. The war hastened the emergence of industry in the region, particularly textile manufacturing, and it created a boom in the cotton market, making some Southerners temporarily wealthy. World War I devastated Europe and made the United States a superpower, but Southern writers were mostly ambivalent about the changes taking place in the region. Faulkner's first novel, *Soldiers' Pay* (1926), portrays the postwar South as a place detached from modernity, leaving the physically and psychologically wounded returning soldiers alienated. In most stories by Southerners set during World War I, including Walter White's *The Fire in the*

Flint (1924) and Katherine Anne Porter's "Pale Horse, Pale Rider" (1939), the war takes place outside the text, a metaphor for the external forces of modernity operating on the region.

World War I initiated the migration of millions of Southerners out of the region. According to the 1910 census, almost 90 percent of African Americans lived in the South, where they were economically exploited, politically disenfranchised, legally subjected to segregation, and lynched with impunity. Wartime labor shortages in Northern industries attracted nearly half a million African Americans to jobs in Northern cities, a population shift that significantly changed the culture of the urban North, and by 1930, nearly 1.5 million black Southerners moved to cities such as Chicago, Detroit, Cleveland, and New York. The shift led to an eruption of African-American literature, often called the Harlem Renaissance, and to the spread of jazz and blues music and black culture into the North. However, as Richard Wright's novel *Native Son* (1940) illustrates, many black Southerners found the urban North disorienting, inhospitable, and dangerous. In the novel, Bigger Thomas, whose family migrates north from Mississippi, accidentally kills the daughter of a wealthy white family, and he meets the same fate there that he would have in Mississippi, except that in Illinois he is executed in an electric chair while in Mississippi he would have been gruesomely lynched. While much attention has been given to the movement of African Americans, many more white Southerners followed the same migratory path, and by 1930, almost 3 million white Southerners were living outside the region. Many Southern writers, both black and white, lived outside the region, many temporarily and some permanently.

While millions of workers left the South, those who remained chafed under the rigid system of social stratification. Textile mills were built across the South to process the cotton grown in the region, and many sharecroppers became millworkers, or lintheads, where they worked on peculiarly Southern factories, often in isolated enclave communities composed of hastily constructed row houses where entire families, including young children, worked together in the mills. Demand for textiles boomed during World War I, creating a large market for workers at good wages, but the market contracted in the 1920s, leading to tension between workers and mill owners. In 1929, workers at the Loray Mill in Gastonia, North Carolina, organized a union and went on strike. The National Guard and local law enforcement broke the strike, and it failed to improve conditions for workers, but it inspired several novels about the industrializing South, including Erskine Caldwell's *God's Little Acre* (1933), Olive Tilford Dargan's *Call Home the Heart* (1932), Grace Lumpkin's *To Make My Bread* (1932), and Myra Page's *Gathering Storm* (1932). These books indicated a proletarian turn in Southern literature that shifted projections of Southern poverty from abject ridicule to sympathy.

When the stock market crashed in 1929, the South was devastated. Cotton prices had been in decline for several years since World War I, so the economy was already in a precarious condition, and during the Depression many farms were foreclosed, unemployment skyrocketed, and thousands of sharecropping families were evicted. The tenuous advances of modernity in the region receded and poverty deepened, leaving Southerners with few opportunities for social progress. In 1934, a small, interracial group of farmers in Arkansas organized the Southern Tenant Farmers Union to advocate for the region's poorest farmers. They were met with violent resistance, but they persevered until World War II and demonstrated that not all Southerners were resigned to poverty. Charlie May Simon dramatized the union in *The Share-Cropper* (1937) in which a sharecropper and a lawyer organize a union, but the landowners have the striking workers arrested for vagrancy and force them to work out their fines chopping cotton in the same fields. The strike fails, but the eponymous sharecropper looks forward to a day when there would be "an honest system, one that would not drag them down to where they could never rise up."[7] Although the Southern economy suffered during the Depression, Southern writing flourished: many volumes of Southern proletarian fiction were published, the "Southern Renaissance" that Allen Tate described reached its zenith, and Faulkner published his major novels, including *The Sound and the Fury* (1929), *As I Lay Dying* (1930), *Light in August* (1932), and *Absalom, Absalom!* (1936). The Depression challenged the notion of modernity as an unfolding process of social progress, and the South symbolized the unevenness of modernity in the American imagination.

President Franklin D. Roosevelt's New Deal invested heavily in government programs for unemployed Southerners during the Depression. Many of his programs created job opportunities for communities across the country, such as the Civilian Conservation Corps and the National Recovery Administration, but the Tennessee Valley Authority and the Rural Electrification Administration had specific impacts on the South, where less than 5 percent of rural homes had electricity in 1930. The spread of electrification and running water to Southern homes marked the most distinct intervention of modernity in many people's daily lives. Of even greater significance for the South, however, was the Agricultural Adjustment Act, a bill that paid farmers to limit their production of cash crops in order to stabilize the commodities market. The bill favored landowners, many of whom evicted sharecroppers and plowed their fields under to increase their subsidies. The displaced sharecroppers, however, were a favorite subject of photographers from the Farm Security Administration, a group of photographers working for the federal government who generated propaganda for the New Deal. Many of the greatest documentary photographers of the time worked for the administration, including Walker Evans, Dorothea Lange, and Ben Shahn, and the images they took visually defined the experience of Southern poverty. Their work influenced a wave of creative nonfiction documentaries about poor Southerners, in particular the photographic and textual collaborations *You Have Seen their Faces* (1937) by Erskine Caldwell and Margaret Bourke-White and *Let Us Now Praise Famous Men* (1941) by James Agee and Walker Evans.

The South emerged from the Great Depression slowly. In 1938, President Roosevelt called the South "America's number one economic problem," and the region did not show significant signs of growth until World War II. The war ultimately propelled the South into modernity, closing the development gap between the regions substantially. Several hundred thousand Southerners served in the war, thousands more worked into massive factories built in the South for war materials, and even more left the South to work in factories in the North. Harriette Arnow's novel *The Dollmaker* (1954) tells the tragic story of Gertie Nevels, a woman from Kentucky who moves with her husband to find work in Detroit, where they are dehumanized, turned into virtually mechanical devices in a harsh urban landscape. After the war, the South urbanized rapidly and agriculture mechanized on a large scale, finally bringing sharecropping to an end. The effect of these changes was to detach the region from its traditional, antimodern way of life, which led to changes in the rigidly stratified social structure, including the slow, inevitable end of segregation. John Oliver Killens's novel *And Then We Heard the Thunder* (1963), however, explores the ways in which the war exported Southern racism both domestically to military encampments outside the South and to bases overseas. Killens's novel, and a wave of postwar Southern writing, suggested that the term "Southern" referred more to a complex set of antimodern social relations than to a specific region.

While massive social upheaval changed the South in the first half of the twentieth century, the region remained a site of social problems that seemed to be detached from the more progressive nation. As modernity developed in the United States, the notion of the American Dream emerged as a model for class mobility and social progress predicated on participant democracy and free enterprise. The model did not always work in practice, but it resonated strongly in the American imagination, yet it did not seem to apply to the South. The feudalistic system of landowners and sharecroppers defied free enterprise and impeded class mobility, and the one-party system of politics prohibited participant democracy. These systemic problems were exacerbated by the South's well-deserved reputation for ignorance, poverty, and violence, and by Southerners' oppressive tendency to enforce social and intellectual conformity, which W. J. Cash labeled the "savage ideal" in *The Mind of the South* (1941). To many Americans, the South was an exotic, coercive, dangerous, and inhospitable alternative nation.

The most obvious sign of Southern savagery in the first half of the twentieth century was lynching. Between the end of the Civil War and the beginning of World War II, more than three thousand African Americans, and some whites, were lynched in the South. Many were accused of violent or sexual crimes, but they were denied the right to trial by jury and were violently murdered by mobs, usually after being tortured and often in public. The gruesomeness of lynching revolted many Americans – although many audiences outside the South cheered the lynching of Gus in *The Birth of a Nation* in 1915 – but Southerners argued that lynch law was essential to maintaining racial hierarchy. African-American modernists exposed the consequences of racial violence: Sutton Griggs's novel *The Hindered Hand* (1905) describes the hideous torture of an African-American couple; Jean Toomer depicts a lynching as the result of a romantic triangle in *Cane* (1923); and a lynching convinces the protagonist in James Weldon Johnson's *The Autobiography of an Ex-Colored Man* (1912) to pass for white. Lynching loomed in the background of many Southern texts, and the pretexts for lynching became a national cause célèbre during the trial of the Scottsboro Boys, nine black teenagers accused of raping two white women in 1931. William Faulkner's novel *Light in August* (1932), published during the trial, concludes with the makeshift lynching of Joe Christmas, his most racially ambiguous character.

Lynchings were an outrageous extralegal form of justice, but the South's institutionalized legal system of justice also shocked Americans. The Reconstruction-era laws known as the Black Codes set substantial sentences for African Americans who violated arbitrary laws, but the South did not have sufficient facilities to incarcerate inmates. An expedient system developed in which contractors leased inmates from the states to use their labor, often in dangerous occupations. Convict leasing created a revenue stream for the states and an incentive to incarcerate as many men as possible. One of the most odious characters in Charles Chesnutt's *The Marrow of Tradition* makes his fortune by exploiting leased convict labor. The leasing system lasted from Reconstruction until the 1920s, when accounts of inmate brutalization finally led to reforms. The only significant change, however, was that states assumed direct responsibility for inmate labor, using them on chain gangs that built roads and bridges, on prison farms such as Parchman in Mississippi or Angola in Louisiana, or in prison mines such as Brushy

Mountain in Tennessee. Robert Burns's sensational autobiography *I Am a Fugitive from a Georgia Chain Gang* (1932) became a blockbuster movie that focused national attention on chain gangs, and John L. Spivak's novel *Hard Times on the Southern Chain Gang* – originally titled *Georgia Nigger* (1932) – exposed the connections between sharecropping and incarceration as forms of racial domination and labor control.

The most effective forms of social control used in the South, however, were not legal but religious. In the first half of the twentieth century, as scientific discovery challenged religious doctrine and as social gospel supported liberal progressivism, Southern religious fundamentalism enforced strict adherence to literal interpretations of scripture and rigid conformity to social mores. The 1925 trial of John Scopes on charges of violating the Butler Act, which made teaching religious heresy illegal, for teaching the theory of evolution in Tennessee public schools is the highest-profile example of public conformity to fundamentalism. The trial focused national attention on the South, and H. L. Mencken, the nation's most famous journalist, who had previously labeled the South a dried-up civilization in "The Sahara of the Bozart" (1920), heaped criticism on the region.[8] John Crowe Ransom initially found Mencken's ridicule persuasive, but his attitude became more conservative over time, and he decries the creeping secularism of modern American life and longs for a return to fundamentalism in *God Without Thunder* (1930). In spite of Ransom's worries about secularization, Biblical standards of moral judgment permeated Southern culture, often in contradictory ways. Southerners, for example, overwhelmingly supported the temperance campaign that led to the prohibition of alcohol in the United States, and they simultaneously supported a vast and lucrative culture of moonshining and bootlegging. Faulkner explores these contradictions in his ironically titled novel *Sanctuary* (1931), in which a wayward Ole Miss coed descends into the underworld of speakeasies and brothels. Erskine Caldwell also exposes the contradictions of Southern fundamentalism in *Journeyman* (1935), his novel about a philandering itinerant minister in Georgia, and Zora Neale Hurston tells a similar story about a conflicted preacher in *Jonah's Gourd Vine* (1934), a novel that demonstrates the relationship between Christian fundamentalism and conjure in African-American folk religion.

Far from embracing the scientific and social progress of modernity, many Southerners looked to a mythological Southern past to construct an ideology and way of life that defied modernization. Although the cult of the Lost Cause that venerated Confederate veterans waned in the twentieth century, it did not disappear, and many Southerners continued to replicate hazy notions of the Old South and to indulge in obsessive historical revision. Several Southern novels betray this type of past gazing, usually focusing on the Civil War as the apotheosis of Southern civilization. Allen Tate rewrites and refights the Civil War in *The Fathers* (1938), as do Stark Young in *So Red the Rose* (1934) and William Faulkner in *The Unvanquished* (1938). These novels, written during the Great Depression, romanticize a version of the South that predates the impoverished, savage South of the twentieth century and thus escapes the challenges of modernity. Faulkner, however, exploded many myths of the Old South in *Absalom, Absalom!* (1936), the story of poor white Thomas Sutpen's single-minded and self-destructive rise to plantation gentry in Mississippi. The most famous account of modern historical imagination, however, is Margaret Mitchell's *Gone with the Wind* (1936). The best-selling Pulitzer Prize–winning novel and the blockbuster Academy Award–winning movie have effectively reconstituted the war, and the Lost Cause in Southern history in the popular imagination.

The cultural ascendancy of *Gone with the Wind* epitomizes the inherent irony of Southern modernism. By the middle of the twentieth century, Southern writers significantly influenced mainstream currents of American literature on a broad scale, arguably for the first time, achieving both commercial and critical success even though – or perhaps because – the region that they represented lagged behind the rest of the nation in other areas of social, cultural, and economic development. The South's delayed development may actually explain its literary success because the region represented an alternative version of nation, one that resisted and evaded the consequences of modernity and acted as a field for Americans to project visions of ignorance, backwardness, pastoralism, and rebelliousness onto a space of alterity. In this sense, the South has always been a figment of the American imagination, but focusing on the imaginary, alternative South can distract readers from the real South – the one where sharecropping and poverty actually existed. The social context matters because in Southern modernism the culture of cotton is just as important as the culture of cubism.

NOTES

1 William Faulkner, *As I Lay Dying* (1930, New York: Vintage, 1991), p. 219.
2 Allen Tate, "The New Provincialism," *Essays of Four Decades* (Chicago: Swallow Press, 1968), p. 535.
3 Richard Gray, *The Literature of Memory: Modern Writers of the American South* (Baltimore: Johns Hopkins University Press, 1977), pp. 2–3; Richard King, *A Southern Renaissance: The Cultural Awakening of the American South: 1930–1955* (New York: Oxford University Press, 1980), p. 7.
4 Matthew Guinn, *After Southern Modernism: Fiction of the Contemporary South* (Jackson: University Press of Mississippi), p. xviii.
5 Scott Romine, *The Real South: Southern Narrative in the Age of Cultural Reproduction* (Baton Rouge: Louisiana State University Press, 2008), p. 4.

6 Allen Tate, "The New Provincialism," *Essays of Four Decades* (Chicago: Swallow Press, 1968), pp. 543–545.
7 Charlie May Simon, *The Share-Cropper* (New York: E. P. Dutton, 1937), p. 247.
8 H. L. Mencken, "Sahara of the Bozart," *Prejudices: Second Series* (New York: Knopf, 1920), p. 137.

7

SARAH ROBERTSON

Poverty and Progress

The South, historically home to high percentages of those living on or beneath the poverty line, and with its turbulent history of slavery and segregation, continues to be synonymous with both poverty and progress.[1] For every progressive step taken toward bringing greater equality among its heterogeneous citizens, reactive moves come into effect to uphold a homogenous narrative about the South that bypasses its complex history and the diverse micro-regions that constitute its whole. In such a climate, economic and political changes neither run smoothly nor without controversy, with the benefits of changes slow to materialize. In the twentieth century, Southern blacks faced the difficult and long journey to bring an end to the region's racial segregation laws. The Southern poor also came to the attention of the nation in startling fashion during the 1930s Depression and President Johnson's War on Poverty in the 1960s. More recently, Hurricane Katrina that devastated large areas of the Gulf Coast in 2005, along with the ongoing global recession, has highlighted the high density of poverty still apparent in southern states.

This essay considers the various ways in which Southern authors explore the social, economic, and political imperatives of their time, moving from the 1930s through the twenty-first century. While the roots of Southern poverty reach back further than the Depression, it was during the 1930s that Southern poverty entered the national consciousness with unprecedented force as the plight of the nation's poor was repeatedly captured through documentary media. Poverty did not end as the nation moved out of the Depression, and the fictions discussed here may be read as telling a continuous story about economic deprivation in the South. While I focus on the experiences of poor blacks and poor whites, the South is, and always has been, a region with more categories than black and white, and Southern Studies now recognizes those Native Americans and immigrants whose narratives had often been written out of the South.

Despite nationwide levels of poverty during the Depression, certain regions and groups more forcefully captured the national imagination. In 1936 and 1937, Mississippi author Eudora Welty's photography was exhibited in New York, underlining the national interest in the South's impoverishment. Certainly, while novels such as John Steinbeck's *The Grapes of Wrath* (1939) and the widely distributed Farm Security Administration's (FSA) photographs, including Dorothea Lange's famed "Migrant Mother" (1936), brought the plight of displaced Midwesterners to the foreground, the FSA lens was directly pointed toward the South where the inherent inequalities in the sharecropping and tenant systems were intensified during this period of economic decline. The Southern annual income during the 1930s was half of what it was in the North and, as Stephen Pimpare explains, for many Southerners "it was worse: $73 for the average tenant farmer, and from $38 to $87 for sharecroppers."[2] Even the introduction of the New Deal did little to advance the lot of poor tenants and sharecroppers as it tended to support landowners and large-scale farmers.[3]

As a result, Southern poverty loomed large in key publications that merged descriptive and visual accounts of poor lives to distinctive effect. In particular, rural poverty was captured time and again in images that have come to dominate cultural perceptions and misconceptions of the region from the Deep South to Appalachia. Such images were intended to highlight the effects of abject poverty in these rural, outlying areas, with writers and photographers often attempting to merge artistic and political ends. In 1937, for example, Erskine Caldwell and photographer Margaret Bourke-White published *You Have Seen Their Faces*, a photo-essay focusing on the lives of black and white sharecroppers throughout the Deep South. Shots of poor blacks and whites litter the text, supported throughout by descriptive prose, but readers do well to read the explanatory note: "The legends under the pictures are intended to express the authors' own conceptions of the sentiments of the people portrayed." In effect, although Caldwell sought to expose inherent inequalities in the sharecropping system, he and Bourke-White privilege their own authorial and artistic interpretation of what they see, denying their subjects the ability to articulate their own plight.

James Agee and Walker Evans's *Let Us Now Praise Famous Men* (1941) is seemingly more nuanced. Perhaps the most renowned of a number of photo-essays, it provides detailed and balanced insights into the lives of three white tenant families in Alabama, with Agee agonizing at length about the difficulties of capturing the lives of others in prose. As an outsider looking in, he asks, "How am I to speak of you?" worried that he might "betray" the tenant farmers.[4] Some of Agee's observations draw sharp attention to his outsider perspective, including his assertion that "'sense of beauty,' like nearly everything else is a class privilege."[5] The struggle to move beyond an "us and them" dynamic was nowhere more apparent than in Caldwell's novel

Tobacco Road (1932), where, despite his efforts to make a searing attack on the tenant system, the descriptions of the debauched Lester family depended on notions of the generational defects of poor whites: ideas expounded by his father, Ira Sylvester Caldwell, in his eugenicist claims for the sterilization of "poor white trash." Unlike William Faulkner's *As I Lay Dying* (1930) that offers a complex portrait of the poor white Bundren family, in *Tobacco Road* Caldwell's description of the facially deformed Ellie May rubbing herself along the ground like a dog in heat sets the tone for the text, with the cyclical nature of the Lesters' lives compounded by Dude's final ruminations on following in his father's path. As Leigh Anne Duck suggests, "Caldwell's stagnating grotesques enabled audience members to manage fears of their own economic and social decline by projecting them onto the bodies of a spatially and temporally distanced population."[6]

Such a distant glance at an othered poor white body is reflected in the novel through the three black characters who watch the Lesters with intrigue, humor, and repulsion. This is a clear reminder of the fraught relationship between poor whites and blacks as both groups tried to advance beyond the bottom rung of the Southern social ladder, with black slaves having been attributed with coining the term "poor white trash," and with poor whites often involved in racial violence against blacks. Even during the Depression, despite the common experiences of sharecropping and tenancy, the antagonism between poor whites and blacks did not diminish.

When authors depicted poor whites in the Depression-era South, they commonly relied on derogatory labels including "white trash," "redneck," "cracker," or "dirt-eater," and their associated traits such as laziness, drunkenness, and violence. Fictions that attempted to move beyond the stereotypes were few and the absence of a strong poor white literary voice to counteract these negative labels only strengthened disparaging interpretations of the class. While class outsiders focused on poor whites during the Depression, black writers were giving voice to their own experiences of Southern poverty and racial discrimination.

Since the publication of nineteenth-century slave narratives, black authors have made important moves into the literary arena, a move strongly enhanced during the Harlem Renaissance throughout the 1920s and 1930s that celebrated black authors, musicians, and artists, including Zora Neale Hurston. Hurston's work, notably her novel *Their Eyes Were Watching God* (1937) and her autobiography *Dust Tracks on a Road* (1942), dropped from view, only resurrected during the 1970s as she was championed by writers such as Alice Walker. During the Harlem Renaissance, Hurston came into conflict with fellow black writer Richard Wright, with Wright claiming in his review of *Their Eyes Were Watching God* that Hurston had created minstrel show characters to please white readers of the novel.[7] Wright's own writing offered a searing portrayal of the limits imposed on black lives in the United States, as exemplified in his photo-essay *12 Million Black Voices* (1941). In this work Wright focuses on poor blacks, with the continual employment of "us," "we," and "our" highlighting his own experiences of poverty and racism. His deep connection with his subject stands in stark contrast to the distance apparent in Caldwell and Bourke-White's photo-essay. In *12 Million Black Voices*, as well as his novel *Native Son* (1940) and autobiography *Black Boy* (1945), he charts the black migration from the South to the North, deliberating on the failure of Northern migration to enhance black lives.

The great migration of Southern blacks to the North was a prominent subject for black writers in the Depression era. Although the migration had begun after the end of the Civil War in 1865, the Depression's dramatic economic downturn and its direct impact on Southern agriculture meant that this period saw a significant rise in those leaving the region. In 1910, the South was home to 89 percent of the country's black population, but by 1970 that percentage had dropped to 53 percent.[8] While writers such as Caldwell risked presenting poor whites as static, of the 9 million people who left the South between 1910 and 1960 the number of whites was marginally higher than the number of blacks. Jacqueline Jones explains that "the migration histories of the two groups ran together, shaped by common forces of displacement and dispersal, and then apart, as a result of contrasting circumstances and historical consciousness."[9] Nevertheless, black migration is more widely recognized and it was a topical issue for many black writers.

In *Native Son*, the Thomas family, having left the segregated South, encounters not a freer, but rather a more subtly segregated society in Chicago. Living in rooms that his mother labels as a "garbage dump," Bigger Thomas hates his family "because he knew that they were suffering and that he was powerless to help them."[10] Such terrible living conditions were captured in *12 Million Black Voices* where he details the extensive problems in Northern cities, and goes so far as to claim that unsanitary living conditions might mean "black folks who dwell in northern cities would die out entirely over the course of a few years."[11] As Bigger continues to experience poverty and racial discrimination in a Northern setting, his pent-up rage is made manifest in his desire for, and murder of, the daughter of his white employer. With acute sensations of fear, Bigger ineffectually burns her body in a furnace but evidence of her white body still remains to incriminate him. Facing the death sentence at the close of the novel, readers leave Bigger behind bars as he hears "the ring of steel against steel as a far door clanged shut."[12] Whatever personal realizations Bigger may experience during the

SARAH ROBERTSON

trial, this final image reflects his complete caging, underlining the denial of any future progression.

Alongside Wright's photo-essay, his autobiographical *Black Boy* (1945) captures direct experiences of poverty and inequality in a racially segregated South. He ruminates on an itinerant childhood spent in various Southern locations, with overwhelming experiences of hunger, both literal and metaphorical, as he dreams of a life outside of the South. As he matures he sees the ways in which black lives are molded and distorted by white society and the challenges of breaking out of such a predetermined existence. By extension, William Attaway's *Blood on the Forge* (1941) captures in vivid detail the plight of Southern black migrants to Northern industrial towns and cities, highlighting "the limited gains that African Americans made in organized labor during the New Deal era."[13] His central characters – three half-brothers, Mat, Melody, and Chinatown – play a "wishing game," but as they are lured North their wishes are either killed with them, as with Mat who is crushed to death during labor unrest, or left unfulfilled, with Melody and Chinatown moving farther North at the end of the novel, still hoping for a better life. While Melody has a keen understanding of the fact that "share-cropping and being hungry went together," Mat's love of land, a love as futile and doomed as Jeeter Lester's, reverberates in his mind long after he and his brothers have moved off the land to take up industrial labor in a place of "limestone and black coke" where they have to *leave off tending green growing things to tend iron monsters.*[14] These iron constraints are like the steel bars that contain Bigger Thomas.

While World War II galvanized the U.S. economy and moved it out of the Depression, the return of black servicemen to the South added fuel to black political demands for the end of segregation and for voting rights, with the civil rights movement gaining momentum. Nevertheless, Alice Walker's key question, "The Civil Rights Movement: What Good Was It?" echoes through a number of novels written during the period. Sarah E. Wright's *This Child's Gonna Live* (1969), is a novel "informed by the dual influences of Black Power and women's rights."[15] This alignment of civil rights and women's rights or feminism was common in a period that witnessed not simply a resurgence of black novelists, but a celebration of black women writers, including Toni Morrison, Maya Angelou, and Alice Walker. In Wright's novel, set in Maryland, the central character, Mariah, continually desires a better life for herself and her children. However, her hopes and desires are restricted by the realities of her daily life, with the family's poverty exemplified in the death of her son, Rabbit. In gruesome detail Wright depicts the parasitic worms that take over Rabbit's body, crawling "right out of his behind" and his nose.[16] Wright's forthright depiction of the poor diet and living conditions of the family is echoed in later works by writers from poor white backgrounds. Harry Crews, for instance, recalls the "worms that would sometimes rise out of their children's stomachs and nest in their throats so that they had to be pulled out by hand to keep the children from choking."[17] These authors describe the daily horrors of poverty, and in Wright's novel Mariah finally finds no escape.

Representations of such restricted lives are legion in Walker's *The Third Life of Grange Copeland* (1970). Her characters typically experience "a feeling of progress," but it is merely a sensation of possibility rather than seismic improvement in their lived experience. The eponymous Grange flees northward, abandoning his family, but like his counterparts in *Blood on the Forge*, Grange discovers the North offers no escape. His eventual return sees him living a better quality of life in the South, but while he helps and supports his granddaughter, Ruth, his return cannot undo the tragic life of his son, Brownfield, who is devastated by poverty and false hope, and who even as a child felt filled with discontent. It is this discontentment that carries violent ramifications as he grows up to beat and then murder his wife. It is in their child Ruth that Walker places hope to break out of the poverty trap. Ruth stands up to her violent father even as a young child, and later, when she lives with Grange, she expresses a willingness to see beyond stereotypes. When she and Grange discuss the poor whites that are their close neighbors, Grange decides to take her to "inspect" them, with this scene drawing attention to the repeated failures of poor black and poor whites to join together in concerted and lasting ways to challenge the Southern class system.

These groups did briefly work collectively to tackle poverty in the 1968 Poor People's Campaign that brought together poor people of various racial backgrounds, including Native Americans, to demand political change with a new "economic bill of rights." Together they marched on Washington in May 1968 after Martin Luther King's death, and set up an encampment, known as Resurrection City, on the Washington Mall. With the camp's closure a month later, in June 1968, the campaign stands as one of many thwarted efforts to bring the poor together to enact change. So, although historically racial barriers are not commonly or easily overcome in the pursuit of class advancement, in Walker's novel, Ruth challenges Grange's assumptions about their poor white neighbors, asking, "Did anybody ever try to find out if they's real *people*," and insisting, "'I want to see and hear them face to face; I don't see no sense in them being looked at like buzzards in a cage.'"[18]

In a period in which black writers were engaging with issues including civil rights and feminism, significant political steps were also being taken to tackle poverty. In 1960, President Kennedy had visited coal towns in

West Virginia, encountering stark levels of economic deprivation that were fully brought into the national consciousness when Michael Harrington published *The Other America* (1962) in which he challenged Americans to lift the veil that kept poverty one of the nation's best-kept secrets. In 1964, President Johnson introduced his War on Poverty that instigated the rollout of numerous initiatives, programs, and legislative reforms to combat poverty. Appalachia, with its isolated communities and hills savaged by coal and timber operators, was a primary target. Initiatives such as the educational program Head Start, launched in 1965 and still operating today, were central to the administration's plans for rejuvenating local communities. The forms of Appalachian poverty that such programs sought to tackle were captured across various publications in the years following the War on Poverty, notably in Harry M. Caudill's photo-essay *My Land is Dying* (1971), and in fiction, as in Breece D'J Pancake's posthumously published work as *The Stories of Breece D'J Pancake* (1977). Despite such thoughtful accounts, in fiction poor whites continued to be written about in negative and debilitating ways. Published in 1970, James Dickey's *Deliverance* offered a slice of Southern gothic in which deformed, frightful, and violent poor backwoods whites act as foils to four city men seeking a retreat into the natural heart of Southern Appalachia before its ruination by the construction of a nearby dam. With the trip becoming an excursion into a heart of darkness, with Dickey's presentation of degenerate, sexually crazed backwoodsmen, readers were returned to the unrestrained behavior of Caldwell's Lesters.

While Cormac McCarthy's early Southern gothic novels, *The Orchard Keeper* (1965), *Outer Dark* (1968), and *Child of God* (1973), are considered to offer more thought-provoking and nuanced depictions of poor whites,[19] in *Child of God*, descriptions of Lester Ballard depend heavily on stereotype and are heightened through his depiction of the dumpkeeper's family living among "levees of junk and garbage" in a "rank and fetid" environment.[20] Members of Ballard's community consider him a member of a lower-evolved species, and while McCarthy appeals to readers to see Ballard's humanity, degeneracy looms large. Even in Harper Lee's *To Kill a Mockingbird* (1960), for all its concern with racial inequalities in both the story's Depression-era setting and in the contemporary world of its production, it depends on long held ideas about the "good poor" and the "bad poor." So low are the poor white Ewells that even judicious lawyer Atticus Finch deems it appropriate to take Scout to see "where and how they lived." Like Alice Walker's Ruth, Scout can see that the Ewells are people, but she does not share the same ability to look beyond her initial assumptions that the Ewells live "like animals."[21] Such assumptions find no challenge from the adults in Scout's life, with Atticus's belief in the generational defectiveness of the

Ewells carrying strains of eugenicist thinking. Lee goes some way to redeem the Ewells through the tragically flawed Mayella, but as a counterpoint to the death of Tom Robinson, she offers up a sinister Bob Ewell to satisfy a sense of justice. With the poor white threat expelled, life in Maycomb is restored to some semblance of order, highlighting the expendability of poor whites. In such novels, poor whites provide the gothic moment of horror that prompts self-reflection in fellow characters and readers.

In *The Other America*, Michael Harrington called for authors to "record the smell and the texture and quality" of poor lives, and while many black writers had already done so, from the late 1970s writers from poor white backgrounds also emerged.[22] The civil rights movement propelled the careers of minority writers, and in conjunction with increased educational opportunities, poor whites turned to literature and autobiography in order to tell their stories. Harry Crews's *A Childhood: The Biography of a Place* (1978) stands as a seminal text, with his uncompromising account of abject poverty setting a precedent for poor white writers who succeeded him. Crews acknowledged the significance of an autobiographical voice for telling his story, professing that he decided to write "naked, without the disguising distance of the third-person pronoun."[23] For poor whites, written about for so long by class outsiders, late-twentieth-century autobiographical writing finally allowed their voices to be heard. Significantly, in *A Childhood*, and across Crews's fiction, he draws attention to the fact that poor whites still experience hard lives shaped by harsh extremities.

Writers including Rick Bragg, Tim McLaurin, Janisse Ray, Sheri Reynolds, Barbara Robinette Moss, and Dorothy Allison have followed in Crews' path, offering up counter-narratives to debilitating stereotypes. Allison, in the Introduction to her collection of short stories, *Trash* (1988), states that writing allows her "to join the conversation," to participate in and to destabilize the dominant narratives that have defined poor white lives. Allison's tone reverberates with the anger, humor, and compassion found across this body of writing as she challenges assumptions about the "bad poor."[24] Allison does not completely dispel negative stereotypes: her male characters often drink to excess, are violent and abusive, their female counterparts are often broken, beaten-down, and resigned to cyclical rounds of poverty. In "River of Names," the opening story in *Trash*, the narrator recalls the terror of a childhood in which violence, death, and sexual abuse passed by unremarked. Yet Allison's writing adds depth and dimension to poor white stereotypes. Indeed in her semi-autobiographical novel, *Bastard Out of Carolina* (1992), the poverty and sexual abuse suffered by the central protagonist Ruth Anne "Bone" Boatwright is partially set into relief by strong characters, particularly her Uncle Earle and Aunt Raylene. Whereas Earle spends the majority of his time between women and prison sentences, Bone gains a sense of pride from his family loyalty. More significantly, she learns from Raylene that "trash rises" and while this phrase refers ostensibly to objects in the river that Raylene retrieves and recycles, it comes to stands as a future objective for Bone.[25]

Childhood poverty has been the subject of many novels and memoirs by both white and black writers, including Maya Angelou's *I Know Why the Caged Bird Sings* (1969), in which she looks back over her childhood in 1930s Arkansas. More recently, poor white memoirists detail poor childhoods during the 1950s and 1960s, offering narratives that form a backstory to the idea of nationwide prosperity in the wake of World War II, filled as they are with children who are hungry for sustenance and improved living conditions: hunger reminiscent of that which plagues Richard Wright in *Black Boy*. The hunger haunting Allison's young protagonist Bone is echoed in the opening lines of Connie May Fowler's *Before Women Had Wings* (1996), where Bird Jackson confides her "craving spells" and how she is "chock-full of wishes."[26] These authors make manifest the complexity of hunger through first-person narrators, as in Kaye Gibbons autobiographical novel *Ellen Foster* (1987). In many of these texts cross-racial friendships are explored, and they typically reveal how the divisive racial hatred that kept poor blacks and whites apart restricts the formation of friendships. As Sharon Monteith demonstrates, a number of contemporary white Southern white writers have turned their attention to exploring "the traditional obstacles that have worked to circumvent cross-racial support, enterprise, and love," and the limits to those friendships mirror wider failures to eradicate racial tensions and widespread poverty.[27]

On the surface, the huge influx of blacks to the South during the economic boom period of the late 1960s and 1970s, commonly referred to as the Sun-Belt South, tells a story of improved economic and social conditions, yet during that period, "[a] black bourgeoisie fared well, while ordinary blacks struggled to make ends meet."[28] While this highlights the ongoing restrictions for those on the poverty line, the return of blacks to the South in a reverse of the great migration is often regarded as offering a positive reevaluation of the region. For Thadious Davis, "black southerners are both literally and imaginatively returning to the region and its past, assuming regional identification for self and group definition."[29] Davis draws attention to the role of the South in writing by non-Southern authors, including Ntozake Shange, Gloria Naylor, and Toni Morrison. Morrison, born in Ohio, has repeatedly gone southward in her work, in particular in *Song of Solomon* (1977) and *Beloved* (1988), as Pearl McHaney describes in her essay in this volume. In

Song of Solomon, protagonist Milkman Dead is propelled on a southern trajectory, first in pursuit of mercantile desire, then in search for his family's past. For a character initially ignorant of the history of slavery, his southern journey allows Milkman to connect with his family's history, one with African and Native American roots. Despite the tensions that arise in registering the South as homeplace, these literary moves, and the actual return of blacks to the region, signal a progressive move to address the region's history for its horror as well as its complexities.

If the South now demands to be read and understood as a heterogeneous place, it still remains troubled by its past. This tension may never be fully resolved, given that for every step toward progress there are strong markers of racism and poverty that still plague the region. When Hurricane Katrina hit the Gulf Coast and the world watched the abandonment of New Orleans's poor citizens, any sense of progress was sharply brought into question. Indeed, in 2005, Louisiana had "the second-highest rate of deep poverty among children" with "almost 40 percent of all New Orleans children" living in poverty.[30] The Depression once made all Americans aware of extensive poverty throughout the South, and Katrina reminded both the nation and a global audience, that in New Orleans, and all along the Gulf Coast, those living on or beneath the poverty line had no means to escape the unfolding natural disaster and the subsequent man-made catastrophe as they were left among the detritus. Katrina produced a wide range of documentary footage, with Eric Gay's photograph of eighty-four-year-old Milvertha Hendrick's wrapped in an American flag outside the Convention Center on September 1, 2005 becoming as iconic as Dorothea Lange's "Migrant Mother." Spike Lee's documentary film *When the Levees Broke: A Requiem in Four Acts* (2006) brought into focus the racial tension between New Orleans disenfranchised blacks and whites, and Dave Eggers's biography, *Zeitoun* (2009) celebrates Abdulrahman Zeitoun who helped fellow citizens in the wake of Katrina, but also highlights the racism Zeitoun encounters as a Muslim and as a Syrian who made his home in New Orleans.

For all the political, social, and economic progress that has radically altered the South since the Depression, the 2010 U.S. census revealed that nationwide, the highest density of poverty is in the South. Such statistics risk being subsumed in a contemporary world where Depression-era chic takes center stage on the catwalk, and where "white trash" is at once still an acceptable slur and a commodified term. In effect, the slick, shiny, and ultimately elusive surface of progress daily subsumes the realities of poverty. In all their horror, events such as Hurricane Katrina break the veneer and show the continual abjection of the poor.

NOTES

1 *Poverty and Progress in the U.S. South since 1920*, ed. Suzanne Jones and Mark Newman (Amsterdam: VU University Press, 2006) is a series of illuminating essays on the dynamics of poverty and progress in the region.
2 Stephen Pimpare, *A People's History of Poverty in America* (New York: The New Press, 2008), pp. 180–181.
3 For a useful overview of the limited successes of the New Deal for poor rural Southerners see chapter 7 in Gilbert C. Fite's, *Cotton Fields No More: Southern Agriculture, 1865–1980* (Lexington: University Press of Kentucky, 1984), pp. 139–162.
4 James Agee and Walker Evans, *Let Us Now Praise Famous Men*, 1941 (New York: Ballantine Books, 1960), p. 92.
5 Agee and Evans, p. 285.
6 Leigh Anne Duck, *The Nation's Region: Southern Modernism, Segregation, and U.S. Nationalism* (Athens: University of Georgia Press, 2006), p. 87.
7 Richard Wright, "Review," *New Masses* (October 5, 1937): 22–23.
8 See James C. Cobb, "Introduction," in Craig S. Pascoe, Karen Trahan Leatham, and Andy Ambrose, eds., *The American South in the Twentieth Century*, p. 3.
9 Jacqueline Jones, *The Dispossessed: America's Underclasses from the Civil War to the Present* (New York: Basic Books, 1992), pp. 205–206.
10 Richard Wright, *Native Son* (1940; London: Picador, 1995), pp. 46, 48.
11 Richard Wright, *12 Million Black Voices* (1941; New York: Basic Books, 2008), p. 107.
12 Wright, *Native Son*, p. 462.
13 Mark Noon, "'It ain't your color, it's your scabbing': Literary Depictions of African American Strikebreakers," *African American Review* 38:3 (Fall 2004): 434.
14 William Attaway, *Blood on the Forge* (1941; New York: Anchor Books, 1993), pp. 1, 52; italics in the original.
15 Jennifer Campbell, "'It's a time in the land': Gendering Black Power and Sarah E. Wright's Place in the Tradition of Black Women's Writing," *African American Review* 31:2 (Summer 1997): 211–222.
16 Sarah E. Wright, *This Child's Gonna Live* (New York: Delacorte Press, 1969), p. 253.
17 Harry Crews, *A Childhood: The Biography of a Place* (1978; Athens: University of Georgia Press, 1995), p. 11.
18 Alice Walker, *The Third Life of Grange Copeland* (1970; London: Phoenix, 2004), p. 233.
19 For favorable interpretations of McCarthy's poor whites, see Vereen M. Bell, *The Achievement of Cormac McCarthy* (Baton Rouge: Louisiana State University Press, 1988) and Gary M. Ciuba, *Desire, Violence, and Divinity in Modern Southern Fiction* (Baton Rouge: Louisiana State University Press, 2007).
20 Cormac McCarthy, *Child of God* (London: Picador, 1989), pp. 26–27.
21 Harper Lee, *To Kill a Mockingbird* (London: Minerva, 1993), p. 34.
22 Michael Harrington, *The Other America: Poverty in the United States* (1962; London: Penguin, 1969), p. 24.
23 Crews, *A Childhood*, p. 25.

24 Dorothy Allison, *Trash* (New York: Plume, 2002), pp. xv, vii.

25 Dorothy Allison, *Bastard Out of Carolina* (New York: Plume, 1993), p. 180.

26 Connie May Fowler, *Before Women Had Wings* (New York: Ballantine Books, 1997), p. 1.

27 Sharon Monteith, *Advancing Sisterhood?: Interracial Friendships in Contemporary Southern Fiction* (Athens: University of Georgia Press, 2000), p. 51.

28 Numan V. Bartley, *The New South, 1945–1980: The Story of the South's Modernization* (Baton Rouge: Louisiana State University Press, 1995), p. 470.

29 Thadious Davis, "Reclaiming the South," in John Lowe, ed., *Bridging Southern Cultures: An Interdisciplinary Approach* (Baton Rouge: Louisiana State University Press, 2005), p. 66.

30 Pimpare, p. 229.

8

JOHN T. MATTHEWS

The Southern Renaissance and the Faulknerian South

"The Southern Renaissance" was a concept meant primarily to designate a remarkable surge of literature originating in the U.S. South from the early 1920s to at least the mid-1940s, and secondarily to identify some of its principal shared features. Bursts of fresh literary art appeared in the South during the first decade after World War I. Innovative periodicals such as *The Double-Dealer* in New Orleans (1921–1926) and *The Fugitive* in Nashville (1922–1925) proclaimed a new era of culture in the South and published avant-garde fiction and poetry. Many important writers associated with the South started their careers during the 1920s: Jean Toomer, William Faulkner, Zora Neale Hurston, Erskine Caldwell, Allen Tate, and Thomas Wolfe were among the most prominent, while a second generation included Eudora Welty, Flannery O'Connor, Lillian Smith, Robert Penn Warren, Ralph Ellison, Tennessee Williams, and many more. The canon of the Southern Renaissance has been debatable since the idea of a definable movement was first proposed, and compelling arguments have been made recently for expanding the Renaissance chronologically, geographically, and ideologically. There are also good reasons to question its continued usefulness altogether.

It was not until 1945 that Allen Tate designated this phenomenon a "Southern literary renascence" in his essay "The New Provincialism." Looking back at the interwar years, Tate noted the number of authors whose works were of permanent value, and who wrote as Southern "traditionalists": "Stark Young, Elizabeth Madox Roberts, Katherine Anne Porter, Robert Penn Warren, Caroline Gordon, Ellen Glasgow ... and William Faulkner, who is the most powerful and original novelist in the United States and one of the best in the modern world."[1] Tate considered such writers traditionalists not because they all celebrated the South's traditions (in fact, many

I gratefully acknowledge the research assistance of Joyce Kim, a doctoral candidate in English at Boston University, in the preparation of this article.

were critical of them), but because they understood the region as possessing distinctive features. As the concept of a Southern Renaissance hardened, however, those distinctive features became more and more associated with the purported virtues of Southern life. In 1930, Tate and a like-minded set of writers and intellectuals had issued a manifesto entitled *I'll Take My Stand*, which, while acknowledging grievous mistakes like slaveholding, nonetheless touted the South's superiority over modern Northern industrialism, market capitalism, materialism, lack of cultivation, and irreligiousness. The so-called Agrarians never saw their views adopted as policies, but their success as academics led to another kind of influence – in institutions of higher education. Tate, John Crowe Ransom, Cleanth Brooks, Robert Penn Warren, and others were responsible for developing a method of literary interpretation called the New Criticism that minimized historical context as well as social content in the analysis of literary works. The New Criticism translated certain kinds of traditional Southern values like the centrality of spiritual truth (particularly a Christian sort), formal beauty, love of nature, and the importance of community into general principles of literary judgment.

Faulkner may have won first place in Tate's original ranking of Southern Renaissance writers, but his fiction has always presented difficulties for those wanting to recruit him to "traditionalist" concerns. For one thing, Tate was being disingenuous in suggesting that *what* got said about the South did not matter so long as the South was treated as distinctive. Faulkner's imaginative engagement with Southern history proves so despairing, that whatever regard for the South's distinctiveness most readers recognized in his writing, they were hardly surprised by Quentin Compson's hysterical protest in *Absalom, Absalom!* (1936) that, "I dont hate [the South]. I dont hate it." Early critics of Faulkner congenial to Agrarian sensibilities found affirmations of reputed Southern values like faith, courage, honor, pity, and love – some of the "eternal verities" Faulkner sometimes spoke of, and which Faulkner's most insightful early critic, Cleanth Brooks, claimed formed Faulkner's moral vision. The bias of such critics still may be seen in a collection of essays on Faulkner and the Southern Renaissance from 1981, *Faulkner and the Southern Renaissance* edited by Doreen Fowler and Ann J. Abadie, which presents the author as keeping Southern traditions alive while exposing flaws in their past exercise. According to Michael Kreyling in *Inventing Southern Literature* (1999), even when a subsequent generation of Southern critics began to acknowledge that the greatest chronicler of the South found no basis of redemption in the region's tragic misbegottenness, they made Faulkner's shame itself the source of essential modern Southernness and identified as melancholic intellectuals of the Quentin Compson sort.

Faulkner's writing, however, transcended the criteria that Agrarian-rooted critics wanted to apply to him and other Southern moderns. Although his fiction obviously deals with the South, and his imaginary Yoknapatawpha County parallels Lafayette County, Mississippi, where Faulkner lived, Faulkner's writing also appealed to readers with little interest in its regionalist aspects. European readers, especially the French, immediately responded to Faulkner's fiction, even before it was appreciated in the United States.[2] Faulkner's modernist features – his exploration of alienated identity, the influence of modern developments in psychology (Freud) and philosophy (Bergson), and his regard for European moderns like Thomas Mann, James Joyce, and Joseph Conrad – all sprang him from strict categorization as a writer treating the South as wholly distinctive, at least in the sense the Agrarians meant. Differently, Faulkner's obsession with Southern history actually made him more of a world novelist. His thick description of Southern plantation life revealed affinities with Caribbean New World plantation society, as well as with Africa and places in Latin America. Faulkner's importance as a world writer comes as much from his depiction of colonial consequences in the global South – slavery, race and racism, colonization, plantation agriculture, proletarianization and mechanization, and removal to towns – as the presumed "universal" subjects of individual identity and consciousness.[3] Therefore, this essay examines several of the topics Faulkner's fiction maps as primary themes of modern Southern literature – but in the conviction that they reveal how falsifying simple definitions of a Southern Renascence may once have been, and how the complexities of Faulkner's writing correspond with much-expanded definitions of this broad event in modern culture.

The Faulknerian South is first of all the South as imagined by Faulkner. This does not mean his version is wholly imaginary, only that Faulkner's fiction highlights the unusual degree to which the South has been the object of fantasy, the creation of *ideas* about what it is or should be. When Thomas Jefferson wanted to persuade a European audience in 1785 that his native Virginia was the epitome of the new American republic (in his *Notes on the State of Virginia*), he insisted on the South's superiority – particularly its rejection of commerce and its opportunities for yeoman farmers to commune daily with nature. That his pastoral vision was contradicted by the reality of a slaveholding plantation culture already entrenched in Virginia suggests how much the South operated in the realm of desire and dream. When northern colonies, by contrast, began thinking about how the new free republic would be distinguished from its European origins, they took to projecting the slaveholding South as feudal, barbaric, and tyrannical – the nation's other. Faulkner's writing about the South, his use of his Southern heritage and habitat as subject matter because he knew it best, repeatedly explores how the South is produced through the interplay of common or competing fantasies.

The Plantation

... himself and his cousin juxtaposed not against the wilderness but against the tamed land which was to have been his heritage, the land which old Carothers McCaslin his grandfather had bought with white man's money from the wild men whose grandfathers without guns hunted it, and tamed and ordered or believed he had tamed and ordered it for the reason that the human beings he held in bondage and in the power of life and death had removed the forest from it and in their sweat scratched the surface of it to a depth of perhaps fourteen inches in order to grow something out of it which had not been there before and which could be translated back into the money he who believed he had both it had had to pay to get it and hold it and a reasonable profit too .... (*Go Down, Moses*)[4]

Antonio Benítez-Rojo describes the plantation system created by European colonials as a "repeating island." By this he means that what Holland, England, France, and Spain established in their "New World" agricultural colonies was a set of wealth-producing machines that could have been (and were) developed anywhere conditions warranted, and that ignored as much as possible the cultures and activities of indigenous peoples (when they did not exterminate them). The passage from *Go Down, Moses* above occurs in a long conversation between two descendants of a prominent cotton planter in one of Faulkner's family sagas. Old Carothers McCaslin comes to frontier Mississippi early in the nineteenth century, buys land from the Indians whom the government recognizes as holding title to it, builds a house, and begins a dynasty. As with Thomas Sutpen, however, McCaslin's efforts to reproduce his name and "blood" go awry; in his case, after fathering male twins and a daughter by a wife unnamed in the novel, he takes a slave woman as a mistress, fathers a daughter by her, then, obscenely, goes on to take that young woman as his mistress. Such open immorality exposes the callous rapacity of the plantation system. Ike McCaslin, whose father is one of the twins, revolts against the legacy of ownership and violation represented by taking title to land and people by renouncing his right of inheritance. His cousin, Cass, another descendant of Old Carothers, argues instead that he should take custody of the land (and its legacy) and use it humanely to furnish employment for the ex-slaves. The dilemma suggests how the plantation South was inhumane at the origin, nothing but a profit-machine that abused the land and those forced to labor on it.

Faulkner's style captures several dimensions of the planter mentality. The narrator underscores the self-delusion in planter ideology by attaching qualifiers like "or believed he had" to almost every assertion, as if there is nothing Old Carothers thought he was doing that was not discredited by what was really happening, or what Ike/Faulkner can now see was happening. The unstopped rush of words may be felt as the headlong impatience of planters like McCaslin and Sutpen (who, Rosa insists, "tore violently" his plantation out of the earth). They hurl themselves at their project before reality catches up with them, yet all the while they know their "heedless[ness]" has already begun to destroy their dreams of dynasty. The paratactic syntax ("and" and "and" ...) suggests the indivisibility of agriculture and commerce, crops no sooner grown than sold.

More defensive of the plantation ideal, Allen Tate in his novel *The Fathers* (1938) identifies a strain of mercantile greed and "foreign" religious and cultural values as contaminants of the plantation ideal coming from the outside. Faulkner's take on the plantation as a machine of commercial capitalism, with side effects of ruinous sexual predation and monetized patrimony, comes closer to those of Southern writers sometimes left on the fringes of the Southern Renaissance. So argued Jean Toomer, who refused to have his experimentalist work *Cane* (1923) publicized as the work of a New "Negro," might better be understood as writing a plantation (or anti-plantation) novel. It presents the interrelated but only partially connected stories of rural Georgians who continue to negotiate industrial and racial institutions structured by slavery; *Go Down, Moses* may be in its debt thematically and formally. Erskine Caldwell's fiction about desolate cotton and tobacco plantations in the early 1930s (*Tobacco Road* [1932] and *God's Little Acre* [1933]) scandalizes readers with the obscenity of farmers reduced to subhuman destitution. Edith Summers Kelly, Elizabeth Madox Roberts, and Ellen Glasgow focus on farm wives in the tobacco agriculture of Kentucky and the dairy regions of Virginia to consider how modernization might prompt new liberties for women.

Land and Labor

He would lie amid the waking instant of earth's teeming minute life, the motionless fronds of water-heavy grasses stopping into the mist before his face in black, fixed curves, along each parabola of which the marching drops held in minute magnification the dawn's rosy miniatures, smelling and even tasting the rich, slow, warm barn-reek milk-reek, the flowing immemorial female, hearing the slow planting and the plopping such of each deliberate cloven mud-spreading hoof, invisible still in the mist loud with its hymeneal choristers. (*The Hamlet*)[5]

In contrast to the Agrarians' unrealistic and halfhearted urging on the modernizing South of a return to subsistence farming, Faulkner unfolds the layers of desire, dependence, and deprivation that make Southerners' love of the land so hopeless. In *The Hamlet* (1940), Faulkner chronicles the sorrow farmers felt after the Civil War when they saw their places falling into mortgage debt, the land increasingly the object of financial speculation, agricultural production replaced by mercantile consumption. Faulkner depicts a radical attachment to the land through Isaac Snopes's idyll in the novel; the man-child is in love with a cow, and the two spend their days wandering the countryside. In the description above, Ike is enveloped by the "earth's teeming minute life;" his senses enliven, and the prose slows nearly to a stop. Faulkner's luxurious imagery and leisurely participial syntax relax away from a modern world running on standardized work time, anxious to make the land produce profit, insisting that labor never ceases. Here, by contrast, Ike worships a farm animal for her inherent beauty as a creature, lives in a fantasy in which work may be left behind; land and labor afford forms of pleasure rather than alienated assets for sale.

The wish to live on land you love and work only to provide your needs corresponds to Thomas Jefferson's ideal of the yeoman farmer. Such a dream appears in many permutations throughout the novel: the fantasy that is "Eula" serves as a collective fantasy for the farmers' wish that the sensuous earth might somehow be immune to the indecencies of monetary valuation and commercial transaction. Her ripe body symbolizes the fertile land, now clouded by the fear that some mercantile creature will show up backed by "the dead power of money" to put his "owner's name" on her exactly as one "might own" "a field": "the fine land rich and fecund and foul and eternal and impervious to him who claimed title to it."[6] Faulkner's extravagant prose indicates the excess of longing required to imagine the land as transcending puny claims to title, commercial use, and speculative profiteering.

Such a dream arises elsewhere in Faulkner: in *Go Down, Moses* (1942), Ike McCaslin and his part-Native American mentor Sam Fathers conduct a somber ritual of mourning for the wilderness they realize is vanishing before the encroachments of railroads, timber mills, and automobiles. Their fantasy of primordial wilderness, however, also suggests a longing to deny the history of slavery that accompanied Southern landownership. *The Hamlet*, ostensibly focused as it is on what happens to white farmworkers at the turn to the twentieth century, is haunted by a past in which work on the land was coerced and black. Its opening pages survey a deserted plantation that many decades later still preserves traces of the massive labor demanded of slaves to make the foreigner's "dream" of a "tremendous" cotton plantation real. The Old Frenchman's Place encrypts a New World history of European settlement, commercial plantation speculation, and agricultural production, along with slaveholding and slave resistance. In *As I Lay Dying* (1930) the next phase of Southern attachment to the land involves its final loss to small farmers just hanging on in the decades of deep economic troubles between the world wars. The novel conducts a funeral for the family-owned subsistence farm as if it were the corpse of a remote, begrudging mother, a trope that captures male longing for the maternal nurture long projected on the land, now vanishing below the rising flood of economic crisis and agricultural modernization. Yet while the Bundren men gaze mournfully at their slipping land, they look right past the women and children commandeered to work on family-run farms.

Predictably, fiction by women about the plight of rural working-class women was neglected in forming the canon of the Southern Renaissance. Sexism was involved, but so was the fact that such fiction tended toward radical leftist politics and realist aesthetics. Half a dozen important novels were inspired by mill strikes in the textile industry of North Carolina and elsewhere: Olive Tilford Dargan (Fielding Burke) examined how Southern familial and racial habits obstructed political mobilization in *Call Home the Heart* (1932), while Grace Lumpkin's *To Make My Bread* (1932) presents a narrative of conversion to class consciousness. The Southern Renaissance and the project of proletarian literature intersect here, and point as well to the many works about labor conflict with Southern connections, such as William Attaway's *Blood on the Forge* (1941). Richard Wright's *Native Son* (1940) and Ralph Ellison's *Invisible Man* (1952), perhaps the country's greatest novels about race, both map the connections between blackness, the South, and labor under industrial capitalism in mid-century America. Wright's protagonist from Mississippi gets treated like a fugitive slave in Chicago, whereas Ellison's Southern émigré joins a communist brotherhood in New York City. Both novels brood on the persistence of social and economic injustice as a legacy of Southern slaveholding and racism. Faulkner's own exploration of the heavy burdens of a racist past made him an appreciative reader of both novels (he sent a note of congratulation to Wright), although he protested when fiction on these subjects veered into what he considered racial partisanship.[7]

Race

> But he could not move at once, standing there, smelling the woman smelling the negro all at once; enclosed by the womanshenegro and the haste, driven, having to wait until she spoke: a guiding sound that was no particular word and completely aware. Then it seemed to him that he could see her – something, prone, abject; her eyes perhaps. (*Light in August*)[8]

Robert J. M. Young argues that the idea of race was largely an invention of European colonial societies that needed a "scientific" justification for the subordination and enslavement of darker peoples. Historians of the United States anticipate this view in demonstrating that the notion of whiteness was forged to consolidate economic advantage around racial difference during late colonial times. Race, then, is a precipitate of coerced labor. The event of traumatic self-comprehension for Thomas Sutpen, the prototypical planter in *Absalom, Absalom!*, involves the youth's realization that he and his poor white family of plantation field hands have no greater standing in the master's eyes than his Negro slaves. Sutpen is sent by his father to Pettibone's mansion to deliver a message; the child is met at the door by a black butler, who admonishes him and sends him to the back door. Sutpen comes to understand that his enemy is not the obvious one, the Negro who looks down on poor white "trash," but the white planter himself, who considers all his laborers subhuman. Sutpen's whiteness is whiteness of a different color. Faulkner describes the intricate mechanisms by which racial identity is reproduced socially to satisfy the needs of a particular economic system.

Faulkner's most celebrated novel of race is *Light in August* (1932), a formally ambitious work that attempts to sort out the intertwined elements of racial violence in the 1920s South. One protagonist, Joe Christmas, embodies the post-Reconstruction South's determination to define racial identity through the concept of naturally distinct black and white "blood," and its abiding dread that this presumed natural fact was nothing but a "legal fiction," to use Mark Twain's term for the ideology of racial difference. Faulkner catalogs the toxic racism of bigots like Doc Hines, Joe Christmas's hate-filled grandfather, and Percy Grimm, the deputized vigilante who hunts down the fugitive and kills him. Faulkner's panorama of a Southern small town reveals how race-sex ideology took on a life of its own. By the 1920s, the fiction of race had permeated almost every walk of life: the way men and women behaved sexually, the religious faith that descended from the defense of the peculiar institution, and the state's violent enforcement of segregation and disfranchisement.

In the preceding excerpt, Joe Christmas famously balks as he is about to lose his virginity to a young black girl who has been coerced into servicing a gang of Joe's friends. Joe suddenly feels trapped by the physical sensation of racial difference, a spell more vertiginous should he be wondering if the smell of blackness is his own. Already confused by the racial insults directed at him in childhood, Joe empathizes with the girl's weakness and humiliation, even as they repulse him. "Womanshenegro" fuses the two categories of social denigration – femaleness and blackness – into a connector category of "she." Her eyes betray "abject[ion]" because blackness is what must be expelled from white bodies to make them white. Faulkner captures the dynamic by which whatever is extraneous to the socially coded identity of white maleness must be actively denied and rooted out.

Joe Christmas's relationship with Joanna Burden, the descendant of Northerners who move to Mississippi to get involved in racial uplift during Reconstruction, illuminates the staying power of racial ideology. Race may originate in the crucible of slavery, but its sorry history throughout the nineteenth and twentieth centuries demonstrates how it has been crossed with matters of sexuality. When Joe makes his way to the dark house, where he knows Joanna awaits him, he realizes she has staged a fantasy involving the seduction of a slave by a plantation mistress, one that will result in a mad reenactment of assault, violation, and the violent release of repressed desire.

In one of the most influential reconsiderations of the Southern Renaissance, Richard King devises a model for it based on Freud's family romance; given prominent Southern fiction's preoccupation with the past, King reads writers like Tate, Faulkner, and Warren in terms of Oedipal anxiety toward Southern tradition. King acknowledges that white women and blacks are by definition marginal to this construct. More recently, however, Andrew Leiter has argued that the Harlem and Southern Renaissances might be read in tandem, as a dialogue over the transfixing myth of the "black beast" concocted during the Jim Crow era. Considering Faulkner, Margaret Mitchell, and Erskine Caldwell in the company of James Weldon Johnson, George Schuyler, and Richard Wright, Leiter suggests points of convergence between renaissances that customarily have been segregated.

Expanding the Southern Renaissance laterally to include more writers of the period is one consequence of recent scholarship in the field; another is extending it chronologically. Carol Manning has argued that the movement ought properly to be dated from the 1890s, when a generation of black women were taking up the question of what a modern South would look like after the Civil War and Reconstruction: Anna Julia Cooper, Ida B. Wells, and Belle Kearney all contributed to serious reflection on the problem of racial division that Du Bois would later call *the* problem of the twentieth century. Two novels whose extraordinary power argues for this reconception of the Southern Renaissance, Frances W. Harper's *Iola Leroy* (1892) and Paula Hopkins' *Contending Forces* (1900), fearlessly portray the extent to which women's lives continued, tragically, to be diseased by American racism. Iola Leroy suffers her mixed racial ancestry as the sexual vulnerability it is for a nonwhite woman under Jim Crow; she shapes her romantic life around her determination to work on behalf of the black race with which she chooses to identify. Hopkins imagines characters wracked by racial and sexual shame, thwarted by romantic prohibitions, both the consequences of slavery's manifold transgressions and humiliations. In works like these, women writers of color (joined by white contemporaries like Kate Chopin) delineate the radiating damage of historical racism in the modern South. Faulkner is one of the few male writers of the next generation who imagine sympathetically, if with obvious limitations, the crushing aftereffects of the plantation South on the private lives of women as well as many men in the wake of the plantation south.

Desire

> ... (I did not love him; how could I? I had never even heard his voice, had only Ellen's word for it that there was such a person) ... that shape without even a face yet because I had not even seen the photograph then, reflected in the secret and bemused gaze of a young girl: because I who had learned nothing of love, not even parents' love – that fond dear constant violation of privacy, that stultification of the burgeoning and incorrigible I which is the meed and due of all mammalian meat, became not mistress, not beloved, but more than even love; I became all polymath love's androgynous advocate. (*Absalom, Absalom!*)[9]

Faulkner repeatedly represents even the most immediate forms of desire and intimacy as inescapably determined by the community's interests. Love is structured by the dictates of family, by matrimonial restrictions, by racial imperatives, by sexual and reproductive orthodoxies, and so on. In the case of Judith Sutpen and Charles Bon, they are hardly free to "fall in love." As much as Ellen Sutpen wants Charles as a trophy for her provincial family, her husband sees racial menace in Bon's uncertain ancestry. As much as the sexually repressed Rosa Coldfield fantasizes about her niece's fiancé, Judith's brother Henry indulges homoerotic fancies for a man who is nearly his brother. Before all that, as much as Charles may be attracted first to Henry, his classmate, then to Judith, the sister, Charles has been put into this position by the machinations of his own mother, who intends to take revenge on Thomas Sutpen for spurning her. As a love object, Bon proves to be less a person than a contested abstraction, an "effluvium" of Sutpen blood.[10]

Similarly, the romantic lives of numerous characters in Faulkner's fiction are governed by abstractions. In *The Sound and the Fury* (1929), Caddy Compson is loved by her brothers – but for reasons that have little to do with her as a person: Benjy loves her for protecting him, Quentin for embodying the ideals of family honor and "purity" (ostensibly sexual, but also racial), Jason for her trading on the financial value of the Compson name (she attracts a prosperous fiancé, who promises Jason a job in his bank). In

Sanctuary (1931), Horace Benbow still identifies a certain kind of female behavior as the guarantor of a social order's legitimacy. Yet when that novel peers into the depths of the traditional Southern family, it can see nothing but disease: the overweening rule of fathers over their daughters' minds and bodies, bordering on incest; the deputized surveillance of brothers over sisters' sexual lives; the hypocrisies of female chastity; the tyranny of heteronormative desire; the contradiction of the excessive value of heirs and the disregard for children's nurture.

Love becomes a matter of instrumentalization in so much of Faulkner – with characters wanting some ulterior object through their romantic designs. Rosa might serve as the paradigmatic case, unfortunate that she is, given that she falls in love not with the person Charles, but with the idea of him. Rosa uses Charles as a fantasy, something like a little machine on her dressing table, which will compensate her for the lack of parents' love, and later as a memory that will console her for her jilting by Sutpen (who sees love as nothing but a pretext for the main business of manufacturing heirs). Rosa embraces the role of "polymath love's androgynous advocate" in a flourish of polysyllabic creative abandon. Rosa becomes the poet not only of the Confederacy, but of her own doomed secession: the breathtaking prose she produces when she finally does tell her story marks women's longsuffering outrage – a way of protesting against love that is singularly heterosexual rather than polymath (while "polymath" generally means widely informed, here I think it also implies knowing about desire in many forms), punishingly gendered rather than androgynous, and self-accusing rather than self-advocating.

Rosa is deformed by the injuries of "love," as are others in comparable circumstances. Both Caddy Compson and her "illegitimate" daughter Quentin act out extremely to make a bid for control of their erotic lives and bodies. Elly in the short story of the same name experiences independence in romance through the scandal of a black lover, and Miss Emily Grierson in "A Rose for Emily" theatricalizes her own victimization by romantic love – at the hands of an authoritarian father and a lover who toys with her – by killing her man and making love to death. Temple Drake seeks to escape a family phalanx of judgmental fathers and protective brothers by abandoning herself to the violation that misogynistic paternalism has always already committed on her. Even Charlotte Rittenmeyer, the female lead in *If I Forget Thee, Jerusalem* (1939), plays out a version of romantic love that gains its transcendent value to her because she must sacrifice husband and children to get it. Charlotte recruits Harry to a Hollywood romance, in which true love involves the cheap fantasy of defying bourgeois mores. These are all counter-fantasies to the ideals imposed on women by masculine needs.

Other Southern writers of the 1920s wrote about the strictures women faced in traditional Southern society. Although they have only recently been understood as significant figures of the Renaissance, two satirical novelists take on the myth of the Southern belle from the standpoint of women – not the too-beautiful-for-words sort (as Faulkner characterized Caddy Compson), but the too-annoyed-not-to-say-something-outrageous sort. Anita Loos composed send-ups of a dimwitted Southern flapper in *Gentlemen Prefer Blondes* (1925) and *But Gentlemen Marry Brunettes* (1927). The novels construct a split discourse between two female characters – one a helpless innocent who somehow always gets what she wants, the other her witheringly ironic companion. Frances Newman's novels *The Hard-Boiled Virgin* (1926) and *Dead Lovers are Faithful Lovers* (1928) puncture the stifling idiocies of life as a Southern belle, and create a space for their hugely cultured, sharp-tongued narrator. If only Temple Drake had read her, instead of movie magazines. The evidence of a women's tradition within modern Southern writing is established by Anne Goodwyn Jones in *Tomorrow Is Another Day* (1981), her study of Newman, Margaret Mitchell, Grace King, and others. Patricia Yaeger focuses on a particular feature of such a tradition in her wide-ranging study of the grotesque in writing by modern Southern women; this has been a trope traditionally used to belittle women's writing, but Yaeger demonstrates how the idea of nonconformity and irregularity are embraced by black and white women writers to explore alternative sensibilities and expressions of dissent. Eudora Welty and Flannery O'Connor are the best-known representatives of women's writing of the grotesque, but Yaeger includes many others in her study of the extreme female body in Southern literature, including Carson McCullers, Caroline Gordon, and Zora Neale Hurston.

The counter-desires suggested by Henry's attraction to Charles, doubled by Quentin's to Shreve, represent all that is excluded by the orthodoxies of hetero-normative sexuality and family reproduction that colonize sexual pleasure and intimacy. Faulkner's fiction imagines numerous possibilities for homoerotic desire: the domestic partnership of the bachelor twins Buck and Buddy McCaslin; the ménage of Roger Schumann, Jack Holmes, and Laverne in *Pylon* (1935); Joes Christmas and Brown, and Rev. Hightower in *Light in August*. Michael Bibler has argued that in plantation fiction of the U.S. South, same-sex pairing, often across the color line, gives characters the chance to experience desire and gratification outside the requirements of racially homogeneous reproduction. Works by Faulkner, Tennessee Williams, Ernest Gaines, Lillian Hellman, Katherine Anne Porter, Margaret Walker, and others suggest how various and extensive such counter-desires are in modern Southern fiction. Gary Richards contends that the canon of the Southern Renaissance reflected the male heterosexual biases of its first commentators, and that the overdue inclusion of writers like James Baldwin, Truman Capote, Carson McCullers, and others not only properly restores queerness to the Southern Renaissance, but also resets its endpoint a decade later.[11]

Oneself

> You get born and you try this and you don't know why only you keep on try-ing it and you are born at the same time with a lot of other people, all mixed up with them, like trying to, having to, move your arms and legs with strings only the same strings are hitched to all the other arms and legs and the others all trying and they don't know why either except that the strings are all in on one another's way like five or six people all trying to make a rug on the same loom only each one wants to weave his own pattern into the rug: and it cant matter, you know that, or the Ones that set up the loom would have arranged things a little better, and yet it must matter because you keep on trying or having to keep on trying.... (*Absalom, Absalom!*)[12]

These words are attributed to Judith Sutpen, the planter Sutpen's daughter, in a scene imagined by Quentin Compson's father, as he tells his portion of the saga. The story must have come to Mr. Compson from his mother, however, given that she is being presented with a letter sent to Judith by her fiancé, Charles Bon. Through this multiplication of filters and relays, Faulkner suggests how Judith's bleak sentiments represent a whole com-munity's sense of futility at how hard it is to find individual personhood in a system that lashes you to those who precede you. The syntax connects units "and" by "and," creating the sensation of stickiness between people in a closed society; you can no more disentangle attached arms and legs than you can phrases and clauses. (Here paratactic style does different work than in the passage on Carothers McCaslin quoted earlier.) The simile shifts sub-tly, from puppetry to weaving. But the difference between being worked by threads or working threads yourself amounts to nothing – you are as much a made object as a frustrated maker.

In *The Sound and the Fury*, Quentin oscillates between being and not-being, *is* and *was*, whereas Darl Bundren in *As I Lay Dying* confronts a similar crisis, one caused not by an annihilating past, however, but by a strange future in which selves no longer "are" but have been segmented and distributed schizophrenically into functions of the modern market and state. Elsewhere in Faulkner, too, the self shatters under the pressures of intensifying sheers between past and present: think of Temple Drake, whose modern waywardness under authoritarian upbringing smash her to smithereens in *Sanctuary*. Pieces of her – legs, lips, eyes – are strewn everywhere, metaphorically, after her crash into an underworld of violence and rapacity about which she had known nothing. Addie Bundren's extremely personal interior monologue begins by quoting her father: "The reason to live is to get ready to stay dead a long time." She cannot make the life she lives under the hand of male authority coincide with her desire for something all her own; doing and saying zoom off at perpendiculars, as she too multiplies schizophrenically – as woman and mother (each new child subdividing her further), as living and dead. Even Cash observes that every individual carries two "fellas" in his head, one trying to outtalk the other. Joe Christmas splits into black and white, alternating madly between life-forms, tortured by feeling he is two or neither, while his lover, Joanna Burden, doubles and subdivides into separate women sharing a single body, or separate genders warring within it.

The seething confusion of Faulkner's characters points to the intense contradictions or conflicts around which selfhood is formulated, the self seemingly constituted by a primordial divide. Faulkner's sensitivity to the duress of modern subjectivity affiliates him with other international modernists – Freud, Conrad, T. S. Eliot, Joyce, Woolf: all of them poets of psychic fission – even as his version maintains its Southern particularity.

Language

…language (that meagre and fragile thread … by which the little surface corners and edges of men's secret and solitary lives may be joined for an instant now and then before sinking back into the darkness where the spirit cried for the first time and was not heard and will cry for the last time and will not be heard then either) … (*Absalom, Absalom!*)[13]

There is much talk in Faulkner but little communication. In this last excerpt, from *Absalom*, language is likened to a single thread that draws together ever so briefly just the outermost surfaces of individuals. Language functions as gossip, knowingly false speculation, commercial weaponry, blackmail, perjury, moral evasion, racial deception, religious delusion, historical ideology, and solitary lament. It is significant that the characterization of language as a "meagre and fragile thread" actually refers in context to Sutpen's difficulty in learning French creole when he is a plantation overseer in Haiti at the beginning of his career. Language is always "a language" too, and here Faulkner takes what appears to be a universal generalization about the nature of all language and exposes an historical dimension. The languages of the New World, his Mississippi English included, are haunted by a long history of hemispheric colonial encounter.

As a modern literary movement, the Southern Renaissance, broadly defined, took a great deal of interest in how the medium of literature might respond to modern circumstances. Jean Toomer's experiments in form make *Cane* one of the richest modernist texts produced in the United States. It proceeds with a mindfulness that words in the South are "[m]isshapen, split-gut, tortured, twisted," and that the effort to make art amid the still-living remnants of plantation slavery mangles utterance on the tongue.[14] Formal experimentation is also important to counter-imagining a traditional South in authors like Evelyn Scott, in her innovative narrative of the Civil War, *The Wave* (1929); Hurston, in her experiments with mixed genres and dialects; and even Gertrude Stein, whose efforts to abstract the rhythms and textures of conversation led her to the idiosyncrasies of black Southern speech in "Melanctha" (1909), a work Richard Wright pointed to as indispensable to his development as an artist.

Robert Brinkmeyer suggests there is still utility in Tate's original conception of the Southern Renascence as defining a moment at which the South moves with anxiety into the modern world as it looks back at a disappearing past. He argues, however, that our understanding of the varieties and extent of the crisis needs to be expanded to include many formerly neglected writers. I might supplement this sensible view by noting that one source of anxiety apparent in most of the writers mentioned here is the worry that aspects of the traditional South, far from disappearing, were actually being revived, and were shaping the modern nation – in the form of templates for imperial ambitions, domestic racial policy, industrial agriculture, labor management, and modern mass culture nostalgia. It is not that the past is dead, Faulkner observed famously; it is that it is not even past. While this essay treats Faulkner as the major interlocutor of the Southern Renaissance – reflecting a centrality his work has (arguably too) long held in Southern studies generally – Faulkner's paramount stature as a world writer today might reinforce reasons to continue to rethink the Southern Renaissance in transnational contexts. As the New Negro Renaissance is now understood as one of several modern anticolonial cultural projects, so it, as well as the contemporary Southern Renaissance, may be compared to nationalist cultural renaissances elsewhere in the world: the Irish Renaissance also confronts a history of foreign plantation colonialism, for example, as do later movements in the West Indies, Latin America, and Africa. A twenty-first-century version of Faulkner, in a maximized conception of the Southern Renaissance, might reveal how both figure in cultural representations of global modernity.

NOTES

1 Allen Tate, "The New Provincialism," in *Essays of Four Decades* (New York: Swallow Press, 1968), p. 545.

2 Maurice Coindreau published an appreciation of Faulkner's fiction in 1931 *La Nouvelle revue française*, and translated *As I Lay Dying* in 1934, *The Sound and the Fury* in 1938, and numerous works after that. Jean-Paul Sartre wrote two essays on Faulkner in the late 1930s.

3 On this topic, see Edouard Glissant, *Faulkner, Mississippi*, trans. Barbara B. Lewis and Thomas C. Spear (Chicago: University of Chicago Press, 2000).

4 William Faulkner, *Go Down, Moses*. The Corrected Text (New York: Vintage, 1990), pp. 243–244.

5 William Faulkner, *The Hamlet*. The Corrected Text (New York: Vintage, 1991), p. 183.

6 Faulkner, *The Hamlet*, pp. 131–132.

7 As in almost every public comment Faulkner made about race, the strains of his complicated and often contradictory positions are obvious. In remarks he made in Japan during a visit there in the mid-1950s, he praised both writers but expressed disappointment that Wright's fiction after *Native Son* adopted a more strictly black standpoint. See Karl Zender, *William Faulkner: American Writer* (New York: Weidenfeld & Nicholson, 1989), p. 919.

8 William Faulkner, *Light in August*. The Corrected Text (New York: Vintage, 1990), p. 156.

9 William Faulkner, *Absalom, Absalom!* The Corrected Text (New York: Vintage, 1990), p. 117.

10 Faulkner, *Absalom, Absalom!*, p. 82.

11 Gary Richards, "'With a Special Emphasis': The Dynamics of (Re)claiming a Queer Southern Renaissance," *Mississippi Quarterly* 55 (Spring 2002): 209–229.

12 Faulkner, *Absalom, Absalom!*, p. 105.

13 Faulkner, *Absalom, Absalom!*, p. 202.

14 Jean Toomer, *Cane* (New York: Norton, 1988), p. 111.

9

PEARL AMELIA MCHANEY

Southern Women Writers and Their Influence

In 1999, twenty-two writers contributed brief essays or poems regarding their first encounters with the language, mystery, or emotional import of Eudora Welty's writing. The occasion was Welty's ninetieth birthday and the pieces were published by Hill Street, an independent press. In 2000, Hill Street published a similar volume of twenty pieces for Flannery O'Connor, "a genuine reflection of the diversity of O'Connor's influence, as well as an indication that O'Connor continues to make a strong impact on young writers."[1] Together, *Eudora Welty: Reflections upon First Reading Her Work* and *Flannery O'Connor: In Celebration of Genius* attest to the overwhelming power of these writers' work, especially for other writers. Doris Betts, who contributed to both volumes, sums up the distinctions of these two writers: "There was a time when critics compared new Southern writers, if male, with William Faulkner, while females were given two options by whom they could be outclassed. If philosophically inclined to Athens, they were measured against Eudora Welty; the slightest whiff of theocentric Jerusalem meant that Flannery O'Connor would become the plumbline."[2] Carson McCullers completes this mid-twentieth-century triumvirate of Southern women writers, although none of them touted such a brand. Welty (1909–2001), McCullers (1917–1967), and O'Connor (1925–1964) occasionally crossed paths, and they read one another's work in publication (with neither acrimony nor applause), but they were not literary friends or even what one might term acquaintances.

Heretofore, many scholars have considered the formidable strengths and literary merits of these and many other Southern women writers, but nearly always the category intones middle-class white writers. Southern women writers outside the brand thrive under labels of African-American, Latina, "white trash," lesbian, and/or feminist writers, and poets and nonfiction writers of any sort are rarely included in discussions of Southern women writers, although this essay will go some way to address this omission. Furthermore, the category of Southern women writers, once its efficacy is accomplished, can occasionally be regrettable. The intentions of any such categorizations must be to create fellowship, recognition, and audience. In *Liberating Voices: Oral Tradition in African American Literature* (1991), Gayl Jones, one of many underread and understudied Southern women writers, summarizes that "the voices of the less powerful group, 'the other,' must always free themselves from the frame of the more powerful group, in texts of self-discovery, authority, and wholeness."[3] The Southern white woman writer was once such an "other," but in the Southern Renascence she found support and audience. Welty and O'Connor, in particular, survived in part because they were well mentored, but more importantly because the power of their writing communicated universal truths that cut through personal, regional, and even national prejudices and preoccupations. With the publication of Margaret Walker's *Jubilee* in 1966, Toni Morrison's *The Bluest Eye* and Alice Walker's *The Third Life of Grange Copeland* in 1970, and Walker's recovery of Zora Neale Hurston's *Their Eyes Were Watching God*, Southern African-American women writers began to be read, and in the wake of changes wrought by civil rights legislation, they escaped confinement of the regional categorization that had been liberating for the white women writers. Yet others have been forgotten until recently, like Sarah E. Wright whose *This Child's Gonna Live* (1969) is reclaimed by Jennifer Campbell and who Sharon Monteith argues enters the Southern literary tradition "as a neglected novelist of despair and survival and as an exponent of rural black Southern speech" following Zora Neale Hurston and preceding Alice Walker. In *Dirt and Desire* (2000), Patricia Yeager insists that critical reading of both white and black writers (including those not out rightly Southern such as Rita Dove and Toni Morrison) helps us foreground the traditions that afford or impose a "Southern" label.[4] For some Southern women writers, "Southern" has been a necessary category for publication, marketing, and canonization but has been limiting rather than freeing. Where the "Southern" label has fallen away, the writing has either succeeded on its aesthetic merits and resisted any limitation in readership or has remained a near-niche production with Southern characteristics that do not resonate beyond the South or beyond their contemporary audiences.

In this essay, I discuss the influence of Welty and O'Connor and the lesser, but still significant, import of Carson McCullers to Southern women writers who followed. Second, I consider the important legacy of Alice Walker and Toni Morrison, who are still too often left out of discussion of Southern women writers, as well as their reflections on Welty and O'Connor. Third, I highlight the writing of a diverse set of writers across different genres including poetry and memoir – Gayl Jones, Judith Ortiz Cofer, Melissa Fay Greene, Janisse Ray, Natasha Trethewey, Dorothy Allison, Jesmyn Ward, and Nikki Finney – to argue that the category of Southern women writers traditionally and contemporarily refers primarily to white writers and "forgets" or ignores poets, nonfiction writers, African-American, and ethnic women writers.

Eudora Welty and Flannery O'Connor were both outsiders to the Lost Cause, Bible Belt Southern culture. Welty's parents were from the West Virginia mountains and the farm country of Ohio. She studied outside the South and came home from New York in 1931 during the full force of the Depression when her father died. O'Connor spent her childhood in the small Irish-Catholic community centered on St. John the Baptist Cathedral across from her home. O'Connor found publishing success in the 1950s whereas Welty hit her stride in the 1930s and 1940s. Both Welty and O'Connor were bright, ambitious, and refused potential gender, regional, and educational constrictions. After college in her mother's family hometown of Milledgeville, O'Connor studied at the fairly new, but already successful, Iowa Writer's Workshop, still the most prestigious such school for creative writing.

At Iowa, O'Connor was taught by Vanderbilt writer Andrew Lytle who invited Allen Tate and Robert Penn Warren to the workshops. These three plus Tate's wife Caroline Gordon, as well as Cleanth Brooks who coedited the *Southern Review* and *Understanding Fiction* with Warren, were influential mentors and friends to both Welty and O'Connor.[5] Tate who also coedited *Kenyon Review*, Lytle who edited the *Sewanee Review* in Tennessee, and Albert Erskine who joined the editors of *Southern Review* between 1935 and 1940 all published Welty and O'Connor. Katherine Ann Porter, Erskine's wife from 1938 to 1942, championed Welty from the first, recommending her for the Yaddo writers' colony in Saratoga, New York, for Guggenheim Fellowships, and writing the introduction to Welty's first short story collection, *A Curtain of Green* (1941), seven of which were first published in the *Southern Review*. Southern intracultural influence, as described in Rosemary Magee's *Friendship and Sympathy* (1992) and Charlotte Beck's *The Fugitive Legacy* (2001), was prevalent in the South among the white male and female writers, but not for African-American writers. Welty and O'Connor benefited from such connections for visiting writer stints and lecture and reading circuits to colleges and conferences around the country, but especially in the South. From 1962 to 1964, for example, O'Connor delivered more than sixty talks and readings, often on crutches, at universities around the country and confided to a friend that she possessed an "element of ham."

Wry comedy, a hallmark of both O'Connor's and Welty's work, has also been a distraction to serious analysis of Southern women's writing. When reminded that O'Connor once said, "Mine is a comic art, but that does not detract from its seriousness," Welty responded that O'Connor was "absolutely and literally right ... the fact that something is comic does not detract from its seriousness, because the comic and the serious are not opposites .... I think comedy is able to tackle the most serious matters that there are. [T]hat the [*New York Times Book Review*] critic thinks I have a good comic spirit ... that's taking me seriously."[6] Southern women writers, Welty and O'Connor in particular, do leave a legacy of humor, but comedy in all genres is denigrated and disregarded as of lesser value and import. In recognizing humor (a throwback to local color writing?) and its entertainment value, critics often fail to realize its serious commentary.

When the two powerhouses Welty and O'Connor met in April 1962, at a literary festival with Brooks and Lytle at Converse College, in Spartanburg, South Carolina, they had been reading and commenting on one another's work. Welty read her essay "Place in Fiction" (1954) and the short story "Petrified Man" (1939) and reported that O'Connor did not like the way Southernness created barriers and limitations. O'Connor spoke about the Southern grotesques in her fiction, that they were realistic, neither fantastic nor ploys for humor.

Reviewers hardly knew where to place O'Connor and Welty. When Welty published *The Bride of the Innisfallen and Other Stories* (1955), one reviewer wrote, "Miss Welty, in spite of her rewards, must feel an injustice in being labeled 'Southern writer,' for she had no part in the creation of the new fiction South, that South of balmy nymphs, sensitive perverts, lonely sadists and kindly lunatics. In fact, the veteran reader may cry out on first reading Welty, 'Can this be the real South?'"[7] Similarly, a reviewer of *Everything That Rises Must Converge* (1965) concluded, "It is wrong to place Miss O'Connor (or Faulkner or Eudora Welty) in the Gothic School, however freakish and shocking her themes. The astounding surface of her stories, as wildly grotesque as the best Gothic, is but the visual equivalent of the outrage she feels before a world stupid with selfishness."[8]

O'Connor engaged with such observations in critical essays that contribute to a taxonomy of Southern writing, claiming that, "In these grotesque works, the writer has made alive some experience which we are not accustomed to observe everyday or which the ordinary man may never experience in his ordinary life." The characters' "fictional qualities lean away from typical social patterns, toward mystery and the unexpected .... [M]eaning is in the possibility rather than the probability .... Fiction begins where human knowledge begins – with the senses – and every fiction writer is bound by this fundamental aspect of his medium." The writer of the grotesque uses "the concrete in a more drastic way.... He's looking for one image that will connect or combine or embody two points; one is a point in the concrete, and the other is a point not visible to the naked eye, but believed in by him firmly, just as real to him, really as the one that everybody sees."[9] In her early stories, Welty also engaged critically with the device of the Grotesque, using physical qualities as a way of showing the interior feelings of her characters. Welty may write with more subtlety than O'Connor, but both writers believed that the art whether through humor, mystery, or both must articulate truth.

The South, as place, is as double-edged as are the grotesque and gothic for Southern women writers. Although "place" in Southern prose and poetry is much touted, it is also misunderstood. Welty argues that while it is essential that characters are rooted in and tethered to some tactile, historical, cultural place, more important are feelings and truths that are challenged, revealed, made consequential through the fiction. Welty explains, "When we write about people, black or white, in the South or anywhere, if our stories are worth reading, we are writing about everybody."[10] While Southern women's writing is set primarily in the South, the work goes beyond the recognized regional settings and cultural distinctions to explore human relationships worldwide.

In humor, the grotesque, place, and truth, Carson McCullers touches both Welty and O'Connor in kind if not in degree. The success of *The Heart Is a Lonely Hunter* at twenty-three created anticipation of McCuller's significance and accomplishment. She, too, was an outsider to the Southern small-town culture. Unrestrained as were Welty by the Depression and O'Connor by illness, McCullers reveled in physical, geographic, and sexual freedom – at Breadloaf in 1940 where she met Welty, at Yadoo in 1941 where Welty and Porter were also, in New York in the February House in Brooklyn Heights with Auden, Gypsy Rose Lee, and Jane and Paul Bowles – but she also dismissed writers with whom she felt herself in competition and expressed unflattering jealousy of Harper Lee, Tennessee Williams, Truman Capote, and O'Connor. Many Southern women writers, however, attribute their courage and point of view in fictionalizing the grotesque to McCuller's work even though McCuller's success was more of an individual sort than of influence. Her protagonists remain primarily adolescent, and her work, like that of her most successful acolyte Dorothy Allison in *Trash: Short Stories* (1988) and *Bastard Out of Carolina* (1992), while leaving a significant mark, are more about herself than not. In her essays, Allison comments about finding license and courage to write what she lived through reading O'Connor and McCullers. Whereas McCullers and Allison become tangled in their own stories, Welty and O'Connor move beyond their particular lives to succeed as stylists in the short-story form that gives credibility and force to their accomplishments and influence.

One aspect of Welty's and O'Connor's success is the power of the language of their fiction. Poet Rita Dove describes Welty's language as that which can "penetrate subtlety yet deeply into secrets and mysteries of human relationships both black and white."[11] This is the language of O'Connor's fiction, too, as described by another poet who feels her influence – Natasha Trethewey, a Pulitzer Prize–winning poet from Mississippi and Georgia, who values the understatement and wicked stories in which characters get their comeuppance.

Alice Walker also devoured O'Connor's stories until she realized that there were "other women writers – some Southern, some religious, all black – I had not been allowed to know."[12] Walker lived for seven years in Jackson, Mississippi, working for voter registration and the Head Start program, teaching at Jackson State University and Tougaloo College. She interviewed Welty in 1973, a year after Welty published her last fiction, the Pulitzer Prize–winning novel *The Optimist's Daughter*. Discussing truth and modern writing, Walker posits that "much popular poetry, some of it black, engages in clever half-truths, designed to shock only. Or to entertain." When Welty replies that she does not "quite understand the virtue of the idiom they strain so over, the language," Walker answers back, "Oh, I understand the idiom and the language; I can see the passion behind it and admire the rage. My question is whether witty half-truths are good for us in the long run, after we've stopped laughing. And whether poetry shouldn't stick to more difficult if less funny ground, the truth." "That's its real business," Welty responds; "I don't believe any writing that has falsity in it can endure for very long."[13] Walker and Welty agreed that for readers, humor (and the Gothic) too often displaced the significance of the intent of serious writing.

Walker had told Welty that black women writers received little or no critical attention, and so began teaching a black women's writers course in the South and the North. She included Kate Chopin and Virginia Woolf "because they were women and wrote, as black women did, on the condition of humankind from the perspective of women," and although O'Connor was not on the reading list, it was she who "destroyed the last vestiges of sentimentality in white Southern writing; she caused white women to look ridiculous on pedestals, and she approached her black characters – as a mature artist – with unusual humility and restraint." Walker appreciated O'Connor's "cold steely-eyed look at the South," her "cool appraisal of how people actually look; their meanness is intact."[14] Walker's first novels, *The Third Life of Grange Copeland* (1970), which honored Bayard Rustin, *Meridian* (1976), concerning complex interracial lives during and after the civil rights movement, and *The Color Purple* (1982) that won Pulitzer and National Book awards, celebrate the language and sense of community of her South as well as the beauty of the Southern landscape. Yet these same works were criticized for their portrayal of black men, the charge also made of Morrison's novels and Gayl Jones's *Corregidora* (1975) and *Eva's Man* (1976) by jazz writer and self-appointed cultural spokesman Stanley Crouch and novelist Ishmael Reed, for example. Walker's, Morrison's, and Jones's works escape the confines of the Southern label and yet are met with other complications such as gender and race politics and are thus not always included in beneficial discussions and analyses of writing by Southern women. Such elisions render Southern literature bereft of its complex, diverse richness.

In 1977, Walker and poet June Jordan founded The Sisterhood, a group of African-American women writers that included Verta Mae Grosvenor, Toni Morrison, and Ntozake Shange. The intent was "to create a space for black women writers to honor each other, to know each other, so that nothing from outside could make us fight over anything. Or even feel competitive."[15] It was an acknowledgment that they had something in common and that they could achieve more together than individually. The Sisterhood might be considered comparable to the 1920s Vanderbilt Fugitives or the Fellowship of Southern Writers founded in 1987, except that neither of these included African-American women until the 2009 induction of Dove and Trethewey into the Fellowship. (Playwright Katori Hall was inducted in 2011.) A more beneficial community with a goal of support similar to that of The Sisterhood was the Dark Room Collective that began in 1988 and in which Trethewey participated.

From the first, Toni Morrison's reading of world literature including South American and African writers and her editing at Random House for eighteen years, in particular for *The Black Book* (1973), informed her fiction and thus aided her support for and influence on Southern women writers including Toni Cade Bambara and Gayl Jones. Morrison showed herself to be a discerning reader and critic; she admired Nadine Gordimer, Eudora Welty, and Lillian Hellman, positing that "[p]erhaps it's because they are all women who have lived in segregated areas of this country or in an area where there is apartheid. They are fearless. Nadine Gordimer and Eudora Welty write about black people in a way that few white men have ever been able to write. It's not patronizing, not romanticizing – it's the way they should be written about." She explained that the "ability to do it is the marked difference between writing on the surface and writing underneath."[16] Morrison once introduced Welty with the accolade that "there are some writers without whom certain stories would never have been written," and when asked if she had not been "critical" of the way some authors depicted blacks, Morrison replied, "No! Me, critical? I have been revealing how white writers imagine black people, and some of them are brilliant at it."[17] Such challenges highlight the burden of representation, the charges of appropriation of language and culture, the assumption that writers write for audiences of their race only, and deny writers the imaginative leap at the heart of creating fiction.

Morrison imbibed the South through her parents' Alabama and Georgia families, and in her novels, the tracing of one's history through time and space is the imperative journey that one must make to understand the present. Sethe escapes from Sweet Home, Kentucky; Paul D is imprisoned in Georgia; Joe and Violet Trace migrate from Virginia; Paradise is in Oklahoma – the imposed home of southeastern Native Americans; in Maryland, Jacob Vaark is reluctantly paid off with the slave girl Florence and soon succumbs to dreaming of Haitian-bred profits. Halfway through her stint as senior editor for Random House, Morrison read the manuscript pages of *Corregidora* by twenty-four-year-old Gayl Jones. Her instant response was that "no novel about any black woman could ever be the same after this.... She had written a story that thought the unthinkable; that talked about the female requirement to 'make generations' as an active, even violent political act. She had described the relationship between a black woman and black man as no one else had with precision, ruthlessness and wisdom."[18] Morrison's praise suggests that Jones's courage influenced Morrison to be daring beyond what she had imagined up to that point. She went on to imagine that Macon "Milkman" Dead would learn that "[w]hen you know your name, you should hang on to it, for unless it is noted down and remembered, it will die when you die," that Paul D would be "the kind of man who could walk into a house and *make* the *women cry*," that Joe and Violet Trace would fall to hate in order to realize love.[19] Morrison edited Jones's *Corregidora* and *Eva's Man*, realizing that they would cause controversy for their negative portrayal of men. And they did. Staunchly arguing that writers can rise above the constrictions of region, race, gender, and politics, Morrison agreed that Jones's men are "violent, insensitive, greedy, selfish, and mean. Men don't like to be portrayed that way .... Of course, there are women who write for women, and then there are women who just write out of the matrix of what they know as women. But the others, like Eudora Welty and Flannery O'Connor, have just written as people. Sometimes it's about men. Sometimes not."[20]

Jones is an example of a Southern writer who crosses genres, publishing *White Rat: Short Stories* (1977) and *Song for Anninho* (1999), a book-length poem recreating the history of Palmares, a seventeenth-century African state in Brazil; poem collections, critical essays, and novels: *The Healing* (1998), a National Book finalist, and *Mosquito* (1999), the stream-of-dreams-and-observations of a black female truck driver rescuing folks along the Texas-Mexico border. Her critical work emphasizes her belief that the "freeing of voice" is "the essential metaphor for the direction of literature" as evident in the experiments that she carries out her writing. Among Jones's analyses are the "Americanness" of Southern writers such as Welty, Ernest Gaines, and Morrison. These writers' orality, their disregard for political or racial correctness, and balance between tradition and invention catapult them beyond region to the larger arena of American literature.[21]

A Southern woman writer who pays homage to Welty, O'Connor, Walker, and Morrison but who is also one of the "others" that Jones characterizes as of "the less powerful group" is Judith Ortiz Cofer, a Latina born in Puerto Rico who has lived in Georgia since her teen years. Her novels, short stories, poetry, autobiography, and essays for adults and young adults have won O. Henry and Pushcart prizes, an Americas Award, and received a Pulitzer nomination. Cofer confronts the tensions the individual writer may feel between expectation and influence, for critics think only of Latin-American influences, but it was O'Connor who astounded her sensibilities: "Here is a woman writer writing about an area I know, and not dwelling on only male issues. This was a woman writing about her neighbors, but beyond that, she had this genius to know that you can make the particular universal. You can write about a farm in Milledgeville, Georgia, and have it be meaningful to somebody in Paris, France." Living midway between O'Connor's and Walker's homes, Cofer ponders her "place" in a buffer zone between white and black:

> There's a white woman, upper middle class, in her Andalusia, and there's this poor black girl in Eatonton, and I am this misplaced person – a 'displaced person' like Flannery (does she only use first name?) would probably call me. All of us have something in common, which is our sense of strangeness .... My kinship [with Southern writers] has to do with the fact that we share a common landscape. When I read their writing, I know exactly what they're talking about; I know where the characters come from.[22]

Despite Cofer's achievements and being an honoree of the Georgia Writers Hall of Fame (as are O'Connor, McCullers, and Walker), she is not a member of the Fellowship of Southern Writers (as Walker and Jones are not). Lack of attention to Cofer may be the result of her multi-genre canon and the fact that the work is not primarily "about" Southern black and white racial issues, but rather concerns the more contemporary challenges of identity, community, and language for the relatively "new" Southerners not of African descent.

To address that which Southern women writers inherit from Southern women writers before them is to interrogate the concept of "Southern." Cofer confides:

> [A]ll of my years in America ... I have been blending the language of my origin, my dreams, and my imagination, Spanish, with the language of my new life, English, in order to create a new way of being an American.... [Homeland] is not necessarily a geographic location, but rather a state of being that fills me with a sense of belonging ... the imaginary place from which my creative energy arises. Home [is] the place where I am a part of the story being created.[23]

Whereas dialect, idiom, and dialogue bespeak the rich linguistic components in the work of Welty, O'Connor, and Walker, Cofer draws attention to the fusion of languages that enrich the imaginations of writers who have grounded themselves in a place identified as "home."

Nonfiction writers Melissa Fay Greene and Janisse Ray similarly demonstrate the pull of the Southern landscape and the culture's divisions. Greene has written *Praying for Sheetrock* (1992) about bringing changes to segregationist McIntosh County, Georgia; *The Temple Bombing* (1996) set in Atlanta, 1958; *Last Man Out* (2003) in which an African-Canadian miner is paradoxically invited to segregationist Georgia; *There Is No Me Without You* (2006), a biography of the AIDS epidemic featuring an Ethiopian who opens an AIDS orphanage; and *No Biking in the House without a Helmet* (2011), her autobiography of growing a family of nine children, five of whom are from other continents. She wryly asks, "Am I a Southern writer? Am I a Jewish writer? Am I a woman writer? All those things, and yet I believe that it is only a failure of imagination that would pen me into those subjects as my only fair terrain." In her teen years, Greene discovered how Welty's writing revealed "the possibility of bringing a scene to life through the painstaking collection of telling, almost microscopic, details." Greene consciously evokes Welty's "extraordinarily attentive quietness" in lines such as these from *Last Man Out*: "Money couldn't be saved on miners' wages, but a child's bike could be bought brand-new at Christmastime from the hardware store and walked home, the dusky winter trees reflected in the tin fenders, the shiny bike itself reflected in the wife's happy eyes as the two of them wheeled the thing into the woodshed and hid it under a tarp."[24] Greene's nonfiction is comparable to the fiction of Welty, O'Connor, Walker, and Morrison in telling historical truths rich in narrative that are much rooted in and influenced by the South and yet extend beyond southern categorization.

Janisse Ray – *Ecology of a Cracker Childhood* (1999), *Wildcard Quilt: Taking a Chance on Home* (2003), *Pinhook: Finding Wholeness in a*

Fragmented Land (2005), *Drifting into Darien: A Personal and Natural History of the Altamaha River* (2011) – is another distinguished writer of nonfiction who should be included in discussions of Southern women writers. She writes of human relationships (her own and, by extension, everyone's) to the land, ecologies of humans in connection to ecologies of nature, particularly in the South. Ray read the Southern writers who loved the land although they did not write of it as she does. Welty, O'Connor, Walker, and Faulkner are among those who make an especially strong impact on Ray, for she contends that the "most alive people are those who are committed to a place; to be whole is to be connected to the land."[25]

For Natasha Trethewey, crafting poems that narrate erased histories (the lives of women in Storyville, New Orleans; the Louisiana Native Guards; empire as depicted in casta paintings) in confluence with glossed-over personal stories, Southern means "the formative years" and the environment that has an effect on the writing, but Trethewey and others suggest that those who are "deeply engaged in the South" are a "disappearing breed."[26] Dorothy Allison took permission to tell the story of her South from the discovery of James Baldwin, O'Connor, Tennessee Williams, and what she calls "the whole rich worlds of southern, queer, and critical fiction." Allison has an understandable dislike of the categories of Southern and woman. She declares, "Every time I pick up a book that purports to be about either poor people or queers or Southern women, I do so with a conscious anxiety, an awareness that the books about us have been cruel, small, and false."[27] Both Trethewey and Allison recognize the influences of the past, but signal scholars of Southern women's writing to read beyond the old categories.

The 2011 National Book Foundation awards may be read as an apex in Southern women's writing because they confirm the direction that Southern women's writing has taken in the first decade of the twenty-first century. Jesmyn Ward of DeLisle, Mississippi, won the fiction award for *Salvage the Bones* and Nikky Finney, of Conway, South Carolina, won the poetry award for *Head Off & Split*. Both African Americans write out of their personal lives in racial America. Ward says that as a black woman from the South she feels pushed into "a niche that is outside the realm of experience for a lot of literary people,"[28] but, arguably, the National Book Awards spirit Ward and Finney out of the smaller and specialized circles of Southern and African-American literature into a national readership. This is just where Southern women writers of note and influence – Welty and O'Connor, in particular – land when the fetters of regionalism are broken. Both Ward and Finney weave personal experience (home, family, place, racism) with historical records and events (slavery, education, politics, Hurricane Katrina), as have Greene and Trethewey before them. Ward guffaws at the idea of a post-racial America: "I don't know that place." When people "can pick up my work and see those characters as human beings and feel for them, then ... that is a political act."[29] Ward says her intention is to write about "the experiences of the poor, and the black, and the rural people of the South so that the culture that marginalized us for so long would see that our stories were as universal, our lives as fraught and lovely and important as theirs." Finney, likewise, attests to being "drawn to history: personal history, American history, Southern history, family history, the history of community, the history of secrets, the history that has gone missing, the history that has been told by the lion hunter but not the lion, the history of pencils, of loss, of tenderness, the history of what the future just might be."[30] The past for Finney, Trethewey, Greene, and other Southern women writers is not only the present but also the future. The past is not to be ignored, nor to be waited upon to pass.

Welty observed that "[o]ne place comprehended can make us understand other places better,"[31] and Finney, Ward, and award-winning playwright Katori Hall (*Hoodoo Love*, 2007; *Saturday Night/Sunday Morning* 2008; *The Mountaintop*, 2009; *Hurt Village*, 2011) have made the South fundamental to their work in content and in inspiration, for each claims home and family as essential. For Finney, home is South Carolina, Virginia, the Blue Ridge Mountains of Alabama, and the Great Smoky Mountains of Tennessee. Like Jones, Trethewey, and Morrison, Finney works back to the beginnings of slavery and her family. She accepts the honorific and descriptive, but fights against the mantle of Affrilachian poet when it threatens to ghettoize, for all of her "places' are confluent with one another, all the way back to Africa.

Walker is a particular influence on these newest Southern writers, and Ward allows that *The Color Purple* showed her that "a black, poor Southern girl" could write a book: "I saw something of – not myself – but the experience of the people around me reflected in that book, because it's set in the rural South and these people are poor, and just seeing that [Walker] could do that made me .... realize that it might be possible." Ward also cites traditional ideas of place as central to her writing and professes to being honored to follow in a "legacy of great Mississippi writers, from Faulkner to Welty to [Richard] Wright to [Anne] Moody, all whom were marked by living here. Place informs character: it influences how characters see the world, how they experience and react to each other, how they speak about their experiences, how they understand the stories of their lives." Esch, the young pregnant narrator of Ward's *Salvage the Bones*, navigates her place in a world "suffused with the rhythms and terrors and sublime beauties of Mississippi"[32] during the days before and during Hurricane Katrina.

Welty and O'Connor provide a legacy of intense observation. O'Connor and Walker contribute attention to the spirit and soul of humankind. Walker and Morrison demonstrate over and over the need to discover, respect, and learn from one's ancestors. Southern women writers inherit from one another. They demonstrate that if one uses the language and place of one's home to create narratives in prose or poetry that stretch toward the mysterious truths of human relationships with one another and with the land, the writing moves beyond regional confines out into a world unrestrained by time or space.

NOTES

1 Sarah Gordon, ed., *Flannery O'Connor: In Celebration of Genius* (Athens, GA: Hill Street Press, 2000), p. xi.

2 Doris Betts, "Talking to Flannery," in *Flannery O'Connor: In Celebration of Genius*, p. 109.

3 Gayle Jones, *Liberating Voices: Oral Tradition in African American Literature* (Cambridge, MA: Harvard University Press, 1991), p. 192.

4 Jennifer Campbell, "'It's a Time in the Land': Gendering Black Power and Sarah E. Wright's Place in the Tradition of Black Women's Writing on Racism and Sexism" *African American Review* (Summer 1997): 211–222; Sharon Monteith, "The Never-Ending Cycle of Poverty: Sarah E. Wright's This Child's Gonna Live," in *Poverty and Progress in the US South since 1920* (Amsterdam: VU University Press, 2006), p. 84; Patricia Yaeger, *Dirt and Desire: Reconstructing Southern Women's Writing, 1930–1990* (Chicago: University of Chicago Press, 2000), pp. 55–56.

5 *Understanding Fiction*, 1st edition (1943), included Welty's "A Piece of News" and "Old Mr. Marblehall," both from the *Southern Review*; the 2nd edition (1959) replaced "Old Mr. Marblehall" with Welty's "No Place for You, My Love" and "How I Write" plus O'Connor's "A Good Man Is Hard to Find." *House of Fiction* (1950), edited by Tate and Gordon included "Why I Live at the P.O." by Welty. The 2nd edition (1960) included nothing by Welty and added "A Good Man Is Hard to Find."

6 Eudora Welty, "The Interior World," in *Conversations with Eudora Welty*, ed. Peggy Whitman Prenshaw (Jackson: University Press of Mississippi, 1984), pp. 54–55.

7 Pearl McHaney, ed., *Eudora Welty Contemporary Reviews* (Cambridge: Cambridge University Press, 2005), p. 124.

8 R. Neil Scott and Irwin H. Streight, eds., *Flannery O'Connor: Contemporary Reviews* (Cambridge: Cambridge University Press, 2009), p. 272.

9 Flannery O'Connor, "Some Aspects of the Grotesque in Southern Fiction," in *Mystery and Manners: Occasional Prose* (New York: Farrar, Straus, & Giroux, 1961), pp. 40–42.

10 Eudora Welty, "Must the Novelist Crusade?" in *Stories, Essays, and Memoir* (New York: Library of America, 1998), pp. 810, 811.

11 Ross Spears, *Tell about the South* (Riverdale, MD: Agee Films, 1999), part II.

12 Alice Walker, *In Search of Our Mothers' Gardens* (New York: Harcourt Brace/ Harvest, 1984), p. 42.

13 Eudora Welty, "Eudora Welty: An Interview," in *Conversations with Eudora Welty*, p. 135.

14 Walker, *In Search of Our Mothers' Gardens*, pp. 260, 59; Ross Spears, *Tell about the South*, part II.

15 Alice Walker, "On Raising Chickens: A Conversation with Rudolph P. Byrd" in *The World Has Changed: Conversations with Alice Walker*, ed. Rudolph P. Byrd (New York: New Press, 2010), p. 318.

16 Toni Morrison, "Talk with Toni Morrison" and "The Visits of the Writers Toni Morrison and Eudora Welty," in *Conversations with Toni Morrison*, ed. Danille Taylor-Guthrie (Jackson: University Press of Mississippi, 1994), pp. 47, 91–92.

17 Toni Morrison, "Toni Morrison: The Art of Fiction," in *Toni Morrison: Conversations*, ed. Carolyn C. Denard (Jackson: University Press of Mississippi, 2008), p. 73.

18 Toni Morrison, "Toni Morrison on a Book She Loves: Gayle Jones's *Corregidora*," in *What Moves at the Margins*, ed. Carolyn C. Denard (Jackson: University Press of Mississippi, 2008), p. 110.

19 Toni Morrison, *Song of Solomon* (New York: Plume, 1987), p. 329; *Beloved* (New York, Knopf, 1987), p. 17; *Jazz* (New York: Knopf, 1992).

20 Toni Morrison, "I Will Always Be A Writer" in *Toni Morrison: Conversations*, p. 6.

21 Jones, *Liberating Voices*, pp. 178, 10, 13.

22 Judith Ortiz Cofer, "Interview with Yohann Brultey" (Athens, GA, May 26, 2011).

23 Judith Ortiz Cofer, "Introduction," in *Riding Low on the Streets of Gold: Latino Literature for Young Adults*, ed. Judith Ortiz Cofer (Houston, TX: Arte Público Press, 2003), p. vii.

24 Melissa Fay Greene, "Q&A with the Author," *ETUDE* (Spring 2003); e-mail with Pearl McHaney (January 20, 2012); *Last Man Out: The Story of the Springhill Mine Disaster* (Orlando, FL: Harcourt, 2003), p. 178.

25 Janisse Ray, "Interview with Janisse Ray" (Swannanoa, NC, Warren Wilson College Environmental Leadership Center, March 1, 2011).

26 Natasha Trethewey, "Conversation with Pearl McHaney" (Decatur, GA, January 4, 2012).

27 Dorothy Allison, *Skin: Talking about Sex, Class and Literature* (New York: Firebrand Books, 1994), pp. 78, 165.

28 "National Book Award 2011 Winners Jesmyn Ward and Nikky Finney Tackle Race and History," *Huffington Post*, November 18, 2011.

29 Jesmyn Ward, "How Hurricane Katrina Shaped Acclaimed Jesmyn Ward Book," *BBC News*, December 21, 2011.

30 Nikky Finney, "Winner Interview: Nikky Finney" *National Book Foundation* (n.d.).

31 Eudora Welty, "Place in Fiction" in *Stories, Essays, & Memoir* (New York: Library of America, 1998), p. 792.

32 Jesmyn Ward, "Jesmyn Ward, Author of *Salvage the Bones*, Answers Eleven Questions"; "Jesmyn Ward on winning the National Book Award – plus, she takes the EW Book Quiz!"; "Jesmyn Ward, *Salvage the Bones*." Available at: http://www.linussblanket.com/jessmyn-ward-answers-eleven-questions/ and http://shelf-life.ew.com/2011/11/18/jesmyn-ward-interview-national-book-award/

IO

SARAH GLEESON-WHITE

Hollywood Dreaming: Southern Writers and the Movies

For Flannery O'Connor's sham general in "A Late Encounter with the Enemy," "only one event in the past ... had any significance": the 1939 Atlanta premiere of *Gone with the Wind*. Held over three days and attended by Margaret Mitchell, David O. Selznick, and the film's white stars – Vivien Leigh, Clark Gable, and Olivia de Havilland – the premiere included a motorcade, a ball, "various cocktail hours, luncheons, teas [and] tours."[1] For all Selznick's concerns about *Gone with the Wind*'s reception in the South, its Atlanta premiere has lingered in regional memory as the high point of the South's relationship with Hollywood – even with an Englishwoman cast in the role of Scarlett O'Hara – a relationship that has attracted significant scholarly attention in terms of Hollywood redactions of Southern literature and representations of the South. In both contexts, Hollywood comes off rather poorly, typically as an exploitative machine that feeds national and global audiences myths of a magnolia-scented plantation South, or a South that borders on the pornographic, populated by violent, incestuous hillbillies, sex-starved white girls, and lascivious black men. Yet, this is only half the story. As Allison Graham and Sharon Monteith's survey of Southern cinema shows, "sometimes native southerners, like D. W. Griffith, were in the forefront of such representations," as actors, producers, and directors.[2] Southerners have also made significant contributions as writers *in* and *about* Hollywood, engaging directly with that most powerful manifestation of the culture industry to control or influence in some way, at least, the South's mediation and its place in the national imaginary.

This chapter extends existing scholarship on Southern contributions to film culture as it simultaneously shifts the boundaries of "Southern literature" to include two apparently invisible narrative forms: the Southern screenplay and the Southern Hollywood novel. Such a willful misprision of Southern literature enables a set of incongruous practices, writers, and concerns to come into view, compelling us not only to rethink but also to expand the category of Southern literature, something that has, as Michael

146

Kreyling notes, "always been a problem for a discipline with so much of its foundation dedicated to strict borders: who was white and who was not, what was literature and what was not, what was southern and what was not."[3]

The Hollywood novel emerged simultaneously with the motion picture industry, and reached its peak in the 1930s and early 1940s. Examples of the genre continued to appear throughout the twentieth century, "in acts of imitation, transformation and parody."[4] According to David Fine, the Hollywood novel typically explores "the confusion between reality and illusion, the conflict between commerce and art, the commodification of sex, and the erasure of both identity boundaries and an ordered sense of time and place,"[5] with the best-known examples Nathanael West's *The Day of the Locust* (1939) and F. Scott's Fitzgerald's *The Love of the Last Tycoon* (1941). What is not widely acknowledged, however, is the striking number of Hollywood novels written by Southerners – for example, Horace McCoy's *They Shoot Horses, Don't They?* (1935) and *I Should Have Stayed Home* (1938); Speed Lamkin's *The Easter Egg Hunt* (1954); Walker Percy's *The Moviegoer* (1961) and *Lancelot* (1977); Robert Penn Warren's *Flood: A Romance of Our Time* (1963); John Ehle's *The Changing of the Guard* (1976); Mark Childress' *Tender* (1990), based on the life of Elvis Presley, and *Crazy in Alabama* (1990); and James Lee Burke's *In the Electric Mist with Confederate Dead* (1993). William Faulkner came close with the Los Angeles setting of "Golden Land" (1935), and Eudora Welty's 1949 collection, *The Golden Apples*, as David McWhirter has argued, is crowded with allusions to silent cinema. Even Thomas Wolfe's *Look Homeward, Angel* (1929) contains anecdotes pertaining to moviegoing. An acknowledgment of the significance of Hollywood culture to the canon of Southern literature seems especially fruitful in the context of current scholarly interest in the "reel" South. Percy's *Lancelot* and McCoy's *I Should Have Stayed Home* are exemplary here. *Lancelot* underscores the "fake" or movie-made South in its account of a Hollywood shoot in Louisiana. Whereas Percy's novel considers the *proximity* of Hollywood and the New South, McCoy's overlooked novel, set during Hollywood's classical era, enacts a juxtapositional dynamic to suggest that industrial modernity – for all its foibles and worse – is largely preferable to the backward-looking South of the 1930s. Either way, both texts actively participate in the South's entanglement with the nation's culture industry.

The narrator of Percy's *Lancelot*, the world-weary Raymond Chandler-rereading Lancelot Lamar, does not share the enthusiasm of O'Connor's general for Hollywood's incursion into the South. A production team arrives at Belle Isle, Lancelot's ancestral River Road estate, to make a seemingly ludicrous film in which "a Christlike hippie stranger … has reconciled poor white sharecroppers, overseers, sheriffs, blacks, whites and the half-caste girl."[6] Its female lead is a Southern small-town girl who has made good in the Hollywood dream factory, a trajectory familiar from William Wellman's 1937 *A Star Is Born*. Like many Hollywood novels – most famously, *The Day of the Locust* – the novel's critique is focused on Hollywood's manufacture of deceit and illusion with the result that reality can no longer be distinguished from its artful copy. Hurricane Marie, for example, which threatens the film-shoot, seems to mimic the film's manufactured hurricane. As Lancelot watches the oncoming hurricane from the porch, the production's hurricane machine simultaneously "cranks up" and "[t]he live oaks blow inside out." Lancelot observes with some irony that "[i]t is necessary to use a real hurricane machine even though a real hurricane is coming, not just because the real hurricane is not yet here, but because even if it were it wouldn't be as suitable for film purposes as an artificial hurricane" (171).

Lancelot broaches the problem of re-presenting the real in terms of what Scott Romine has described as the South's "fraught and anxious relation … with authenticity."[7] Lancelot's declaration that Belle Isle, now razed to the ground, is "[a]s gone with the wind as Tara" (106) embodies this anxious relationship: he conjures the plantation South (and it seems always to be the antebellum South that is [mis]taken for the real South) via a fake plantation from a Hollywood blockbuster fit for movie consumers. Where *is* the real South then? Romine's answer is that, as "globalizing economies [Hollywood is exemplary here] may have buried 'the South' too deep for recovery by history or memory,"[8] the fake South becomes "the real South through the intervention of narrative." The South, then, is "increasingly sustained as a virtual, commodified, built, themed, invented, or otherwise artificial territoriality."[9]

This perplexing entanglement of the fake and the authentic, and indeed the substitution of the latter by the former, which drives Lancelot finally to burn down Belle Isle – killing his adulterous wife, Margot, and the Hollywood crew in the process – is also confronted by Warren's fictional filmmaker in *Flood*. Yasha Jones and his collaborator, acclaimed Southern screenwriter Brad Tolliver, arrive in Fiddlersburg, Tennessee, to make a feature film about the Tennessee Valley Authority's controlled flooding of the town. The challenge that lies before them is that the South is already "a perfect cliche" with its "dark house,[10] moon, ruined terrace and mockingbirds." Jones "wondered, wryly, what they would say if he … put this in his picture, absolutely as it was. But … he would do something to it so that it would no longer be what it actually was, what it really was, but because it was unreal would be taken for real."[11] While certain tropes – ruined terraces, mockingbirds – might have the power to evoke the "South," it remains fragile, depthless – indeed, as unreal as a film set. Hollywood, then, seems the ideal lens through which to examine the real South: its accessibility or otherwise, and its mediation.

On visiting the film set for the first time, Lancelot concludes that "[w]hat was nutty was that the movie folk were trafficking in illusions in a real world but the real world thought that its reality could only be found in the illusions"(152). This epistemological crisis is played out at the formal level, in the penultimate chapter that is largely a record of the novel's alternative film: "a new kind of cinéma vérité" (128). This is the videotape recording that Lancelot makes to catch Margot in the act with Janos Jacoby, Merlin's assistant. The conventional novel layout is at this moment invaded by marquee advertising ("FRIDAY AFTERNOON AT THE MOVIES: A DOUBLE FEATURE"); the program's intertitles ("FIRST FEATURE: MISS MARGOT'S ROOM" and "SECOND FEATURE: MISS RAINE'S ROOM") as well as, thoughtfully, "INTERMISSION." In another "scene," the barely heard dialogue of Margot and the film's director appears in the format of a screenplay, as if transcribed from the film footage that Lancelot is watching (186–189). The (already fictional) "real" world of the novel becomes enmeshed in the imagined or "reel" world of the film.

Margot – who is, rather conveniently, an actor – lends a further Southern inflection to this most ubiquitous theme of the Hollywood novel: illusion versus reality. Hailing from west Texas, she inhabits the South through a process of accessorization and performance, becoming a belle-guide on the tourist Azalea Trail. Here she meets Lancelot, whose estate is one of the Trail's destinations, and once they are married, she is promoted to Southern belle, "Mardi Gras matron, chatelaine of Belle Isle." Her rapid transformation from Westerner to Southerner suggests that the South, rather than a bounded and mappable place with an "exceptional" organic culture, is constituted by a series of performances that anyone (even a Westerner) can take on and do quite well – although sometimes Margot would "forget and curse like a cowboy" (166). Once she has secured her River Road planter and his plantation, her passion for "old 'authentic' things" emerges as she sets about restoring both house and husband to their original condition (80). Somewhat bemused by this impulse, Lancelot observes that Margot "didn't restore me exactly, she created me according to some Texas-conceived image of the River Road gentry, a kind of gentleman planter without plantation, a composite ... of Ashley Wilkes ... Leslie Howard ... plus Gregory Peck, gentle southern lawyer, plus a bit of Clark Gable as Rhett" (120). Beside *Gone with the Wind*'s Ashley Wilkes, played by the English Leslie Howard, the other two screen Southerners require either no name or a first name only; larger than life, they stand in for the actors who, by contrast, require full names. Implicit here is the idea that it may be *non*-Southerners who best "do" the South: Margot, Leslie Howard (and Vivien Leigh), and Hollywood, all engaged in the production and certification of the South.

Horace McCoy composes a different portrayal of Hollywood and its relationship with the South in *I Should Have Stayed Home*, narrated from the perspective of a Southerner in Hollywood. McCoy, who has fallen under the radar of "Southern literature," tried first to establish himself as a screen actor but then turned to (largely B-film) screenwriting to support his fiction writing. He was contracted to several of the major studios, including Twentieth Century-Fox and Warner Brothers, from 1932 until his death in 1955, the very period in which Faulkner worked on and off in Hollywood.[12] McCoy is best known for his novel *They Shoot Horses, Don't They?* in which two young Hollywood hopefuls compete in a dance marathon. *I Should Have Stayed Home* is more avowedly about the industry in its dark account of a naive Georgia farm boy, Ralph Carston, whose movie-star good looks and Southern accent attract the notice of a Hollywood talent scout during a local theatrical performance of *They Knew What They Wanted*.[13] Carston moves out to Hollywood to join the cast of a film about the South, but instead finds only occasional work as an extra. In exchange for what he hopes will be his big break, he becomes entangled with a wealthy man-eating widow, Mrs. Smithers, a relationship that surely presages that of struggling screenwriter Joe Gillis and Gloria Swanson's Norma Desmond in *Sunset Boulevard* (1950).

Although Carston's experiences are bleak, to say the least – one friend commits suicide and another enters a tawdry marriage of convenience – Hollywood somehow appears the better of two evils, if the alternative is small-town Georgia. "I'd wipe the whole south right off the map. They're stupid and ignorant and illiterate and live in the Dark Ages," he declares, "I'll die before I go back home."[14] He discovers that Hollywood offers a relative degree of moral freedom: everyone minds their own business, which means that men and women can swim naked together in a pool, and a white film star can have an affair with an African American. When Carston spots the couple in each other's arms at Mrs. Smithers's fundraising party for the Scottsboro boys, he exclaims to his friend, Mona Matthews,

> "Why, he's a nigger," .... She turned around to me quickly. "You mustn't use that word," she said. There's no niggers out here. It's colored men. He's a colored man." "Indians are colored, too," I said, still looking at them. "The point is she's a white woman. Why, the – " "Now, wait a minute," she said, ... "You stop being a professional Southerner. You mind your own business – .... They've been sleeping together for months. That's Helga Carruthers.... Don't you know this is one town where nobody pays any attention to what anybody else does?" (35–36).

In mocking Carston for being "a professional Southerner," Mona evokes a crucial function that many Southerners fulfilled in Hollywood during the studio era. Screenwriters such as Nunnally Johnson and Lamar Trotti, as professional Southerners, "provided advice on local color and racial etiquette" to the studios.[15] Perhaps McCoy, whose own screenwriting career seemed only to falter at this time, is here ridiculing these professional Southerners, two of the most powerful screenwriters of his generation.

The exchange between Carston and Mona also reveals the laissez-faire and racially progressive attitudes that she ascribes to Hollywood, at a time when Los Angeles was one of the most segregated cities in the country. Indeed, the portrait of Hollywood the novel provides is of a relative oasis of liberalism. Carston finds himself involved in or eavesdropping on conversations that range over local, national, and international concerns: the blackballing of Writers' Guild members; the studios' exploitation of extras and writers; Hollywood's persecution of Upton Sinclair and Thomas Mooney; James Cagney, Robert Montgomery, Joan Crawford, and Franchot Tone's support of "organizing"; the Sacco-Vanzetti case; the Scottsboro boys; and the rise of fascism in Germany and Spain. As the apparently omnipotent, hard-nosed, and corrupt studio bosses bear the brunt of the novel's scathing satire, McCoy takes care to compose a picture of Hollywood as sophisticated and international in outlook.

We need, of course, to approach with some skepticism the degree and sincerity of the political engagement that McCoy ascribes to Hollywood insiders; they are to some extent "parlor Communists" (30), and the novel is a satire, after all. Nevertheless, however minimal or superficial this engagement might be, the Hollywood of I Should Have Stayed Home is somewhat atypical for a Hollywood novel. By implicit contrast, the South is unattractively insular, perversely obsessed with miscegenation, and as fearful of unionization as it is of communists. For David Fine, I Should Have Stayed Home ultimately fails as a critique of Hollywood because Carston "continues to dream of success in Hollywood" and his "persistent guilelessness mars the book's effectiveness as an indictment."[16] Yet McCoy's novel is intriguing for this very reason; it resists a simplistic or singular perspective of Hollywood, refracted as it is and framed by the experiences of a Southern farm boy. I Should Have Stayed Home, like Percy's Lancelot, stretches the South out of recognizable shape in disclosing the national and global cultural industry in which the region actively participates.

The many Southern screenwriters who have contributed to, and sometimes controlled, the way the South has interacted with the culture industry have extended the important cultural work that these Hollywood novels undertake as part of the South's encounter with modernity and its expressive forms. Indeed, a surprising number of Southern screenwriters have worked in Hollywood, beginning with Griffith who wrote scenarios before his spectacular directorial turn. Indeed, several of the most prolific and powerful screenwriters of the classical era were Southerners, most notably Johnson and Trotti, as well as Virginian Robert Buckner.[17]

Johnson and Trotti had long and productive careers – between them, they received screenwriting credit on approximately 100 film projects – at Twentieth Century-Fox under Darryl Zanuck, renowned for his appreciation of the writer's substantial role in the filmmaking process, unusual in this era of the producer-centered studio. As well as collaborating with Faulkner,[18] Johnson, Trotti, and Buckner wrote several "Southerns" (original screenplays, for the most part) at that moment in studio history when the "myth" of the Southern box office frequently dictated what did and did not make it to the screen.[19]

Between 1920 and 1940, the Southern boxoffice became, according to Thomas Cripps, "a monolithic creature .... After all, the reasoning ran, if it *would not* sell in the South, it *might not* sell in the North. Besides, the profits made in the South, although smaller than those in other regions, could carry a movie 'out of the red'."[20] Southern accents were particularly risky in this regard. Johnson, in his role of professional Southerner on John Ford's *The Prisoner of Shark Island* (1936), warned that "Southerners don't know they've got an accent to begin with until they hear somebody mocking it, and then they get their backs up."[21] And, wanting to ensure the mistakes of *Jezebel* (1938) were not repeated, Johnson advised Selznick on the handling of Southern accents for *Gone with the Wind*.[22] Trotti considered the screenplay of *Judge Priest* (1934), which he co-wrote with Dudley Nichols for John Ford, as "a corrective to all of Hollywood's previous missteps in depicting the South" and was apparently thrilled with the result: "The colored people, Stepin Fetchit et al are really negroes as we know them, played for comedy chiefly but of course human and recognizable."[23] Whether or not the vigilance of these professional Southerners created more authentic depictions of the South on screen is difficult to establish (*Lancelot* and *Flood* suggest this is an impossible task anyway). But, Trotti's career, as Matthew Bernstein argues (and this would pertain to Johnson and Buckner) invites us to consider "the intriguing dynamics of [the] intermediate role played by one white resident southerner in Hollywood across three decades."[24]

Langston Hughes, a highly regarded poet by the late 1930s, seized the opportunity to make his own contribution to the Hollywood South when assigned to co-write, with actor Clarence Muse, the RKO antebellum musical, *Way Down South* (1939). Cripps notes that "Until Wallace Thurman came to Hollywood in the mid-1930's as a contract writer no black man sat in a position to rail against ... stereotypes."[25] The film's director, Bernard Vorhaus, was convinced that "as black people [Hughes and Muse] would get some feeling into this story."[26] Their first draft bore little resemblance to "the Hollywood formula version of the fabled Southland." However, perhaps unsurprisingly, they were impelled to include in later drafts "obligatory images of the Hollywood South" – poor whites, "pickaninnies," bad Yankees, and the "slave situation" – in order to avoid offending the powerful Southern box office.[27] While their original intentions may not have made it to the screen, Cripps argues that Hughes and Muse's collaboration on *Way Down South* was nonetheless of great historical significance: two African Americans "had not only gotten credit – *sole* credit – for a Hollywood screenplay and story but had also gotten credits for two songs."[28]

That Southerners played active roles in the mediation of the South from the early days of the motion picture industry poses a challenge to those who might assume that the Hollywood-South relationship has only been that of exploiter and victim. The incorporation of these screenwriters into the directory of Southern writers, while underscoring their status as Southerners – "professional" or otherwise – also goes some way to challenging accounts of Hollywood that present it as a story of the West and of the traffic of talent East to West exclusively. Furthermore, we can no longer ignore the screenplay within the scope of Southern literary studies.

There is perhaps a perfectly rational explanation for the exclusion to date of the screenplay from the field of Southern literature, and from literary studies more broadly. While extant scholarship includes Bernstein's account of Trotti's career, a handful of essays on Faulkner's screenplays, Jeffrey Couchman's *The Night of the Hunter: A Biography of a Film* (2009), and discussion of the screenplays of Truman Capote and Tennessee Williams, for example, in *The New Encyclopedia of Southern Culture: Media* (2011), there exists the very real problem of accessibility. The majority of Hollywood screenplays remain in manuscript form and are held in studio vaults and archives across the United States. Another obstacle to the incorporation of the screenplay into the canon relates to the question of authorship. Most Hollywood films – and thus, by extension, Hollywood screenplays – are adaptations of novels, short stories, or plays. This creates a problem for literary studies because the screenwriter is not coextensive with the author. Screenwriting is a collaborative practice, often involving multiple writers as well as directors, producers, marketing personnel, and actors, and this too makes it difficult to assign authorship, as does the production of various drafts and versions – by the same or different writers – making it difficult to deem even the final version authoritative.[29] Nonetheless, Hollywood screenplays exist and in great number, and feed fruitfully into the New Southern

Studies' project of seeking alternative modes through which to articulate the region: its texts, networks, images, and identities.

Many Southern authors have either carved out lengthy careers writing in Hollywood or written a single screenplay: Paul Green (who also taught screenwriting courses from his home in Chapel Hill, North Carolina); Faulkner; Erskine Caldwell; James Agee (*The African Queen, The Night of the Hunter*); Capote (*Beat the Devil, The Innocents, Indiscretions of an American Wife*, and an unfinished adaptation of *The Great Gatsby*); James Dickey (who adapted his own *Deliverance*); John Ehle (who adapted his novel *The Journey of August King*); John Grisham; Mark Childress (who adapted his novel *Crazy in Alabama*); Pat Conroy; Anne Rice; and of course Williams, who wrote several original screenplays in addition to adapting his own plays to screen, and who formed a powerful partnership with Elia Kazan.

Other playwrights able to maintain successful, parallel Hollywood careers include Lillian Hellman, who regularly worked with director William Wyler and writer Dashiell Hammett, and adapted Horton Foote's *The Chase* to the screen (Foote apparently loathed it) and her New Orleans-set *Toys in the Attic*. She also wrote an original screenplay, *The North Star*, for director Lewis Milestone, which she had published when taken off the project prematurely. Foote succeeded in Hollywood as well as in television during its golden age, publishing a collection of original teleplays in 1956. He is best known for his adaptation of *To Kill a Mockingbird* (1962) and his original screenplay, *Tender Mercies* (1983), both of which earned him Academy awards. Of his Hollywood career, from the mid 1950s to the mid 1960s, he has said that "any time there was a third-rate, or fourth-rate, or a fifth-rate Southern novel, they'd call me up and everyone thought I was a Southern specialist" – yet another professional Southerner in Hollywood, it would seem.[30] Foote also adapted Faulkner's short story, "Tomorrow," to screen and television, and "Barn Burning," the "Old Man" section of *The Wild Palms*, and Flannery O'Connor's "The Displaced Person" for television.

Carson McCullers almost wrote the screenplay for *Indiscretion of an American Housewife*, which Capote ended up writing (although the extent of his contribution to the project is disputed). Richard Fine claims that Thomas Wolfe "received a substantial offer from MGM," which he turned down to finish a novel, "but not before he repeatedly reassured the studio that 'if Hollywood wants to seduce me, I am not only willing but eager.' The offer was presumably never repeated."[31] Willie Morris describes his experiences as a script consultant on *Ghosts of Mississippi* (1994) in *The Ghosts of Medgar Evers: A Tale of Race, Murder, Mississippi, and Hollywood* (1998), and Richard Wright co-wrote the screenplay adaptation of – and also starred in – *Native Son* for an Argentinean production of his novel in 1951.

Others, such as Cormac McCarthy and Barry Hannah, have worked at the edges of the Hollywood screenplay, and in the process raised interesting questions about the screenplay's relation to other literary genres. Joel and Ethan Coen wrote, directed, and produced *No Country for Old Men*, an adaptation of McCarthy's 2005 novel. What is not widely known is that McCarthy first wrote the narrative as a screenplay, almost twenty years before the publication of the novel.[32] The traces of the screenplay genre are everywhere in the novel he would come to write: the lack of attributions (including speech marks); the present-tense narrative; and the overall sparseness of that narrative, in particular its minimal psychological insights. Over the course of his career, McCarthy's prose has become more and more transparent, a radical departure from the opacity of the earlier Appalachian novels and *Blood Meridian* (1985), so that *No Country for Old Men* bears little resemblance, stylistically, to the Faulknerian flourishes of these earlier novels. Reading his fiction alongside his screenwriting makes sense of this quite radical stylistic shift.

Barry Hannah's collection, *Captain Maximus* (1985), concludes with "Power and Light: A Novella for the Screen from an Idea by Robert Altman," a rather bemusing little story of power-line workers, which would later appear in a single volume as a novella. Set in Seattle, it is the first of Hannah's narratives to take place out of the South, although one of the principal characters, Maureen, is from Hannah's native Mississippi. "Power and Light" is written in continuous present-tense prose that closely resembles a film treatment: it contains suggestions for sound directions, for example, the non-diegetic music that opens the narrative, "A chorus from Tchaikovsky [that] sings the morning," and there are frequent directions as to what readers or spectators are expected to see. These elements contribute to the text's overall generic ambiguity.

However, it is Faulkner's screenwriting career that perhaps best exemplifies the real payoff of the inclusion of the screenplay in the field of Southern literature, because we have to work a little harder to accept him as a collaborative writer who wrote to order for approximately two-thirds of his literary career. Faulkner may not have found pleasure in the work he undertook in Hollywood over an accumulative four years between 1932 and 1955, but according to Meta Carpenter Wilde, "he was, nevertheless, a writer who was incapable of doing less than his best … he did not write down to the medium or hold with the take-the-money-and-run cynicism that was prevalent."[33] Faulkner collaborated with some of the most important screenwriters of the time, powerful producers like Zanuck, and leading American and European directors such as Howard Hawks, John Ford, and Jean Renoir. Over the course of his Hollywood career, he wrote screenplays (chiefly adaptations) with various temporal and geographic settings: the Revolutionary-era frontier ("Drums Along the Mohawk"); World War I Europe ("The Road to Glory"; "Splinter Fleet"); World War II Martinique ("To Have or Have Not"); the Californian Gold Rush ("Sutter's Gold"); postwar China ("The Left Hand of God"); 1930s Los Angeles ("The Big Sleep"); and even ancient Egypt ("Land of the Pharaohs"; original) and a "Mythical Latin-American kingdom" (original). He thereby removed himself from the South, not only physically (to Hollywood) but also imaginatively and, in order to undertake these screen adaptations, he familiarized himself with a variety of American and European literary and popular fictions, not conventionally considered among his influences.

During the hiatus between beginning "The Dark House," an early draft of *Absalom, Absalom!*, and completing that novel, Faulkner wrote a screen adaptation of Blaise Cendrars' *L'Or* (1925; *Sutter's Gold*, 1926), a fictionalized account of Swiss immigrant, Johannes Sutter, and the establishment of his estate, New Helvetia, in 1830s California. The resonances between the plots of *Sutter's Gold* and *Absalom, Absalom!*, as well as in the characterization of Cendrars's Colonel Sutter and Faulkner's Colonel Sutpen (including the homophonic names) are so striking as to prompt us to read *Absalom, Absalom!* anew. Read with Cendrars's novel in mind, Faulkner's novel would seem a transposition onto the Southern landscape of the Far West story of a Swiss colonel, a story of European immigration and westward migration, of the destruction of native peoples and their environment, the attempted establishment of a personal empire, enslaved foreign laborers upon which that empire was founded, and finally the demise of that empire. If *Absalom, Absalom!* is, among other things, both a chronicle of the South and a limit text of "the Southern narrative," then the existence of Faulkner's "Sutter's Gold" makes it increasingly difficult to accept Faulkner's careful surveying and mapping of Yoknapatawpha county as hemmed in as it once seemed by the Tallahatchie and Yoknapatawpha rivers. Its narratives are formed in no small part, it turns out, by encounters with other regions and places, both within and beyond national boundaries.

Turning attention to the interface of the cinematic and the literary, and to the encounter of industrial and literary culture, which the Southern Hollywood novel and the Southern screenplay invite, encourages us to think about Southern literature as a constellation of texts, practices, and cultural modes that frequently lie beyond the region and beyond those forms most conventionally associated with Southern narrative: the novel and the short story. There emerges a relationship of exchange between Southern literary history and that most powerful and international of U.S. mass cultural forms – Hollywood cinema – that exerts irresistible pressure on the borders of that "little postage stamp of native soil."[34]

NOTES

1 Matthew Bernstein, "Selznick's March: The Atlanta Premiere of *Gone with the Wind*," *Atlanta History* 43.2 (1999), p. 8.

2 Allison Graham and Sharon Monteith, ed. *The New Encyclopedia of Southern Culture, Volume 18: Media* (Chapel Hill: University of North Carolina, 2011), p. xix.

3 Michael Kreyling, "Toward A New Southern Studies," *South Central Review* 22.1 (2005), p. 4.

4 David Fine, *Imagining Los Angeles: A City in Fiction* (Albuquerque: University of New Mexico Press, 2000), p. 156.

5 Fine, p. 173.

6 Walker Percy, *Lancelot* (New York: Farrar, Strauss and Giroux, 1977), p. 196. Subsequent references will be included in parentheses. Arthur W. Wilhelm notes that the film "is a loose parody of *The Fugitive Kind*, the 1959 screen version of the Tennessee Williams play *Orpheus Descending*," in "Moviemaking and the Mythological Framework of Walker Percy's *Lancelot*," *The Southern Literary Journal* 27.2 (1995), p. 64.

7 Scott Romine, *The Real South: Southern Narrative in the Age of Cultural Reproduction* (Athens: University of Georgia Press, 2008), p. 3.

8 Michael Kreyling, *The South that Wasn't There: Postsouthern Memory and History*. (Baton Rouge: Louisiana State University Press, 2010), p. 7.

9 Romine, p. 9.

10 "The Dark House" was William Faulkner's initial working title for *Absalom, Absalom!*.

11 Robert Penn Warren, *Flood: A Romance of Our Time* (New York: Random House, 1964), p. 50.

12 See David E. Wilt, *Hardboiled in Hollywood* (Bowling Green: Bowling Green State Popular Press, 1991) for an overview of McCoy's Hollywood career.

13 The ending of *I Should Have Stayed Home* mimics the plot of Sidney Howard's 1924 play.

14 Horace McCoy, *I Should Have Stayed Home* (New York: Garland, 1978), pp. 59, 64. Subsequent references will be included in parentheses in the text.

15 Thomas Cripps, *Making Movies Black: The Hollywood Message Movie from World War II to the Civil Rights Era* (New York: Oxford University Press, 1993), p. 10.

16 David Fine, "Beginning in the Thirties: The Los Angeles Fiction of James M. Cain and Horace McCoy," *Los Angeles in Fiction: A Collection of Original Essays* ed. David Fine (Albuquerque: University of New Mexico Press, 1984), p. 62.

17 All three started out as journalists; Johnson published a short story collection of Southern small-town life, *There Ought to be a Law and Other Stories* (1931).

18 Johnson: *The Road to Glory*; Trotti: *Drums Along the Mohawk* and *Slave Ship*; Buckner: "The DeGaulle Story" (unproduced).

19 Johnson: *The Three Faces of Eve* (adaptation), *Jesse James* (original), and *The Prisoner of Shark Island*; Buckner: *Love Me Tender* (original), *The Santa Fe Trail* (original) and *Jezebel* (uncredited; adaptation); Trotti: *Belle Star* (original screenplay from story), *Slave Ship* (adaptation), *Judge Priest* (adaptation), *Young Mr Lincoln* (original), and *I'd Climb the Highest Mountain* (adaptation).

20 Thomas Cripps, "The Myth of the Southern Box Office: A Factor in Racial Stereotyping in American Movies, 1920–1940," *The Black Experience: Selected Essays* ed. James C. Curtis and Lewis L Gould (Austin: University of Texas Press, 1970), p. 121.

21 Nunnally Johnson, quoted in Tom Stempel, *Screenwriter: The Life and Times of Nunnally Johnson* (San Diego, CA: A. S. Barnes, 1980), p. 55.

22 Matthew Bernstein, "'A 'Professional Southerner' in the Hollywood Studio System: Lamar Trotti at Work, 1925–1952," in *American Cinema and the Southern Imaginary* ed. Deborah Barker and Kathryn McKee (Athens: University of Georgia Press, 2011), pp. 123–124.

23 Quoted in Bernstein, "'Professional Southerner'," p. 129.

24 Bernstein, p. 124.

25 Cripps, "Myth," p. 132.

26 Quoted in Thomas Cripps, "Langston Hughes and the Movies" in *Montage of a Dream: The Life and Art of Langston Hughes* ed. John Edgar Tidwell and Cheryl R. Ragar (Columbia: University of Missouri Press, 2007), p. 309.

27 Cripps, "Langston Hughes," pp. 311–312.

28 Cripps, "Langston Hughes," p. 316.

29 There is also the question of credit. Many screenwriters work on properties for which they remain uncredited.

30 Foote quoted in Gary Edgerton, "A Visit to the Imaginary Landscape of Harrison, Texas: Sketching the Film Career of Horton Foote," *Literature/Film Quarterly* 17.1 (1989), p. 5.

31 Richard Fine, *West of Eden: Writers in Hollywood 1928–1940* (Washington, DC: Smithsonian Institution, 1993), p. 11.

32 To my knowledge, the Coen Brothers did not draw on McCarthy's screenplay to write their own. McCarthy also wrote *Cities of the Plain* (1998) first as a screenplay 1978. His other screenplays are "Of Whales and Men" (unpublished; mid-1980s), and, for PBS, *The Gardener's Son: A Screenplay* (Hopewell: Ecco Press, 1996).

33 Meta Carpenter Wilde and Orin Borsten, *A Loving Gentleman: The Love Story of William Faulkner and Meta Carpenter* (New York: Simon and Schuster, 1976), p. 27.

34 Interview with Jean Stein in *The Paris Review*, 12 (1956).

11

SHARON MONTEITH

Civil Rights Fiction

In the summer of 1963, literary critic Granville Hicks asserted: "All around the fringes of the movement, and on both sides of the barricades, magnificent dramas are taking place."[1] He cited Eudora Welty, Bernard Malamud, and Ralph Ellison in his review of Junius Edwards's *If We Must Die* (1963). If Hicks missed something as he read, it was that in perceiving African American Edwards to be exceptional, or at least unusual, in writing about the civil rights movement of the 1950s and 1960s, he turned automatically to critically acclaimed writers in seeking out stories. Ellison, who suffered criticism for a lack of overt engagement with the movement, felt similarly – "I think that revolutionary social political movements move much too rapidly to be treated as the subjects for literature in themselves" – and when pushed in an interview to examine that idea, he stated his belief that if it were possible to find the "imaginative equivalents" of Rosa Parks and James Meredith, it would not be in fiction by black writers but in Faulkner.[2]

Faulkner did create archetypal characters to portray the region's racial complexities, like Lucas Beauchamp who with pride and courage faces down those whites who would keep him in his place, and Clarence Snopes whose rise as a politician and a Klansman is an early dramatization of what journalist Robert Sherrill would describe in 1968 as the "gothic politics" of the Deep South. In 1963, Eudora Welty had gone further than most in her story "Where Is the Voice Coming From?" where the dramatic action is the assassination of the NAACP leader Medgar Evers and she explores the psychology of his murderer as hardened by hate and fear. Welty made vivid a reactionary individual supported by anti-movement forces (as Byron De La Beckwith's first two trials for Evers's murder would make manifest), creating a disturbingly deadpan portrayal of a very matter-of-fact sniper: "I seen what little time it takes after all to get a thing done like you really want it," he confides, and his wife's sole concern is whether he has been bitten by insects while waiting to commit murder.[3] In 1964, poet Robert Lowell's "For the Union Dead" would expose how the legacy of the Civil

War haunted massive resistance struggles in the 1960s, but most white writers, Shelby Foote and Joan Williams among them, would turn to civil rights only much later.

However, Hicks and Ellison both miss the shift – signaled by books like *If We Must Die* – toward representing movement goals, the courage of those who pursued them in the civil rights–era South, massive resistance to those initiatives, and racial terrorism. Louisiana-born Edwards's novel is a disturbing tale of the escalating civil rights movement. A black veteran of the Korean War returns home to a small southern town and attempts to register to vote. It is an early example of fiction in which voter registration, the cornerstone of movement strategy to enfranchise black Southerners, is the fulcrum of the action, and, when read today, a reminder of the continuing need to defend voting rights against legislative efforts to redistrict black voters in order to sap their political strength. Nevertheless, the novel received scant critical attention in the 1960s and continues to be neglected despite republication in 1985. Civil rights fiction can be a tough and dispiriting read when, as in this case, the outcome is violent and tragic. It can also be controversial when black characters struggle with whether they could kill for the cause in novels by Alice Walker and Julius Lester, or when writers imagine the private lives of public figures, notably Dr. Martin Luther King in John A. Williams's *The Man Who Cried I Am* (1967) and Lester's *And All Our Wounds Forgiven* (1994).

In *If We Must Die*, Will Harris watches a refugee from a communist country register to vote while he is denied the same privilege. When interviewed by the local press, the newcomer's words ring true but feel like a taunt to Will who suffers spurious disqualification by the same registrar: "Just like you all. I'm American … America means freedom. Today I came down here to do the biggest thing that any American can do, register to vote."[4] Fired from his factory job, Will's reputation as a troublemaker for having tried to register leads to his being dismissed from each job he secures. In this sense he is a precursor to the veteran protagonist of *Nothing But A Man* (1964), the small-budget independent film that Malcolm X acclaimed as the most important film made about the black experience in the United States, whose veteran protagonist also feels like "just half a man" on coming home to the South.

Will spirals inexorably toward a fate worse than death. A white mob ambushes him and debates the many ways of killing black men like him, who step out of their place. One man states that he would "rather just hang them," whereas an illiterate poor white who fails to understand Will's "crime" because he does not understand what voting is confides that he would like to choke them. He is dispatched to perform the "honor" of castration that will be his induction into racial terrorism, and the horror of the novel's denouement derives from a farcical situation, described with chilling simplicity, when he is unable to undertake the task but cuts and bludgeons Will in the attempt. Although Robert Penn Warren felt able to observe in 1956 that poor whites were "only the cutting edge of violence" in the segregationists' arsenal,[5] here that edge is shown to be hideously sharp. Finally left to die from wounds sustained to his wrists, Will's "rescue" by an old black man is saturated with cruel irony; he believes he is telling his rescuer not to remove the makeshift tourniquet that holds in his life's blood, but in reality he has been rendered silent by shock or a stroke. Having loosened Will's bonds for comfort, as he thinks, the old man lifts him into the back of his wagon, and the reader leaves Will there bleeding to death. Edwards's novel encapsulates the courage, frustration, rage, fear, and tragic irony that animate much writing about civil rights – fiction that Granville Hicks underread and emotions that were overlooked by James McBride Dabbs, the only critic in the period to publish a study of novels that incorporate civil rights as a theme.

This essay explores the ways in which literature that focuses on the movement – stories about civil rights organizations, voter registration and demonstrations, and activists in the African-American freedom struggle – differs from fiction that locates "civil rights" within the broad theme of race relations, as was usually the case with the writers that Hicks revered. It differs again when the civil rights era is revisited, because novelists who write beyond the historical "ending" of the movement enter a more imaginative discursive terrain and undermine the dominant representation of the movement as being truly over by the end of the 1960s.[6] It has become a critical commonplace to state that fictional responses to the movement were deferred, with critics citing Alice Walker's *Meridian* (1976) and Rosellen Brown's *Civil Wars* (1984) as the first works to explore activist characters.[7] But, in fact, much fiction and poetry was published in the era and written by those who served on the movement's front line, including members of the Student Nonviolent Coordinating Committee (SNCC), journalists on the civil rights beat, and writers – black and white, young and old – for whom the drama of the movement was too important not to try to capture its political force and social momentum in imaginative writing.

However, by the 1960s, another assumption had come close to critical consensus: that when black writers portrayed race relations, it was in the form of "protest" fictions or "problem" novels, and that "moral" fictions about the civil rights–era South were written by whites coming to consciousness of the movement's destabilizing of the racial status quo. In *Civil Rights in Recent Southern Fiction* (1969), Dabbs surveyed renowned and new writers but conflated attention to "civil rights" with what he discerned as a "tendency to see the Negro with new eyes," with writers helping to "create the new image of the Negro as a human being." Aside from a nod to Wright and Ellison, Dabbs focused only on white writers and so missed Junius Edwards, but also James Baldwin, John O. Killens, John A. Williams, Gwendolyn Brooks, Alice Walker, Ernest Gaines, and, indeed, any and all black writers of the period for whom civil rights was more than a "problem" or a theme. Dabbs never discusses the reason for his lack of attention to black writers, although he may be reworking an observation he made in 1964 that the white Southern fantasy of the black Southerner had been "not the Negro of today but that mythical figure that arose out of the turmoil of Reconstruction and Redemption. The Negro still appears before the white as in a frozen moment of the South's history."[8] In attributing this shift in consciousness specifically to white writers, he assumes a position that was still very much the case in the 1960s: that a Southern writer would be white and that the story of a changing South would be told by them. Dabbs deemed a writer's attachment to movement tenets misleading: "It would lift the race problem out of the total tissue of Southern life and by so doing would give to it an importance that it does not deserve." In this sense, his study was typical of cultural work undertaken to contain race relations within a larger, more positively curated image of the region, as epitomized by Louis Rubin's declaration in 1961 that "important though the race problem may be, most people, even in the South, do not spend every waking moment thinking of it."[9] Dabbs criticizes novels such as Jesse Hill Ford's *The Liberation of Lord Byron Jones* (1965) for drawing "too dark a picture of the South."[10] Despite the promise of its title, Dabbs's study undermines its own premise because, in disaggregating civil rights from the movement and in seeking balance between what he saw as the "cruel" and the "gentle" Souths, his survey suffers a racial imbalance and, consequently, a lack of intertextual weave between authors exploring the region from both sides of the barricades, to borrow Hicks's revealing metaphor. The result is a study of civil rights that tempers and tames the ways that a changing racial landscape was explored in the region's fiction.

In fact, balance was anathema for many Southern writers in the *sturm and drang* of the political moment, especially for those who saw the era as a Second Reconstruction, with segregationists returning to the antebellum past and the myth of heroic Klansmen to underline the "Again" in "Never Again." Undertaking a historical survey of the Klan in 1963, novelist Ben Haas stated ominously, "Ninety seven years after its birth ... the Ku Klux Klan ... not only exists, but is fattening on the hatreds generated by the current battle for integration."[11] The Klan revival to battle the movement was so central to Haas's depiction of civil rights struggles that the narrative pace of his novel *The Troubled Summer* (1966) is slowed by a contextual history of the Reconstruction Klan provided by the director of a civil rights organization visiting a southern town. "If a civil rights movement does get started here," he warns, "it'll have the Ku Klux Klan to deal with." Two black boys who spy on a Klan meeting are awed: "There was something absurd about them, but something evil and dangerous too; they could have been ghosts or demons who had crawled from some dark underworld to enact weird and profane rites."[12] It is axiomatic to describe the civil rights era as both an unfinished Civil War and a Second Reconstruction, so it is not surprising that fiction should tell two stories at once – the first of the bellicose battles of the movement, with allusions to civil rights workers as "scalawags" and "carpetbaggers" in the era's fiction, the second a postmortem for integrationist hopes epitomized in the Reconstruction era. While *The Troubled Summer* focuses on a moment, in *Look Away, Look Away* (1964), Haas creates an epic that spans the 1930s through the 1960s and traces a political dynasty battling against the fact that black Southerners could alter the sociopolitical structure of the region, an idea that had so frightened their forefathers during Reconstruction and that underpinned the movement's goals in Haas's moment of writing.

Thomas Haddox is one of the few critics to formulate how the "white civil rights novel" understands civil rights as a theme; explicating his thesis via Elizabeth's Spencer's *The Voice at the Back Door* (1956), he asserts that such fictions are "set in small southern towns and their environs, all foreground the mores and politics of race relations, and all present these relations not as a metaphysical given (as earlier Southern novels did) but as a problem that requires attention."[13] He records similarities between the themes of this "genre" and the racial conversion narratives that Fred Hobson identified in his study *But Now I See* (1999). However, when Spencer returned to Mississippi from Italy in 1955, she found the racial attitudes she depicted from memory had hardened and sharpened; the white sheriff's hopes to promote a better life for Southern blacks as imagined in the novel were being thwarted by anti-movement forces in her home state.[14] Haddox also considers what may be "postsouthern" about Walker Percy's *The Last Gentleman* (1966) but fails to note that when Will Barrett, a twenty-five-year-old born in the Mississippi Delta suffering from nervous amnesia in New York City, describes himself as dislocated from "the Philadelphia thing," Percy is signaling his relation to the Freedom Summer campaign of 1964, and that when Will meets a "pop-eyed playwright" on his journey back to the South, Percy invokes an ironic echo of James Baldwin whose overarching thesis was that the civil rights "problem" was an illness afflicting whites, which "must be checked, even though it cannot be cured."[15] Haddox successfully teases out how liberal gradualists conceived of civil rights as a theme, but he risks seeing the fictions written by those same "liberal" whites as having no narrative dialogue with the work of African Americans in the era.

Excavating civil rights fiction reveals that many assumptions result from failing to acknowledge the breadth of the genre. When Akinyele O.Umoja argues that "literary and media recreations of the Movement rarely emphasize the significance of armed resistance,"[16] despite nonviolent tactics being underpinned by self-defense and debates over the inevitability of violence, he misses the ways in which this debate textures fictions by African-American writers. Black avengers punish anti-movement forces over and over again: from the black Night Riders in William Demby's *Beetlecreek* (1958); through John O. Killens's *'Sippi* (1967), in which the Elders react with vengeful violence against the white community when a civil rights activist is murdered; to Toni Morrison's *Song of Solomon* (1977), in which a group that calls itself The Seven Days is motivated by the murders of children in Birmingham in 1963 to take revenge every time a black person is killed by a white. In Gwendolyn Brooks's poetry collection, *In the Mecca* (1969), Way-Out Morgan collects guns and his mantra is "Death-to-the-Hordes-of-the-white-men!" because his sister was "mob-raped" in Mississippi. In *Bourbon at the Border* (1997), Pearl Cleage returns to the same debates about nonviolence when she creates a disturbing drama of a mental breakdown precipitated by a false calm and buried anger. Civil rights worker Charlie is jailed and tortured during Freedom Summer and May who will become his wife is raped by three white officers of the law while he is forced to watch. Thirty years later he kills three white men in Detroit; their only possible or imagined relation to the racist violence he and May suffered in 1964 is their whiteness, and he confesses: "I picked out three, just like those three in Mississippi picked us out, and I did what a man is supposed to do."[17]

Charlie is an idealist turned nihilist who advances through a compulsive logic to seemingly logical murder. Cleage's play *Bourbon at the Border* and Lester's novel *And All Our Wounds Forgiven* both explore individuals traumatized by what happened to them as they struggled for the African-American franchise. As Cathy Caruth has argued, the enigma of trauma is that "it is both destruction and a survival."[18] Even though he is tortured and terrorized, Lester's civil rights worker, Robert Card tries but fails to take violent revenge. Instead, he spends thirty years learning how to survive, having lost his youth to the movement, mourning others who lost their lives fighting for change. He learns to endure, in the same way that Lester – a student at Fisk when the sit-ins began in 1960, photographer for SNCC, folk singer, and activist – described in autobiographical terms in the 1990s: "To live where the presence of death was as palpable as the smell of honeysuckle lacerated the soul in ways one dared not stop to know until a decade or two had passed."[19]

Depictions of retaliatory violence provoked controversy, especially in the 1960s. James Baldwin's *Blues for Mister Charlie* (1964) is dedicated to the memory of Medgar Evers and the African-American children murdered in Birmingham in 1963. It focuses on the trial of a white man who murders the black pastor's son when the latter returns from New York to fight for civil rights in his hometown. Whereas the *New York Times*' reviewer described it as "a play with fires of fury in its belly, tears of anguish in its eyes and a roar of protest in its throat," that "brings eloquence and conviction to one of the momentous themes of our era," theater critic Robert Brustein asserted Baldwin's play was "the embodiment of everything he once professed to deplore, being 'notoriously bloodthirsty' propaganda of the crudest sort, with little existence either as truth, literature or life … it is a play of thumbs – fashioned, I would guess, to gouge the eyes of the audience."[20] Equating anger only with protest rather than also with soul-searching "tears of anguish," the effect of this flawed but explosive play is lost on Brustein.

That not only depictions of armed resistance but also startlingly violent responses to segregationist logic find place in a chameleonic range of fictions is testament to the force of African-American feeling that Dabbs chose not to consider. Narrative excess could convey an apocalyptic sense of a racialized society coming apart, and pointed satire could depict a society in free-fall. White supremacy was shaken by civil rights initiatives, subverted and ridiculed by political performance in the form of sit-ins and by the exposure of supposedly secret societies such as the Klan and the Mississippi State Sovereignty Commission. There is no reason to assume that racial segregation would not also be exposed as warped in literature. Ossie Davis, African-American actor-writer of the Broadway play *Purlie Victorious* (1961), filmed in 1963, avowed: "I can imagine no other institution on the face of the earth more ridiculous than the institution of segregation."[21] He used folk humor, slapstick, and farce to unpick a system that was cruel and violent but also, and finally, shown to be ludicrous. Davis comments obliquely on the movement with characters "getting all non-violent" and taking their cues from Dr. Martin Luther King; his play was a rare example of a civil rights–themed comedy although white supremacists are lampooned by Faulkner and in the 1960s Donald Harington and Michael Thelwell would publish comic stories that revealed serious flaws in the Southern system.

Melodrama infused civil rights fictions of the era. Ann Fairbairns's *Five Smooth Stones* (1966) is a 900-page soap opera in which the death of his grandfather in New Orleans is the turning point for David Champlin returning from New York to work for civil rights and embarking on a love affair with a white woman. Although consistently popular with readers, melo-drama is the scourge of critics, with a *Washington Post* review dismissing Fairbairns's best-selling formula as "grab a liberal cause, say civil rights in the Deep South, precisely as you would an acoustical guitar; strum it for all you're worth on the strings marked sentiment, martyrdom and moral outrage; keep two fingers firmly pressed on the frets of dialect and cliché."[22] Civil rights stories were not limited by genre, but when they were told in genre fictions and other popular forms they risked such negative reviews.

Much more successfully in the 1960s, the baroque plots of civil rights thrillers sometimes began as scoops with journalists transforming news into fiction. Jay Milner in *Incident at Ashton* (1961) and Elliott Chaze in *Tiger in the Honeysuckle* (1965) turned what they witnessed in Mississippi into novels set in small towns with local newspapermen, civil rights organizers, and summer volunteers playing key roles. News features and photojournal-ism influenced fiction then and later. In *Music of the Swamp* (1991), for example, Lewis Nordan's character Sugar Mecklin discovers a dead body caught in "a drift of brush" while fishing. The body is that of an elderly white man rather than the young black boy Emmett Till, but the image per-sisted for Nordan, who grew up close to where Till was murdered in 1955, until in *Wolf Whistle* (1993), in reimagining Till's murder, he realized that the phrase "drift of brush" that had haunted him was from a news article he read when Till's body was found in the Tallahatchie River by the white boy whose fishing trip triggered the trial. The tragedy of fourteen-year-old Till's murder by white supremacists was a spur for activists joining the movement and remains emotive decades later, as Nordan's novel and other fictions explored in *Emmett Till in Literary Memory and Imagination* (2008) make clear. The symbolic center of Elizabeth Nunez's *Beyond the Limbo Silence* (1998) is another murder: the notorious abduction of civil rights workers Michael Schwerner, James Chaney, and Andrew Goodman by a posse of Klansmen on a deserted Mississippi back road in the dark of night in 1964. In a narrative of magical hyperreality, Africanist conjuring locates the bodies of the young men, but Nunez's description of a dam in which their bodies were hidden closely follows journalist Claude Sitton's report in which he detailed how "the dam had collected no water despite heavy showers."[23] In the novel, the mantra "*rain will make rivers but no water*" is a mystical clue to recovering the young men who gave their lives for the civil rights cause.

Nunez's novel is a fascinating if flawed creative intervention into civil rights. Spinning off into the surreal is unusual and risky when sensitivity and fidelity to the experiences of civil rights workers are a structuring principle in many fictions, especially by those who labored in the movement. In turn, civil rights workers celebrated and memorialized the courage of Southern blacks. SNCC's Michael Thelwell exposes the effects of fear, tragedy, sheer commitment, and hard work on the body and mind of a civil rights worker in the short story "The Organizer" (1966), which is the most detailed and evocative fictional distillation of this role.[24] His protagonist Travis Peacock is representative of the cadre of black field secretaries who embedded themselves in rural communities to facilitate voter registration, and Peacock is devastated by the murder of a courageous local leader – killed when his house is firebombed – whom he admires and loves like a father. Thelwell tells what Julius Lester described as the "real stories" of the movement, with Lester's 1964 journal recording similar tales of bravery by black Southerners who lost their jobs for trying to register, or for taking civil rights workers into their homes, leading Lester to speculate then that "courage is the norm in Mississippi."[25] In her essay "Silver Writes" (1982), Alice Walker polishes a poetic image of the Southern freedom struggle: "Although I value the Civil Rights Movement *deeply*, I have never liked the term itself. It has no music, it has no poetry. It makes one think of bureaucrats rather than of sweaty faces, eyes bright and big for *Freedom!*, marching feet.... Older black country people did their best to instill what accurate poetry they could into this essentially white civil servants' term ... so that what one *heard* was '*Silver*.'"[26]

Walker's novel *Meridian* also celebrates black Southern culture and explores the loss of self to the movement in political and philosophical terms. Such stories have something of an autobiographical specificity, with Thelwell a field secretary (1963–1964), director of the Mississippi Freedom Democratic Party from 1964 to 1965, and a SNCC strategist, and Walker working for voter registration in Liberty County, Georgia, and later for the Head Start school program in Jackson, Mississippi. Civil rights fictions written in the aftermath of the movement signal a painful adjustment to the times. *Meridian* also makes a case for the role of the movement poet, "singing from memory songs" that former activists "will need once more to hear."[27] Teddy Carll in Rosellen Brown's *Civil Wars* with his livid facial scar a continual reminder of the toll of his activism, is an example of a character clinging grimly to memories of the movement having found nothing to replace its meaning in his life, his marriage to a civil rights volunteer collapsing amid declensionist feelings in the 1970s. Brown returns to the movement again, and her own experience as a teacher at Tougaloo College in Mississippi, in *Half A Heart* (2000), where she explores an interracial relationship forged between two teachers in the civil rights era and traces its breakdown in the life of their child. In each novel a private relationship disintegrates with the loss of movement idealism or in the struggle to find oneself in its aftermath.

While Alice Walker wrote about her experience tangentially in *Meridian*, she commented obliquely and symbolically on the freedom struggle in the fable "The First Day: After Brown" (1974), only adding the subtitle in a late draft to make the context achingly clear for readers. Over barely three pages she explores the extended metaphor of the magnolia jungle that conflates the psychic (a black child Stanley's traumatic experience of running the gauntlet of snarling segregationists standing at his schoolhouse door) with the social (the Supreme Court's *Brown vs. Board* decision as it affected the children who tested it). The NAACP had described "the state of jungle fury" in Mississippi around Emmett Till's murder when his death and the murders of others, including Lamar Smith and Rev. George E. Lee, led the NAACP to ask the federal government to intercede in the state.[28] Fables operate according to metaphor and metonymy to make a political point a moral lesson, and Walker's metaphor of the jungle lends this tale menace. In black folklore, animals are configured as creatures whose meaning carries the weight of the tale in etiological stories. In this civil rights fable, Stanley plunges into a jungle of lionesses and hyenas (crazed white mothers snarling and scratching him) and thinks desperately of his multiplication tables as he negotiates the cordon of police (depicted as fat blue vultures) before finally and safely entering the school.

The foundations on which a civil rights fable rests are usually concrete but the meaning it projects can be elliptical. In an aside that she never pursues in her study of Southern allegory, Jan Whitt muses on the fact that "[n]either Christ nor his characteristics are embodied in a Gandhi or a Martin Luther King in Southern literature; rejecting a historical parallel or typology (which is strange enough considering the South's penchant for history) …"[29] Such examples remain hidden from a critic who focuses only on well-known writers. Henry Dumas was born in Arkansas and moved to Harlem aged ten but returned to the rural South as the setting of fables such as "Fon" (1968) whose moral legibility is as clear as the long legacy of slavery that underpins the story, even though the event depicted is murky and magical. Todorov argues in his study of "the fantastic" that the intervention of a supernatural element in a text "always constitutes a break in the system of pre-established rules."[30] On a lonely Mississippi road in the South that Flannery O'Connor called "Christ-haunted," a young boy called Alfonso (Fon) assumed to fit the stereotype of "uppity" is taunting a "cracker" called Nillmon (no kind of man) who then returns to the road with a lynching party to kill the boy. But the ritual is broken when black rocks like fists rain from the sky and just as Fon is about to be lynched his "brothers" rain down arrows that kill the white men. Fon walks away toward a black church, having stamped out the torches the men would have used to burn it, thinking of *"four centuries of black eyes burning into four weak men.*" In my reading Dumas fuses the boy with legends of the Fon, the peoples of Dahomey whose African belief system included reincarnation and vodoun, Old Testament vengeance, and Black Power forces about to "set the whole earth on fire."[31]

"Fon" echoes an idea that Carson McCullers posited, namely that in a disorganized society, "individual Gods or principles are likely to be chimerical and fantastic."[32] She too would turn to civil rights in her final novel, *The Clock Without Hands* (1961). Reading the novel for poet Muriel Rukseyer's course on contemporary Southern writers at Sarah Lawrence, student Alice Walker raised a question: "How does one explain the seeming paradox of a man like the Judge in *Clock Without Hands*?" McCullers's Judge is sickened by the idea of racial integration and upholds white supremacy at every turn, but, as Walker notes, the white judge treats black Sherman "as if he were his own son allowing him liberty after liberty" but then orders the bombing of Sherman's home.[33] These are the apparent paradoxes with which white writers grapple most revealingly. A troubled conscience is the determining factor of novels by Erskine Caldwell, Hodding Carter, Lillian Smith, and Elizabeth Spencer, among many others. Walker Percy once observed that the white South had formed "one big kinship lodge," wherein the state's rights were those of the white Mississippi family. When James Meredith enrolled at the University of Mississippi, he argued, "It was as if he had been quartered in [the students'] living room."[34] The white family is the lynchpin to which black (nationalist) and white (Republican) conservatives return in criticism of affirmative action programs that were a consequence of efforts made in the 1960s to ensure the inclusion of racial and ethnic minorities in university admissions. The perception that a black student stole the place of a white family member is the underlying factor in white resentment, and the white family under segregation is explored in novels by white Southern writers with real insight.

Typically writers scrutinize the white moderate whose "moderation" is held back to gradualism by the fear of change. In Madison Jones's quiet novel *A Cry of Absence* (1971), a mother who knows her son to be guilty of a racist murder slowly pushes them both toward suicide. Jones captures a world being extinguished for Hester Glynn, symbolized by her home and by the curtain at the window that "partially obscured her view of the world around her"; she retreats into the past as a defense against a changing present: "In such a world, what could a person do except cleanse his house and shut his door against the stink of dissolution." Hester's efforts to remain untouched fail in a town where racial anger seethes. Mother of two sons whom she both relies on too heavily and treats with distant or dismissive grace, Hester is the novel's controlling figure, but she fails to control Cam's violent attempt to stop the world from turning in a small town by murdering another boy he sees as a representative of the forces that would change it. Such narratives reveal much about fear as instrumental in the ideological complex that was massive resistance; as one character summarizes, "I have no doubt your boy when he murdered that Negro, had some kind of idea that he was upholding society, carrying out its will."[35]

Hester is a quieter version of the mother in Flannery O'Connor's "Everything That Rises Must Converge" (1965) who reminds her son: "Your great-grandfather was a former governor of this state.... Your grandfather was a prosperous landowner. Your grandmother was a Godhigh." Hester's nostalgia for her slave-owning grandfather also recalls Mrs. Turpin in O'Connor's "Revelation," who enumerates the class distinctions she believes set her apart:

> On the bottom of the heap were most colored people, not the kind she would have been if she'd been one, but most of them; then next to them – not above, just away from – were the white-trash; then above them were the home-owners, and above them the home-and-land owners, to which she and Calud belonged. Above she and Calud were people with a lot of money and much bigger houses and much more land. But here the complexity would begin to bear in on her, for some of the people with a lot of money were common and ought to be below she and Calud and some of the people with good blood had lost their money and had to rent and then there were colored people who owned their homes and land as well.[36]

Mrs. Turpin's nonsensical litany is made more so because of the perfect irony of her husband's name, but where O'Connor is comedic in her treatment of a lady whose thoughts condemn her as clearly as the homonym Calud and colored, Jones's tragic fiction teaches that even someone as demure as Hester is coarsened by living in a racially segregated society and carries its guilt.

Coming to consciousness of the civil rights movement is a trope in much fiction written in its aftermath by black and white writers. In Marita Golden's *And Do Remember Me* (1992), black Jessie Foster comes of age in the Mississippi Delta against the emotionally murky and politically dangerous moment of the Freedom Summer demonstrations in 1964; Anthony Grooms's *Bombingham* (2001) depicts characters who originate in an unruly and violent moment in civil rights history in Birmingham in 1963; the shooting of Walter's friend Lamar mirrors the murder of Virgil Ware on the same Sunday that four little girls were killed in a churchbombing, with the African-American owned *Birmingham World* describing the seventh-grader as "a very quiet and Christian little boy" shot by two sixteen-year-old Eagle Scouts as he rode his bicycle across town.[37] Grooms reclaims the child from the shadows of civil rights history and Sena Jeter Naslund dedicates her epic novel *Four Spirits* (2003) to Addie Mae Colins, Denise McNair, Carole Robertson, and Cynthia Wesley, the girls killed in the bombing of Sixteenth Street Baptist Church on that same Sunday of September 15, 1963.

The children of those young people who fought in the civil rights revolution are beginning to tell their stories in memoirs, including Rebecca Walker's *Black White and Jewish: Autobiography of a Shifting Self* (2001) and John Blake's collection *Children of the Movement* (2004), and are portrayed in fiction such as Rosellen Brown's *Half A Heart* and Danzy Senna's *Caucasia* (1998). The movement has provoked a surplus of meanings still being explored, and writers have begun to complicate its legacy in quite daring fictions. The protagonist of Adam Mansbach's *Angry Black White Boy: The Miscegenation of Macon DeTournay* (2005), was conceived in Macon, Georgia and is studying in New York in 1998. Mansbach imagines Macon's grandfather as Cap Anson, the major league ballplayer whose white supremacist views were renowned, and imagines a white mob setting out to kill Fleet Walker, the first African American to play in the Major Leagues, in his final game before Anson led the decision to segregate the league in 1889. In the story whereas Walker escapes, another player dies in his stead. Macon feels an emotional continuity with the civil rights era that is based on a keen sense of familial guilt but which also acts as a prosthetic memory and a form of commodity fetishism. In *Angry Black White Boy*, civil rights activism becomes high theater in the media age when Macon writes a "Letter from a Birmingham Bus," and organizes a "Black Like Me'" rally and franchise on MTV. The tragedy of this clever and surprising novel is that Macon is murdered by "crackers" for being an "outside agitator"; he is killed on a deserted southern country road, that loaded image epitomized on the cover of SNCC's photography collection, *The Movement* (1964), recalled in memoirs by organizers who drove those roads at breakneck speed to evade attacks – and the place where God shows himself to man in Dumas's "Fon." Fictions like Mansbach's indicate how flexible – and even satirical – the "civil rights story" can be. They are also a tacit reminder that, as Lillian Smith presciently declared, after "the flood of protests, the powerful words spoken or written by a few poets and novelists, the decisions of the courts .... There are images that can never be forgotten, sounds that echo through a lifetime: bind these with the searching truth of a few who have written and spoken and acted – and the past becomes a catalyst which the future cannot escape the effect of."[38] Civil rights stories are as heterogeneous as their authors; they cross periods and genres and historical momentum and their continuing relevance carries them into the twenty-first century.

NOTES

1 Granville Hicks, *Saturday Review*, August 3, 1963.
2 Ralph Ellison, *Going to the Territory* (New York: Vintage, 1986), pp. 295, 302.
3 Eudora Welty, "Where Is the Voice Coming From?," *The Collected Stories* (London: Penguin, 1989), pp. 603–607.
4 Junius Edwards, *If We Must Die* (New York: Doubleday, 1963), pp. 11–12.
5 Robert Penn Warren, *Segregation: The Inner Conflict in the South* (Athens: University of Georgia Press, 1994), p. 64.
6 Sharon Monteith, "The Sixties and Its Cultural Legacy," *American Culture in the 1960s* (Edinburgh: Edinburgh University Press, 2008), p. 187.
7 Richard H. King, "The Discipline of Fact/ The Freedom of Fiction?" *Journal of American Studies* 25 (1991), pp. 171–188; Christopher Metress, "Making Civil Rights Harder: Literature, Memory, and the Black Freedom Struggle," *The Southern Literary Journal*, 40:2 (Spring 2008), pp. 138–150.
8 James McBride Dabbs, *Who Speaks for the South?* (New York: Funk and Wagnalls, 1964), p. 331.
9 Louis D. Rubin, *South: Modern Southern Literature in Its Cultural Setting*, eds. Rubin and Robert D. Jacobs (New York: Doubleday, 1961), p. 383.
10 James McBride Dabbs, *Civil Rights in Recent Southern Fiction* (Atlanta: Southern Regional Council, 1969), pp. iv, 127, 108.
11 Ben Haas, *KKK* (New York: Tower, 1963), p. 5.
12 Ben Haas, *The Troubled Summer* (New York: Grosset and Dunlap, 1966), pp. 49, 98.
13 Thomas F. Haddox, "Elizabeth Spencer, the White Civil Rights Novel, and the Postsouthern," *Modern Language Quarterly*, 65:4 (2004), p. 561.
14 Editors' Preface, *The Voice at the Back Door* (New York: Time Inc., 1965), p. xii.
15 James Baldwin, "Many Thousands Gone," *Notes of a Native Son* (Boston: Beacon, 1984), p. 25.
16 Akinyele O Umoja, "1964: The Beginning of the End of Nonviolence in the Mississippi Freedom Movement," *Radical History Review*, 85 (2003), p. 201.
17 Pearl Cleage, *Bourbon at the Border* (New York: Dramatists Play Service, 2005), p. 61.
18 Cathy Caruth, *Unclaimed Experience: Trauma, Narrative, and History* (Baltimore: Johns Hopkins University Press, 1996), pp. 68–72.
19 Julius Lester, "Black and White – Together" in *Falling Pieces of a Broken Sky* (New York: Little, Brown and Company, 1990), p. 125.
20 Howard Taubman, "Theater: Blues for Mister Charlie," *New York Times*, April 24, 1964, p. 24; Robert Brustein, "Everybody's Protest Play," in *Seasons of Discontent: Dramatic Opinions, 1959–1965* (London: Jonathan Cape, 1966), p. 162. Brustein is quoting, of course, from Baldwin's own essay, "Everybody's Protest Novel" (1949).
21 Ossie Davis, "The Wonderful World of Law and Order," *Anger and Beyond: The Negro Writer in the United States*, ed. Herbert Hill (New York: Harper and Row, 1966), p. 156.
22 Robert F. Jones, "The Latest in Civil Rights Soap Operas," *The Washington Post*, December 29, 1970, p. C4.

23 Claude Sitton, "Graves at a Dam: Discovery Is Made in New Earth Mound in Mississippi," *New York Times*, August 5, 1964, p. 1.

24 Monteith, "SNCC's Stories at the Barricades," *From Sit-Ins to SNCC: Student Civil Rights Protest in the 1960s*, eds. Philip Davies and Iwan Morgan (Gainesville: University of Florida Press, 2012), pp. 97–115.

25 Julius Lester's journal, July 11, 1964, Biloxi, Mississippi, *All Is Well* (New York: William Morrow, 1976), p. 112.

26 Alice Walker, "Silver Writes," *In Search of Our Mothers' Gardens: Womanist Prose* (London: The Women's Press, 1984), p. 336.

27 Alice Walker, *Meridian* (London: The Women's Press, 1985), p. 205.

28 The *Memphis Commercial Appeal*, September 8, 1955.

29 Jan Whitt, *Allegory and the Modern Southern Novel* (Macon, GA: Mercer University Press, 1994), p. 66.

30 Tzvetan Todorov, *The Fantastic: A Structural Approach to a Literary Genre*, trans. Richard Howard (Cleveland, OH: Case Western Reserve, 1973), p. 166.

31 Henry Dumas, "Fon," *Black Fire: An Anthology of Afro-American Writing*, ed. Amiri Baraka and Larry Neal (New York: Morrow, 1968), p. 465.

32 Carson McCullers, "Author's outline for 'The Mute' (*The Heart Is a Lonely Hunter*)" published in 1966, *The Mortgaged Heart*, ed. Margarita G. Smith (New York: Mariner, 2005), p. 124.

33 Alice Walker, "Compilation of Questions," p. 8, Box 72, Folder 30, Alice Walker Papers, MARBL, Emory, Atlanta. With thanks to Alice Walker and to Emory University.

34 Walker Percy, "Mississippi: The Fallen Paradise," *Harper's Magazine*, April 1965.

35 Madison Jones, *A Cry of Absence* (London: André Deutsch, 1971).

36 *The Complete Stories of Flannery O'Connor* (London: Faber, 1990), pp. 407, 195–196.

37 "Funeral for Virgil Ware, Allegedly Killed by White Youth, Set for Sunday, Sept. 22," *Birmingham World*, September 21, 1963, p. 1.

38 Lillian Smith, *Our Faces, Our Words* (New York: W. W. Norton, 1964), p. 110.

12

GARY RICHARDS

Southern Drama

With the exceptions of the justly celebrated works of Tennessee Williams and the selective output of a small handful of other playwrights, the U.S. South has rarely been scripted as central to the nation's history of writing, producing, and attending drama. And yet, when playwright and stage manager William Dunlap opened his monumental *A History of the American Theatre from Its Origins to 1832* (2005), he immediately reminded readers that some of the earliest professional English-language dramatic productions took place in the southern British colonies of North America and soon found widespread favor in that region. Facing the uncertainties of London's theatrical markets, William Hallam organized the London Company of Comedians, directed by his brother Lewis Hallam, and sent them to Virginia, working, Dunlap speculates, "from the knowledge that Episcopalians were then more liberal in regard to the drama than most other sects."[1] With a repertory consisting primarily of Shakespeare and Restoration standards supplemented with farces, the company landed at Yorktown, progressed to Williamsburg, the colonial capital, and offered the "first play performed in American by a regular company of comedians,"[2] *The Merchant of Venice*, with the popular farce *Lethe* as an afterpiece.

Although still highlighting the southern colonies, twentieth- and twenty-first-century theater historians have augmented Dunlap's history, as when Jeffrey Richards notes in *Early American Drama* (1997) that the "first play known to have been performed in English-speaking America was *The Bear and the Cub* (or as it was written down in the court records, *Ye Bare and Ye Cubb*), acted in a tavern in Pungoteague, on the Eastern Shore of Virginia, in 1665."[3] Moreover, by the late 1740s, "professional actors from England via Jamaica – Walter Murray and Thomas Kean's Company of Comedians from Virginia – began to play in American cities."[4] Nevertheless, most historians agree that early companies like Murray and Kean's and Hallam's (reconfigured after his 1756 death by his widow and her second husband, David Douglass, as the famous long-lived American Company) became fixtures in the late-eighteenth-century South. However, as theater historian Larry Stempel adds, "They led precarious existences. With no cities in the colonies able to support them for a full season, they toured in varying orbits from Halifax, Nova Scotia, to the Leeward Islands in the Caribbean."[5]

By the Revolutionary War, permanent theaters to host and, in growing instances, to house these companies appeared not only in New York, Newport, and Philadelphia but also in Annapolis, Baltimore, Charleston, and Richmond. As Charles S. Watson has chronicled, Charleston, with its Dock Street Theatre, was a major eighteenth-century theatrical center that rivaled Philadelphia and New York. At the same time, Richmond became "the rising sun of Virginia, and our histrionics appear to shun the sinking towns as naturally as rats fly floundering ships."[6] And yet, in the period that saw theaters rebound from wartime bans and other disruptions, Richmond uniquely faced dual theatrical tragedies. On December 8, 1811, the city withstood the death of adored actress Eliza (Arnold) Hopkins Poe, whose fame would eventually be eclipsed by her son Edgar's. Then, on December 26, holiday playgoers, still mourning Poe's death, found themselves within the inferno that the Richmond Theatre became when curtains caught fire and the building was "enveloped in hot scorching smoke and flame."[7] Seventy-two persons died, including Virginia's sitting governor, and the event was one of the most horrific urban disasters in the early United States.

And yet, as other urban spaces developed during this period, including territorial acquisitions such as the Old Southwest and the Louisiana Purchase, developers, reacting to and instigating demand for professional theatrical productions, constructed more theaters. By the Jacksonian era, professional dramatic productions in permanent theaters had spread to Petersburg and Norfolk, Virginia; Savannah, Georgia; Lexington, Kentucky; Saint Louis, Missouri; Nashville, Tennessee; Natchez, Mississippi; and Huntsville, Alabama. Although no permanent theater seems to have been constructed in New Orleans under French and Spanish rules, the city hosted French theatrical performers as early as the 1790s, and French-language productions flourished from this time well into the nineteenth century, especially after the construction of the short-lived Théâtre St. Pierre in 1807 and subsequent theaters featuring French-speaking performances. English-language productions began in polyglot New Orleans as early as 1806, and the city's antebellum theater community – unique for the South with its mainstream bilingualism – eclipsed Charleston's, with patrons luxuriating in the gas-lit American Theatre and, after 1835, the fabled St. Charles Theatre, both under the management of James H. Caldwell.

As the repertory of Hallam's troupe documents, British drama was the main colonial fare, but the Revolutionary War infused theatrical tastes with patriotism and demanded native dramas. "To *be* American in the new republic meant laying claim to a distinctive sense not just of place, but of character," Stempel posits, and in the theater this would move "beyond simply performing for audiences in the United States of America, engaging them in plays that addressed American themes and from the perspectives and sensibilities of Americans."[8] The result was a prolific and diverse outpouring of antebellum plays and other types of dramatic productions, most typically comedies of manners, melodramas, pantomimes, and farces. Critically shunned by twentieth-century critics' modern and postmodern aesthetics, these plays continue to be rediscovered, historicized, and reassessed, and some, including *The Octoroon; or, Life in Louisiana* (1859), a melodramatic exploration of the "tragic mulatta" by transplanted Irishman Dion Boucicault, now constitute an emerging reclaimed canon. *The Octoroon* also showcases what arose early in the nineteenth century and continues into the twenty-first as one of the central preoccupations of Southern drama: racial difference and conflict. Although this focus would narrow almost exclusively to blacks and whites by the twentieth century, early Southern drama also featured significant – albeit highly stereotyped – representations of Indians.

A noted group of playwrights emerged in Charleston during this era and grew increasingly politicized, especially in defense of slavery and Southern exceptionalism as secession loomed: William Ioor, author of *Independence* (1805) and *The Battle of Eutaw Spring* (1807); John Blake White, author of *Modern Honor* (1812) and *The Forgers* (1829); and William Gilmore Simms, author of *Michael Bonham* (written 1844; produced 1852) and *Norman Maurice* (1851) as well as popular romances like *The Partisan*, *The Cassique of Kiawah*, and *Woodcraft*. Working in Virginia, which retained its colonial investment in theater, was George Washington Parke Custis, grandson of George and Martha Washington and father-in-law of Robert E. Lee, as well as author of eight popular dramatic works. Anticipating Paul Green's and others' twentieth-century outdoor dramas celebrating regional identity, Custis's plays almost invariably rehearsed "Virginia's colorful legendary" such as Washington in *The Indian Prophecy* (1827) and Pocahontas in *Pocahontas; or, The Settlers of Virginia* (1830).[9]

Of the antebellum theatrical genres, none was more popular than the minstrel show, especially in the 1840s and 1850s, and scholars continue to explore the intricate racial and sexual politics associated with this distinctly American form of drama. A forerunner of the vaudeville revue, these shows developed in northern venues, featured white actors sporting blackface to represent African Americans as buffoonish stock characters, and combined skits, dances, and musical performances. In most of these shows, the South was presented as home to either contented black slaves or ones too foolish for freedom, making minstrelsy broadly anti-abolitionist, despite its occasional subversive elements. Following Thomas Dartmouth Rice, who developed the character of Jim Crow in the late 1820s, were Daniel Decatur Emmett, who led the Virginia Minstrels, and Edwin Pearce Christy, who founded Christy's Minstrels. After the Civil War, white minstrelsy declined even as black minstrelsy – African Americans performing in blackface – developed, as with the popular Callender's Original Georgia Minstrels. These shows eventually led to African-American successes on the vaudeville stage, and shows such as the groundbreaking *In Dahomey* (1903), with lyrics by Paul Laurence Dunbar and performances by comedians George Walker and Bert Williams, began to reshape the content of blackface productions into more positive, nuanced representations of blacks in the South and elsewhere.

Given minstrelsy's antebellum popularity, its preoccupations and devices unsurprisingly informed the dramatizations of *Uncle Tom's Cabin* that began to appear even before Harriet Beecher Stowe finished serializing her enormously successful antislavery novel in 1852. Unrestricted by copyright laws and eager for financial profit, multiple dramatists – Henry J. Conway, Charles Western Taylor, Clifton Tayleure, and others – ignored Stowe's Calvinist disdain for theater, cannibalized her best seller's plots and characters, and, in almost all versions, undermined the novel's serious racial politics while retaining a leavening of Christian morality. (Some, such as Conway's, which played at P. T. Barnum's American Museum, were overtly anti-abolitionist.) Stowe's black characters, freshly complex imaginations in their day, were minimized (defiant George Harris) or rewritten as minstrel figures ("wicked" Topsy) and performed by whites in blackface; spectacle and melodrama – Eliza and Harry crossing the ice of the Ohio River; the deaths of Eva, St. Clare, and Tom – were accentuated; new characters were introduced; and tableaux and songs, such as Stephen Foster's "Old Folks at Home," a staple of Christy's Minstrels, were interpolated.

The most successful of these adaptations – indeed, often described as the most popular American play of the nineteenth century – was by George L. Aiken and initially performed by the company of George C. Howard and his family in Troy, New York, in 1852. A. H. Purdy brought the sprawling six-act play to New York for an astonishing 325-performance run between July 18, 1853 and May 13, 1854. The play follows Stowe's novel closely but, like other versions, minimizes the voices of rebellious slaves (George and Eliza last appear in Act II) and imposes an ending in which Simon Legree dies. Moreover, Aiken freezes the sentimental deaths in act-concluding tableaux, broadens the humor, and creates multiple comic marriage subplots, including several involving Ophelia, now a comic scold. The newly added Phineas Fletcher likewise allows for dialect humor – as Eliza crosses the

Ohio, he asserts, "That thar river looks like a promiscuous ice-cream shop come to an awful state of friz" – as does Gumption Cute, who descends from Royall Tyler's Jonathan and, although from Vermont, parallels, along with Phineas, the darkly comic shifty ne'er-do-wells of Old Southwest humor and *Adventures of Huckleberry Finn*.[10] At almost every turn, Aiken's play and its kindred adaptations both attest to the horrors of black enslavement and white cultural domination and diffuse this critique through humor and stereotype to limn an ultimately benign South. The result was a set of inordinately durable works of popular theater, collectively known as "Tom shows," that toured throughout the nation – including the South – deep into the twentieth century.

By this time, however, a handful of white Southern playwrights, including DuBose Heyward, Paul Green, and Lillian Hellman, found regional and, more important, national success in new theatrical forms that rejected sentimentalism, melodrama, and sectionalism in the face of modernism and often advocated social reform. More sensitively and authoritatively than Stowe and yet with a tendency toward exoticism, the Charleston-born Heyward sought to record Southern African-American lives, doing so repeatedly in fiction that was subsequently theatricalized. First and most famous was *Porgy* (1925), Heyward's debut novel exploring the crippled Porgy and his fellow inhabitants of Catfish Row, a Charleston slum. Heyward and his playwright wife, Dorothy (Kuhns) Heyward, dramatized the novel, and The Theatre Guild oversaw a triumphant 367-performance Broadway run in 1927 and 1928. The play in turn provided the source material for *Porgy and Bess* (1935), the masterpiece "folk opera" by composer George Gershwin and his lyricist brother, Ira, with DuBose Heyward crafting the libretto and providing lyrics that Stephen Sondheim has characterized as the profession's finest. The marital couple next dramatized Heyward's *Mamba's Daughters* (1929), with the play running on Broadway the same year and featuring songs by Jerome Kern. The Heywards' work, however, prompted fierce debate over the politics of white authorship and black representation.

Like the Heywards and the Gershwins, North Carolinian Paul Green was drawn to folk drama, especially as it might be used to represent Southern African Americans from a liberal perspective and call attention to their plight. After garnering attention with *The No 'Count Boy* (1924), he triumphed with his Pulitzer Prize–winning *In Abraham's Bosom* (1926), a play that, with its mixed-race protagonist, Abraham McCranie, both returned to the racial preoccupations of *Uncle Tom's Cabin* and *The Octoroon* and marked the modernist distance from those melodramas. Green's other works include *The Field God* (1927), *The House of Connelly* (1931), *Roll, Sweet Chariot* (1934), and *Native Son* (1941), his co-adaptation with Richard

Wright of his famous novel, as well as numerous outdoor pageants, with the still-running (but heavily revised) *The Lost Colony* (1937) being that most noted. Green was, for Watson, "the central, indispensible figure in the development of southern drama" (*The History of Southern Drama*, 101) before Tennessee Williams.

Equally informed by liberal politics, but less preoccupied with Southern representation than Green was Lillian Hellman. Now perhaps best known for her controversial autobiographical writing, the New Orleans-born Jewish editor-turned-playwright burst onto the theatrical scene with *The Children's Hour* (1934) and became one of the leading Broadway figures of the 1930s and 1940s. Her best plays, many critics hold, are those set in the South: *The Little Foxes* (1939) and its prequel, *Another Part of the Forest* (1946). Here, via the Hubbard family, Hellman explores the collapse of the planta-tion economy and the unethical machinations of white Southerners, paral-lels to William Faulkner's atrophied Compsons and rapacious Snopeses and Margaret Mitchell's indomitable Scarlett O'Hara. Indeed, Regina (Hubbard) Giddens, initially incarnated by famous Southern actress Tallulah Bankhead, proved such a fascinating bitch heroine that, when Marc Blitzstein adapted Hellman's play into opera, he renamed it *Regina* (1949).

For all the significance of the somber works of the Heywards, Green, and Hellman, perhaps the most pervasive imagining of the South on the Depression-era stage was by Jack Kirkland, who adapted *Tobacco Road* (1932), Erskine Caldwell's debut novel that featured the poverty- and pel-lagra-stricken Lester family. In a scathing review in the *New York Times*, Brooks Atkinson offered, "Under Mr. Caldwell's influence it is ... one of the grossest episodes ever put on the stage.... The men of letters have stolen the dramatists' crimson badge; and the theatre has never sheltered a fouler or more degenerate parcel of folks than the hardscrabble family of Lester that lives along the Tobacco Road." And yet, Atkinson conceded, "Caldwell's grossness cannot be dismissed as morbidity and gratuitous indecency. It is the blunt truth of the characters he is describing, and it leaves a malevo-lent glow of poetry above the rudeness of his statement."[11] This uniqueness propelled the dramatization not only to run on Broadway for an astound-ing 3,182 performances between 1933 and 1941, but also to see revivals there throughout the 1940s. Moreover, as with the earlier "Tom shows," numerous road shows carried productions throughout the nation, even as they faced sporadic bans for obscenity, and reaffirmed for countless persons the stereotypes of the benighted South – poverty, illness, brutality, sexual deviancy – presented in largely humorous contexts.

During his lifetime, dismissive critics often pointed to much the same elements in the plays of Tennessee Williams, and yet he, more than any other Southern playwright, has secured what stands to be a lasting place in regional, national, and global literatures. After a substantive apprenticeship, he faced "the catastrophe of success," as he phrased it, with *The Glass Menagerie* (1944), his autobiographically inflected "memory play" that wedded domestic drama with formalist experiment. His New Orleans–set masterpiece, *A Streetcar Named Desire* (1947), was followed by a string of plays written for mainstream audiences and typically – but not exclusively – set in the South: *Summer and Smoke* (1948), *The Rose Tattoo* (1951), *Camino Real* (1953), *Cat on a Hot Tin Roof* (1955), *Orpheus Descending* (1957), *Suddenly, Last Summer* (1958), *Sweet Bird of Youth* (1959), *Period of Adjustment* (1960), and *The Night of the Iguana* (1961). Williams's late career, marred by increasing dependency on drugs and alcohol and the death of his partner, Frank Merlo, was nevertheless prolific, even if Williams rarely recaptured his earlier Broadway successes. Critics such as Annette Saddik have reassessed these late plays and joined David Savran and others to rescue a playwright initially canonized as apolitical, especially in contrast to Green, Hellman, and Williams's political non-Southern contemporaries such as Clifford Odets and Arthur Miller.

With their subtler politics, Williams's plays may be distinguished from earlier works dramatizing the South in a number of ways, including his lyricism, but perhaps most striking is the relative absence of African Americans, whether in his plays or in his critically neglected fiction. (The nameless black woman who opens *Streetcar* and the nameless black man who closes "Desire and the Black Masseur" are emblematic.) Yet Williams seems prescient in acknowledging a nuanced multicultural South in his systematic complication of whiteness and its relation to traditional scriptings of the region. This is particularly true of *The Rose Tattoo*. With its setting of a Sicilian immigrant community on the Gulf Coast, the play's geography is far afield from a biracial South determined by generations of elite European Americans and enslaved African Americans. With an entire community of transplanted Sicilians, *The Rose Tattoo* destabilizes whiteness even beyond the earlier Irishness of Jim O'Connor in *The Glass Menagerie* and the Polishness of Stanley Kowalski in *Streetcar*. As the master narratives of Southern studies continue to shift under the pressures of post-Southernness and twenty-first-century regional multiculturalism, particularly post–Hurricane Katrina, the very elements that left *The Rose Tattoo* underappreciated stand to make it extraordinarily attractive for critical reassessment.

Williams's handling of gender and sexuality was even more provocative and groundbreaking, so much so that his infamous branding by George Jean Nathan as "a Southern genital-man" might now be reconsidered as a badge of honor. Gay identities and male same-sex desires and practices were recurring polymorphous preoccupations throughout Williams's literary career. Although the ill-fated Allan Grey of *A Streetcar Named Desire* exemplifies what Vito Russo termed the obligatory gay suicide, and there is the equally ill-fated Sebastian Venable of *Suddenly, Last Summer*, Williams also created Oliver Winemiller, who displays a cold omnisexuality in "One Arm"; Brick Pollitt, who agonizes over the slippage between homoerotic and homosocial desire in *Cat on a Hot Tin Roof*; Billy, who, in contrast, entertains few anxieties about sexual cruising in "Two on a Party"; and the pedophilic Stephen Ashe, who worships above all gods the divinity of a teenage boy's ass in "The Killer Chicken and the Closet Queen." In addition to these variegated representations of male same-sex desire, these texts also feature a brave array of other sexual practices and identities used to various symbolic ends within an era that often shied away from such depictions: rape, promiscuity, intergenerational sexual activity, interracial sexual activity, eroticized cannibalism, sadomasochism, the prostitution of male and female bodies, masturbation, and bisexuality.

The canonization of Tennessee Williams in both the academy and popular culture – especially through the adaptation of his plays into successful films like *A Streetcar Named Desire* (1951), *Cat on a Hot Tin Roof* (1958), and *Suddenly, Last Summer* (1959) that minimized his radical sexual content – unfortunately eclipsed attention given to other mid-twentieth-century Southern playwrights, such as Horton Foote (1916–2009) and Romulus Linney (1930–2011). Although their deaths have instigated reassessments of their work, these two writers remain critically neglected in comparison to Williams, despite being, according to another Southern playwright, Jim Grimsley, "the best examples of Southern drama in our time."[12] Best known through his screenplays of *To Kill a Mockingbird* (1962), *Tender Mercies* (1983), and *The Trip to Bountiful* (1985), Foote, an actor-turned-playwright, broadened the preoccupations of Southern drama, and Southern literature more generally, by repeatedly turning to his native coastal Texas for inspiration. Just as Faulkner compulsively reworked Oxford as Jefferson, Foote fictionalized his hometown of Wharton as Harrison in play after interrelated play; however, he eschewed Faulkner's and Williams's excesses and instead depicted upper- and middle-class white families with delicacy, humor, and nuance worthy of Trollope or Chekhov. These plays include *Texas Town* (1942), *Only the Heart* (1944), *The Chase* (1952), *The Trip to Bountiful* (1953), and *The Traveling Lady* (1954), as well as nine one-act plays written throughout his career that comprise the acclaimed *The Orphans' Home Cycle* (2009). Professionally active into his nineties, Foote won a Pulitzer Prize for *The Young Man from Atlanta* (1997), a subtle exploration of male sexuality and familial responses to it, and saw new work on Broadway only months before his death with *Dividing the Estate* (1989; 2007), a rejoinder to *The Little Foxes* and *Cat on a Hot Tin Roof*.

Far more wide-ranging was the work of Romulus Linney, whose dramatic outpouring prompted Bruce Weber to offer in Linney's *New York Times* obituary:

> His work was redolent of artistic seriousness but nonetheless intended to entertain, and he often spoke in interviews about the need for dialogue to help propel a story and not simply to explore ideas. He wrote more than 30 plays, many of them one-acts, some comic, some somber, wide-ranging in theme and content and often steeped in literary and historical references. "In terms of scope of ambition, Mr. Linney may be our bravest living playwright," Ben Brantley wrote in *The New York Times* in 1996, "running from rural dramas about hillbilly homicides to lush meditations on Lord Byron's ghost and Frederick the Great."[13]

Staples of off-Broadway and regional theaters, many of Linney's plays, such as *Holy Ghosts* (1977) and *Gint* (1998), are set in Appalachia and draw on his childhood in North Carolina and Tennessee. Other works include *The Sorrows of Frederick* (1966), *The Love Suicide at Schofield Barracks* (1972), and *Childe Byron* (1977; 1981), as well as adaptations of source material ranging from Mary Rowlandson's seventeenth-century captivity narrative to Ernest Gaines's *A Lesson before Dying* and Tim O'Brien's *Going after Cacciato*.

The eclecticism of the theatrical marketplace of the last half-century suggested by Linney's playwriting has also been deepened by the major Southern female playwrights who have emerged to check a professional history dominated by men. Although women garnered sporadic regional attention, the South fostered few nationally recognized female dramatists before the 1960s with the exception of Hellman. Carson McCullers successfully adapted her novel *A Member of the Wedding* for the stage in 1950 and wrote a less successful original play, *The Square Root of Wonderful* (1958), but she was foremost a fiction writer, as was Zora Neale Hurston, though she wrote the minor plays *Color Struck* (1925) and *The First One* (1927) as well as the friendship-ending 1930 collaboration with Langston Hughes, the folk drama *Mule Bone: A Comedy of Negro Life*.[14] In contrast, the 1980s witnessed the emergence of Beth Henley and Marsha Norman, successful professional dramatists who have repeatedly explored Southern locales and themes. In her early work, such as *Crimes of the Heart* (1981) and *The Miss Firecracker Contest* (1985), as well as in her most recent, *The Jacksonian* (2012), Henley has mined her familiarity with southern Mississippi and eastern Louisiana, offering plays that critics have eagerly – if somewhat simplistically – used to position her within a Southern Gothic tradition. Norman has drawn more subtly on her Kentucky childhood in plays such as *Getting Out* (1977) and *'night, Mother* (1983), and in her extensive writing for musical theater, she has returned to Southern material, as with the libretto to *The Color Purple* (2005). The two plays that have become canonical in Southern and U.S. drama – *Crimes of the Heart*, focused on three sisters, and *'night, Mother*, focused on a mother and daughter – evince broadly feminist sensibilities, particularly in the overdue prominent representation of women.

In contrast but not surprising given the region's racial history, a substantive history of African-American non-musical dramatic representations of the South stretches back to William Wells Brown. "From the outset," theater historian Watson posits, "the dramatic impulse has been strong among black southerners who found the stage a platform, for protest and pride."[15] And yet, as his survey evinces even as it attempts to rectify the problem, black playwrights have been more productively explored by scholars working in African-American and theater studies rather than Southern studies, which as a rule remains unconcerned with little drama beyond Williams. Albeit briefly, Watson assesses Willis Richardson and the coterie of black female playwrights (May Miller, Georgia Douglas Johnson, and Mary P. Burrill, among others) working in the nation's capital during the 1920s and 1930s and appearing in important anthologies like Alain Locke and Montgomery Gregory's *Plays of Negro Life* (1927) and Richardson and Miller's *Negro History in Thirteen Plays* (1935). The next generations of black playwrights included Virginia-born Randolph Edmonds, author of *Six Plays for a Negro Theatre* (1934); Louisiana-born Theodore Ward, author of *Big White Fog* (1938) and *Our Lan'* (1947); and Louisiana-born and Texas-raised Ted Shine, author of *Contribution* (1969) and many other plays. Like Toni Morrison in her fiction, several recent African-American playwrights, even from outside the South, have represented the region as crucial to black existence in the United States and have reshaped Southern representations, with August Wilson's *Joe Turner's Come and Gone* (1988) and Suzan-Lori Parks's revised libretto to *Porgy and Bess* (2012) being instances. Other black playwrights, such as Pearl Cleage in Atlanta, flourish within regional contexts.

This diversification within the region's dramatic production also extends to ethnic, religious, and sexual identities, as suggested by Alfred Uhry, Nilo Cruz, Mart Crowley, and Jim Grimsley, all major figures of contemporary U.S. and Southern drama. Especially fitting for a region that saw its first professional theatrical production be *The Merchant of Venice*, Uhry has repeatedly explored the lives of Southern Jews during his prolific career, most significantly in *Driving Miss Daisy* (1987), *The Last Night of Ballyhoo* (1997), and *Parade* (1998), a musical made in collaboration with Jason Robert Brown exploring the 1915 lynching of Leo Frank. With works such as *Anna in the Tropics* (2003), the Cuba-born Cruz has forcefully reminded theatergoers of the Latino/a South. Finally, Vicksburg, Mississippi native Crowley has penned *The Boys in the Band* (1968), the now-classic Stonewall Era exploration of gay male group identity, as well as *A Breeze from the Gulf* (1973) and *The Men from the Boys* (2002). Likewise, Grimsley, though better known for his fiction, has been a prolific writer of plays, including the gay-themed, New Orleans–set *Mr. Universe* (1987), his acknowledged homage to Williams and *A Streetcar Named Desire*.

Over the course of the twentieth and twenty-first centuries, plays have – with a few noted exceptions – increasingly become the fare of the culturally elite, on par with opera, making musicals the theatrical mainstream, especially if one retains narrow definitions before the complications and expansions called for by performance studies. As the adaptations of *Uncle Tom's Cabin* and *Tobacco Road* demonstrate, dramatic representations of the South within this mainstream have been and remain crucial in shaping understandings of the region, and the Broadway musical has indeed long privileged the South in its representations. In the twentieth century, amid numerous shorter-lived shows, major productions such as *Cabin in the Sky* (1940), *Louisiana Purchase* (1940), *Finian's Rainbow* (1947), *Purlie* (1970), and *Big River* (1985) drew on Southern locales, identities, and histories and met with financial and critical success, as did several of the foundational texts within the genre from the first half of the century now ensconced in the musical theater canon: *Show Boat* (1927), the already noted *Porgy and Bess*, and *South Pacific* (1949). This same representational preoccupation has continued into the twenty-first century, and, over the last decade, images of the South have proliferated in the American musical. A partial catalogue of twenty-first-century Broadway and off-Broadway shows set in the South includes *Hairspray* (2002), *Caroline, or Change* (2004), *Dessa Rose* (2005), *The Color Purple* (2005), *The Great American Trailer Park Musical* (2005), *Memphis* (2009), *Million Dollar Quartet* (2010), *Bloody Bloody Andrew Jackson* (2010), and *The Scottsboro Boys* (2010). Moreover, this list easily expands to include successful revivals such as *South Pacific* (2008) and *Finian's Rainbow* (2009).

Despite this proliferation, images of the region remain vexed. With few exceptions, musicals dramatize the South exclusively as a – or perhaps the – site of racial tension between black and white Americans (*Andrew Jackson* does interject Native Americans into this representational field, just as *Parade* includes Jewish characters), freeze the region in a distant past that highlights this tension, quarantine the nation's racial injustices to that geography, and accentuate its violence. Perhaps appropriately, Richard Rodgers and Oscar Hammerstein, the popularizers of the book musical during the so-called Golden Age, provided this template. One of the rare times the duo drew on Southern culture, *South Pacific*'s manifestations of Southern racism are the most insidious, with the racism of Nellie Forbush from Little Rock, Arkansas, troubling in ways that that of Joseph Cable from Philadelphia, Pennsylvania, is not. Anxious though Cable is over his involvement in an interracial romantic liaison, he has a moment of vexed insight and self-chastisement in the bitter "You've Got to Be Carefully Taught." In contrast, Nellie, the "cockeyed optimist," is repulsed merely by the traces of such a liaison, as embodied in Emile de Becque's mixed-race children, and, unlike Cable, she espouses a resolute essentialist stance on racism: "I can't help it; it is something you're born with." Although the musical ultimately redeems Nellie's racial politics, it is via *deus ex machina* and seems largely the era's requisite redemption of a leading lady rather than a thoughtfully delineated evolution of Southern identity.

Even with the impact of postmodernity, musical after musical taking up the South follows this template, with Tracy Turnblad from *Hairspray* and Huey Calhoun from *Memphis* being Nellie Forbush's clearest heirs. Even more daring playwrights have resorted to these representations. To the frustration of many, Tony Kushner's negotiations of the South have extended this pattern, a continuation that seems all the more problematic because he spent his childhood in Lake Charles, Louisiana, and thus, unlike Rodgers and Hammerstein, has an intimate – albeit dated – knowledge of at least one version of Southern culture that stands to temper the pre-dominantly urban Jewish milieus of Rodgers, Hammerstein, and Kushner's own extended family. Despite this formative regional influence, his early drama avoids the South, and his otherwise brilliant *Angels in America*, intent with an expansiveness worthy of Whitman, to capture the entirety of the United States at the mid-1980s onset of AIDS, ignores the region altogether. When Kushner eventually turned to his childhood to create the operatic *Caroline, or Change* with composer Jeanine Tesori, the result – a narrative in which an African-American maid struggles with the racial and economic privilege of the Jewish family that employs her – yet again imagined Hammerstein's racially conflicted South of the distant past. While New York critics enamored with Kushner since *Angels* struggled to find laudatory superlatives for *Caroline* throughout its extended development, a handful of others detected these problematic elements. Ben Brantley, for instance, homed in on the limitedness of these images of the South and its racial politics. "*Caroline*," he offered with damning guilt by association, "might be regarded as the brooding person's *Hairspray*, the Broadway hit that also considers integration in the early 1960's." Even when he clarified that the intricately crafted *Caroline* is far more somber and ambivalent than *Hairspray*, where "no social ill is so vicious that it can't be worked out in an *American Bandstand*-style dance-a-thon," he nevertheless indicted Kushner and Tesori's work as pandering to New York audiences' pre-conceived expectations of the South: "The show deals with, among other things, the relationship between a weary black housekeeper and a mother-less white boy; the growing civil rights movement; and the assassination of President John F. Kennedy – subjects traditionally guaranteed to push New York theatergoers' mist-up buttons." Though guardedly appreciative, Brantley sensed a chilling detachment and concluded that "there's an out-sider's perspective to much of *Caroline*, as if its characters were, above all, pieces of historical evidence to be assessed."[16]

Theatrical negations of the U.S. South, whether musical or not, are thus currently at a moment of distinct tension. On the one hand, their diver-sity suggests the limits of the approach Watson deploys in *The History of Southern Drama* (1997), which remains the only complete survey of the field. Invested in the backward glancing project of Southern Renascence building, he offers an eight-point checklist for Southern drama ostensibly applicable throughout its history: "the presence of one or more distinctive social types," such as the Southern belle; violence; "southern legendary," such as Andrew Jackson and Robert E. Lee; fundamentalist religion; "a highly recognizable form of speech" unique to the region; local color; "a love-hate attitude toward the South"; and a "revisionist nature ... to set right a popularized, inaccurate view."[17] Certainly some of these elements continue to structure contemporary theatrical works, but they often negate other ostensibly requisite elements. *Bloody Bloody Andrew Jackson*, for instance, is revisionist in its skewering of the racial politics of the noted "southern legendary." Similarly, although Southern speech and local color persists, they are not the calcified speech and local color of a monolithic region and can range from the horrifically clichéd accents of *Memphis* to the deliberately homogenized ones of *'night, Mother*, a play that Martyn Bone and other critics would assess as set in a post-Southern South. On the other hand, even as one acknowledges the datedness of Watson's categories, the delineated musicals seem constructed by a new but equally rigid set of categories, especially regarding race. Although some exceptions emerge, such as the nuanced *The Light in the Piazza* (2003), adapted from Elizabeth Spencer's novel, the South of *Memphis* and *The Scottsboro Boys* is virtually the same as that of *Show Boat*, and the contemporary multicultural South – not without its own racial issues – has yet to be sung. If this South is being dramatized in non-musical ways, the representations are unfortunately lim-ited in their circulation to regional venues with circumscribed audiences, suggesting that the South's relation to theater remains a troubled one.

NOTES

1 William Dunlap, *A History of American Theatre from Its Origins to 1832* (Urbana: University of Illinois Press, 2005), p. 10.

2 Dunlap, p. 12.

3 Jeffrey H. Richards, "Introduction," *Early American Drama* (New York: Penguin, 1997), p. x.

4 Richards, p. x.

5 Larry Stempel, *Showtime: A History of the Broadway Musical Theater* (New York and London: W. W. Norton, 2010), p. 22.

6 Dunlap, p. 69.

7 Dunlap, p. 373.

8 Stempel, pp. 23–24.

9 Charles S. Watson, *The History of Southern Drama* (Lexington: University Press of Kentucky, 1997), p. 19.

10 George L. Aiken, *Uncle Tom's Cabin* in *Early American Drama* (New York: Penguin, 1997), p. 382.

11 Brooks Atkinson, review of *Tobacco Row*, by Jack Kirkland, *New York Times*, December 5, 1933.

12 Jim Grimsley, "Muscle Men, Tennessee Williams, and the State of Southern Drama," *North Carolina Literary Review* 18 (2009), p. 73.

13 Bruce Weber, "Romulus Linney, Wide-Ranging Playwright, Dies at 80," *New York Times*, January 15, 2011.

14 This lure continues to exert its power over Southern writers who are primarily not dramatists. Elizabeth Spencer, Reynolds Price, and Cormac McCarthy are three of many fiction writers who have sporadically written plays.

15 Watson, p. 144.

16 Ben Brantley, "Outsiders Bond in a South of Roiling Change," *New York Times*, December 1, 2003.

17 Watson, pp. 4–6.

13

MICHAEL P. BIBLER

Queering the Region

Understanding how Southern writers have explored notions of sexual and gender queerness is not the same as tracing a lesbian and gay canon of Southern literature. As scholars since Michel Foucault have shown, the modern sexual categories "heterosexual" and "homosexual" emerged only in the late nineteenth and early twentieth centuries as ideological tools for classifying individuals, and the terms "lesbian" and "gay" became associated predominately with white, middle-class, homosexual subcultures in metropolitan cities like New York. Because "lesbian" and "gay" still retain these limited connotations, scholars and activists in the 1990s reclaimed the abusive label "queer" as a politically defiant umbrella term that encompasses the full spectrum of sexual and gender expression outside the social norms of any particular place or time, including bisexuality, transsexualism, gender ambiguity, sadomasochism, and more. In Michael Warner's early definition, "queer" "rejects a minoritizing logic of toleration or simple political interest-representation in favor of a more thorough resistance to regimes of the normal.... For both academics and activists, 'queer' gets a critical edge by defining itself against the normal rather than the heterosexual."[1] For scholars working in Southern studies, this expansiveness of "queer" opens possibilities for understanding the complex deployments of gender, desire, and eroticism both prior to the invention of homosexuality as a category and in relation to the region's diverse cultural topographies, where the labels "lesbian" and "gay" may seem foreign or anachronistic, including rural and Appalachian spaces as well as Southern African-American, ethnic, Native, and poor white communities.

However, any analysis of Southern literature and culture must remain attuned to the historical and contextual specificities wherever queerness can be seen or sensed. Critical usage of "queer" obviously draws on the term's wider designation of an unaccountable oddness or strangeness that unsettles the familiar and conventional. Queer theory thus opens rich avenues for exploring the uncanny and grotesque dimensions of what is familiarly called the "Southern gothic," as suggested by Eve Kosofsky Sedgwick's claim that "queer" can refer to the "possibilities, gaps, overlaps, dissonances and resonances, lapses and excesses of meaning when the constitutive elements of anyone's gender, of anyone's sexuality aren't made (or *can't be* made) to signify monolithically."[2] Yet an uncritical approach that simply embraces this openness could drain the term of any value by interpreting every gothic inflection as queer – as would an analysis that flatly posits the whole of Southern regionalism as an aberration of, or deviation from, national normativity. Queering the region requires an acute awareness of historical differences and careful attention to the ways that nonnormative expressions of gender and desire – especially, but not exclusively, same-sex desires and identities – intersect with concepts of nation and other aspects of identity such as race and class.

Indeed, queering the region is more a matter of taking a particular methodological approach (or combination of approaches) to Southern literature and culture than of building something like a ready archive of texts. That is, the kinds of works we identify as queer might shift according to how we understand the peculiar interventions those works (or authors) might be trying to make within their own historical moments, and how we locate those interventions within the contexts of power, identity, and discourse in our own time(s). This essay suggests some of the ways that writers have used models of sexual and gender queerness to resist, revise, or otherwise engage with the dominant cultural narratives of the South. Although my argument follows a linear trajectory beginning in the colonial period, this is by no means an exhaustive list of writers in whose works queerness can be traced. Yet I also do not mean to imply that *every* Southern text can or should be subjected to a queer analysis. Rather, I show how the structures of power and ideology that shape Southern culture become most apparent wherever queer aberrations of gender, desire, and eroticism expose the contradictions and inconsistencies embedded within those power structures. By revealing what does not fit comfortably within narratives of region, literary models of Southern queerness offer powerful sites for critiquing and reimagining the regional ideologies that mark the boundary between "normal" and "deviant," yet that always fail to maintain that boundary with absolute success.

A good example of how queering the region involves the questions and methods we bring to texts, rather than simply textual content, is the written archive of the colonial South. A great deal of research remains to be done regarding the codes of sex and gender within the different Native tribes of the pre-Columbian and colonial southeast. But as Andrea Smith writes, a queer critique can also help "escape the ethnographic entrapment by which

Native peoples are rendered simply as objects of intellectual study and instead can foreground settler colonialism as a key logic that governs the United States today."[3] This kind of scholarship at the intersection between Native studies and queer studies suggests useful ways for thinking about the wider field of intercultural contact during colonialism, including canonical Anglo-American texts like William Byrd II's *The History of the Dividing Line Betwixt Virginia and North Carolina* (1728). Byrd's chapbooks and secret diaries offer frank descriptions of his erotic impulses and sexual exploits with his first wife (including on a billiard table), with genteel women and prostitutes in London, and with his servants and slaves in Virginia. This heteroerotic context helps illuminate Byrd's depictions of his white assistants' sexual escapades with, and assaults on, Native women in *The History of the Dividing Line*. But Byrd also demonstrated a nonjudgmental curiosity about sex between men.[4] Instead of asking simply how Byrd's almost libertine attitudes about sex influenced his humorous depictions of backwoods whites and Natives, we might take Smith's approach and ask how Byrd's apparent complacency with homosex fit with his attempt to assert social dominance as a "gentleman" and construct a colonial subjectivity through his writing. We might then extend this line of inquiry to other colonial southern texts, such as John Lawson's *A New Voyage to Carolina* (1709), which is usually noted for his sympathetic treatment of Native Americans, and Ebenezer Cooke's satirical poem *The Sot-Weed Factor* (1708), which portrays Maryland's leading ladies as prostitutes or sexual opportunists while mocking European assumptions about Native "savagery." How are Eurocentric notions of sexual and gender normativity, transgression, and deviance central to the project of imagining a coherent colonial subject defined in opposition to the "native"? In short, how would queering William Byrd II help us queer the very project of settler colonialism in the southeast?

In the first half of the nineteenth century, Southern writing similarly interrogated the construction of subjectivities at the junctures between gender, race, sexual relations, and persistent concerns about what counted as "native." In the Native South, a queer study might explore how sex and gender were deployed in conflicts over sovereignty, assimilation, and forced relocation. Researchers might consider how marriage and gender conformity figured in debates led by Elias Boudinot and others over the Cherokee nation's struggle to maintain autonomy, or how matriarchal family structures in the Chickasaw nation intersected with U.S. laws governing slave ownership, perversely inspiring a liberalization of married women's property laws in Mississippi – the first state to make such reforms. Irregularities and conflicts between Native and settler forms of sexual and gender expression can also shed light on the cultural politics of frontier fiction and humor of the "Old Southwest." The Davy Crockett Almanacs (1835–1856) comically exaggerate frontier mythologies with tales of grotesquely mannish and powerful pioneer women. And the homoerotic animal imagery in Thomas Bangs Thorpe's "The Big Bear of Arkansas" (1854) and Augustus Baldwin Longstreet's "The Gander Pulling" (1835) unravels the coherency of masculine identities and rituals even while trying to reinforce certain models of masculine prowess. White masculinity is also lauded and lampooned in juxtaposition to (usually) derogatory portrayals of blacks, Natives, women, and naïve city men in works such as Longstreet's *Georgia Scenes* (1835), which includes a story about a male-male married couple entitled "A Sage Conversation," and the pseudonymously published "Fire in the Rear; or, Bill Jones among the Girls" (1851), which comically describes the sadistic punishment the "girls" inflict on the nude protagonist when they catch him spying on them bathing in a stream. While most frontier humor is patently racist and misogynist, a queer analysis could distinguish when and how the portrayals of sex, race, and gender might also work to unsettle the power dynamics of settler colonialism during southwesterly expansion.

Beginning in the 1820s, white writers also took up questions about the masculinity and mastery of plantation owners, spurring the tradition of plantation fiction that remains popular today. Antebellum plantation fiction typically portrayed the planter as a benevolent cavalier who cares for his slaves and white dependents and asserts his masculine supremacy in military conflicts or duels. Plantation romances also deployed a marriage plot whereby the young cavalier must marry a woman of the same class in order to perpetuate the plantation system infinitely into the future.[5] But many Southern writers also questioned the rigidity of gender roles within such a staunchly patriarchal and (what we would now call) heterosexist system. In John Pendleton Kennedy's *Horse-Shoe Robinson* (1835), a novel about the Revolutionary War, the gender ambiguity of the siblings Henry and Mildred Lindsay helps them resist the tyranny of their Loyalist father, rupturing the cycle of patriarchal dominance that would otherwise break their solidarity and destroy the bonds of both the family and, by extension, the new nation.[6] William Gilmore Simms also considered alternative forms of gender and family in *Woodcraft* (1854), in which the hero Porgy eventually gives up on the idea of marriage and turns his plantation into a haven for bachelors. Alongside his neighbor, the somewhat mannish widow Eveleigh, who is the most successful planter and businessperson in the region, Porgy's mild distortion of gender norms destabilizes the roles set for both men and women, opening space for other, queerer forms of identity.

Similar distortions of gender and romance occur in fiction written by Southern women. The heroines of Augusta Jane Evans's novels *Macaria; or, the Altars of Sacrifice* (1864) and *St. Elmo* (1867) defy the conventions of the submissive plantation belle or lady by foreswearing or postponing marriage and instead pursuing the more traditionally masculine paths of education and a career (such as a writer, in the latter text). Furthermore, *St. Elmo* and other works such as Caroline Lee Hentz's *Marcus Warland* (1852) and E.D.E.N. Southworth's antislavery *The Prince of Darkness* (1850/1866) include deeply homoerotic portrayals of male sentimentality, again pushing the boundaries of masculinity, femininity, and hetero-normative romance. While it could be said that, on one level, these works enlist alternative models of gender behavior and romantic attachment to stabilize the authors' visions of what the South should be, on another level those alternative forms inevitably exhibit a queer instability that disrupts those visions of social order and clears room for imagining more radical possibilities.

Not surprisingly, abolitionists offered explicit depictions of gender and sexual perversity to highlight the injustices of the slaveholding South, focusing regularly on the sexual abuse of enslaved women and creating a pervasive image of what Ronald Walters has called "the erotic South."[7] Henry Bibb repeatedly described the sexual threats aimed at his first wife and how her master eventually forced her into concubinage. Harriet Jacobs's narrative even includes a powerful scene of one master's relentless sexual assaults on his male slave Luke. Works such as William Craft's *Running a Thousand Miles for Freedom* (1860) and William Wells Brown's novel *Clotel; or, the President's Daughter* (1853) draw further attention to the way that oppression under slavery can queer gender identities and marital and family relations, including driving enslaved people to acts of cross-dressing in order to escape white surveillance and the South itself. In other abolitionist works, such as Frederick Douglass's novella *The Heroic Slave* (1852), writers mobilized unabashedly homoerotic forms of sentimentality to seduce white men to the abolitionist cause, often by rendering the black male body into an explicit object of male desire.[8] All of these works show how slavery produced a range of queer effects by perverting normative expectations about family, intimacy, sex, and desire in Victorian America.

Nineteenth-century minstrel shows notoriously included homosexual imagery,[9] and sensationalist fiction blatantly sought to titillate readers with scenes of sexual excess. Joseph Holt Ingraham's *The Quadroone* (1841) queers the gaze of white readers by soliciting their erotic investment in the physical beauty of both male and female mixed-race characters, even as the book stokes anxieties about racial and national "purity." Ned Buntline's dime novel *The Mysteries and Miseries of New Orleans* (1851) and Baron Ludwig von Reizenstein's German-language abolitionist novel *The Mysteries of New Orleans* (1854–1855) offer salacious depictions of rape, concubinage, and prostitution, as well as, in the latter text, a surprisingly explicit and sympathetic account of lesbian love. Finally, no discussion of the antebellum period would be complete without mention of the sexual gothicism that pervades the works of Edgar Allan Poe. For example, "Fall of the House of Usher" (1839) famously subverts the plantation romance by remaking the emphasis on aristocratic bloodlines into a matter of incest and degeneration, and "Ligeia" (1838) queers male anxieties about erotic intimacy between women by describing the coexistence of two women's souls within a single body.[10] Further analysis is required to determine the extent to which nineteenth-century readers would have understood any of these works as "queer" in the sense that we might find them, but we can still learn much about the early South by reading these scenes of sexual and gender excess and instability through a queer lens.

In the late nineteenth century, discourses of race, gender, and sexuality increasingly deployed models of codified identity *categories* that defined individuals as discrete and immutable types, giving rise to the split between "heterosexual" and "homosexual" at the same time that Southern authorities instituted stricter methods for segregating "white" from "black."[11] Not surprisingly, Southern writing during this period engaged these discourses by playing with forms of indeterminacy and category confusion, particularly in narratives of racial impersonation and cross-dressing. *Adventures of Huckleberry Finn* (1885) and *Pudd'nhead Wilson* (1894) are just two of the many stories in which Mark Twain links scenes of racial and gender disguise with male homoeroticism to make a "radical challenge to society's accepted and determinative racial binaries," as Linda Morris argues.[12] The prevalence of these dynamics in Twain's work raises questions about whether other narratives of racial impersonation and passing – of which there are countless examples – similarly distort *gender* and *sexual* identities in queer ways. In George Washington Cable's work, scenes of same-sex attraction – especially between Joseph Frowenfeld and Honoré Grandissime in *The Grandissimes* (1880) – emphasize the unpredictable and uncontainable nature of desire in a South where racial mixing and genealogical confusion are rife. In *The Entomologist* (1899), Cable even interrupts his narrative of extramarital intrigue with what can only be interpreted as a scene of homosexual cruising, again stressing how desire and eroticism easily exceed the boundaries of identity and propriety. Finally, queerly sentimental bonds between men are also present in the romanticized attachments between former slaves and their white masters in the works of Thomas Nelson Page and Joel Chandler Harris.[13] While Page and Harris were more interested in reinforcing social and racial boundaries, instead of challenging them as Twain and Cable do, these intimate, sentimental bonds nevertheless trouble the coherency and legitimacy of the identity categories on which these authors' conservative visions of the New South depended.

In other works of Southern writing, eroticized portrayals of black, white, and ethnic bodies – male and female – are suffused within the general exoticism that made local color so appealing to a mass audience. Southern local color writers sought to reveal the peculiarities of a specific locale through intimate portrayals of unusual characters. Yet this emphasis on peculiarity can make it difficult to distinguish the line between "queer" and "normal." Instead of focusing on constructions of identity, a more productive queer analysis might concentrate on scenes where affects and emotions rupture the narrative and ideological coherency of setting and place. In *The Goodness of St. Rocque and Other Stories* (1899), Alice Ruth Dunbar Nelson richly describes the emotional worlds of marginalized, abandoned, and neglected women of color and ethnic women, making pointed challenges to racial and patriarchal dominance as well as what we would now call compulsory heterosexuality. Many of Kate Chopin's stories similarly challenge the regimes of patriarchy and marriage by plumbing the emotional interiors of her female characters. *The Awakening* (1899) dwells on the inchoate feelings of dissatisfaction and desire that set Edna Pontellier at odds with her husband and the bourgeois society around her, and that nurture her homoerotic relationship with the musician Mademoiselle Reisz. As Mary Biggs writes, "autoeroticism, homoeroticism, and homosexual sex" are inseparable elements "in the complex weave of Edna's awakening and in the book's ... sweeping scrutiny of her society."[14] Edna can also be read as an example of the "New Woman" who sought to break out of the constraints of conventional femininity at the turn of the twentieth century, making her an interesting parallel to the mixed-race character Sappho Clark in Pauline Hopkins's *Contending Forces* (1900), which is set partly in the South. These fiercely independent characters experience erotic and emotional connections with other women that defy the rigid classification system separating "homosexual" and "heterosexual," "lesbian" and "straight."

Potentially queer figurations of the New Woman can also be found in the early-twentieth-century fiction of Ellen Glasgow and Katherine Anne Porter. But as clearly defined gay and lesbian subcultures began to emerge in cities across the country – including in the South – writers began to incorporate more direct representations of same-sex desire and identity in their works. This shift corresponds with the wider tendency in modernist writing to push against nineteenth-century forms of middlebrow sentimentality by explicitly depicting sex, violence, rape, and socially transgressive characters, including homosexuals. Porter included gay characters in her novella *Hacienda* (1934), and all of her stories offer a powerful, woman-focused critique of compulsory heterosexuality and marriage. Similarly, Lillian Hellman's exploration of lesbian desire in *The Children's Hour* (1934), and the "Julia" section in her memoir *Pentimento* (1973) supports a queer reading of the critique of marriage and what I have called the "southern kitchen romances" between white and black women in her Southern plays. The largely unknown writer Murrell Edmunds offered a cryptic tale of male homosexuality in his early novel *Sojourn among Shadows* (1936) and continued to emphasize male homoeroticism as a source of liberal political sympathies in his later civil rights fiction. Lillian Smith likewise made lesbian relations central to her condemnation of Southern racism, religion, and conformity in *Killers of the Dream* (1949) and her novels *Strange Fruit* (1944) and *One Hour* (1959). In Smith's view, racial segregation perverted psychosexual relations by forcing arbitrary divisions between "natural" and "unnatural" both in society and on the body, ironically clearing space for homosexuality as an integral, if problematic, part of Southern culture. Jean Toomer's richly atmospheric exploration of racial mixing in his experimental novel *Cane* (1923) is equally invested in troubling racist constructions of normalcy and perversion and the segregation of homo and hetero identities. In profound yet different ways, all of these writers link modernist portrayals of sexual queerness to a direct criticism of the South's racial and sexual conservatism.

Other Southern modernist writers present interesting challenges to queer studies. William Faulkner wove examples of explicit homoeroticism into his early short stories and his novels *Light in August* (1932) and *Absalom, Absalom!* (1936), and a queer subtext can easily be traced in *The Sound and the Fury* (1929), *The Wild Palms* (1939), and *Go Down, Moses* (1940). But as is always the case with Faulkner, the political significance of these depictions is complex: partly linked to liberal ideas about sexual and racial politics and partly linked to his wider use of perversion, violence, and degeneracy to depict the grotesqueness of the human condition, such as in the infamous rape scene in *Sanctuary* (1931) or Ike Snopes's carnal love for his cow in *The Hamlet* (1940). However, what does it mean that Faulkner's work differs significantly from that of one of his contemporaries, William Alexander Percy, and one of his closest mentors, Stark Young? Both men's homosexuality was somewhat common knowledge during their lives, but they did not openly depict or discuss homosexuality in their fiction and nonfiction. Instead of mislabeling Faulkner as a "gay" writer or dismissing Percy and Young as "closeted," we should recognize how they offer unique possibilities for expanding queer studies precisely because their works resist common expectations about (homo)sexual identities and sexual politics.

Similar opportunities exist with other modernist writers whose works incorporate queer dynamics that can help us reconsider the wider appeal of

the Southern gothic. Both Zora Neale Hurston and Richard Wright mobilized forms of queerly charged homosociality to assist their depictions of
black community.[15] Although Erskine Caldwell rarely depicted homoeroticism or homosexuality in his fiction, he regularly queered assumptions about
white superiority with comic scenes of incestuous, predatory, and intergenerational sexual relations. In works such as "Why I Live at the P.O." (1941),
Delta Wedding (1946), and *The Ponder Heart* (1954), Eudora Welty used a
different form of humor to queer assumptions about what should count as
"normal" in a South where powerful white and black women rupture local
patterns of male dominance (as well as conventionally masculine forms of
narration), and where effeminate men unsettle narrow frameworks of marriage and family. The broadly perverse characters of Flannery O'Connor's
fiction further disrupt clichéd and complacent modes of knowledge and
belief by confronting the reader with radically different forms of corpore-
ality and identity. Perhaps the queerest examples appear in the frustrated,
angry, and isolated young men of *Wise Blood* (1952) and "The Enduring
Chill" (1965), as well as the scene of male rape in *The Violent Bear It Away*
(1960). Finally, Ernest J. Gaines included male homosexual characters in *Of
Love and Dust* (1967) and "Three Men" (1968) as part of his meditation on
black masculinity. In all of these works, queerness forms one strand within a
larger exploration of the South's regional peculiarities during a time of rapid
modernization and change.

Some mid-century Southern writers deliberately used their work to validate alternative sexualities in the face of nationwide anxieties about sexual
and gender difference, especially homosexuality. The famously grotesque
characters in Carson McCullers's fiction embody the full complexities of
multivalent desires that do not fit the categories "gay," "straight," or even
"bisexual," not least in *The Member of the Wedding* (1946) and *Ballad of
the Sad Café* (1951), but also in her less popular *Reflections in a Golden
Eye* (1941) and *Clock without Hands* (1961), where same-sex desire is most
unambiguous. Truman Capote's groundbreaking novel *Other Voices, Other
Rooms* (1948) and his early short story "A Diamond Guitar" (1950) gained
widespread notoriety for their positive and unapologetic, if still deeply
gothic, portrayals of homosexuality and gender transitivity. Harper Lee's
characters Scout and Dill in *To Kill a Mockingbird* (1960) echo Capote's
emphasis on gender ambiguity (Dill was famously modeled on Capote) and
add a decidedly queer-positive dimension to her novel. William Goyen's *The
House of Breath* (1950) and Thomas Hal Phillips's *The Bitterweed Path*
(1950) present nonsensational, even tender stories about queer male relationships that stand at odds with the heterosexist parameters of traditional
Southern culture; but, unlike Capote, they associate male homosexuality

more with masculinity than gender transitivity. The most influential writer of the queer South is undoubtedly Tennessee Williams. His major plays *Cat on a Hot Tin Roof* (1955) and *Suddenly, Last Summer* (1958) simultaneously demand sympathy and understanding for homosexuals and other queers while challenging the Cold War tendency to restrict both the psyche and the body to narrow social categories. His minor plays and short stories are even more provocative in the way they use mythical and psychological symbols and cross-gender identifications to validate and explore the illogical connections between desire and alienation, tenderness and violence, and queerness and sociality. While his works also incorporate elements of shame, self-loathing, and internalized homophobia, his wide appeal brought the discussion of homosexuality into the public sphere more than any other writer at the time.

This group of loosely queer-positive, mid-century writers inspired many others after the 1960s to write even more direct and sustained meditations on queer Southern sexualities. Of course, some writers continued to subsume images of queerness within a larger exploration of region. Both William Styron's *The Confessions of Nat Turner* (1967) and James Dickey's *Deliverance* (1970) scandalously made scenes of homosexual sex central to their meditations on race, masculinity, and power. Meanwhile, a lesbian affair in Ellen Douglas's *A Lifetime Burning* (1982) forms a crucial part of the protagonist's attempt to break out of the narrow sexual role scripted for white Southern women. But other writers made queerness more central to their works, especially those involved in lesbian and gay communities and politics in the wake of the 1969 Stonewall riots in New York. Through the story of Molly Bolt, who refuses to be defined or constrained by patriarchy, homophobia, or the lesbian subculture of New York, Rita Mae Brown's bestselling *Rubyfruit Jungle* (1973) offers a humorous and fiercely defiant statement of sexual independence and feminist self-actualization. Minnie Bruce Pratt has also been deeply involved in feminist and lesbian and gay liberation movements since the 1960s and has crafted award-winning explorations of lesbian identity, gender fluidity, motherhood, race, and region in her poems, essays, and other work. The lesser-known African-American poet Doris Davenport wrote about black women's experiences of same-sex love and lesbian identity, although she had trouble publishing her works until the 1980s. And Ann Allen Shockley's stories and novels, *Loving Her* (1974) and *Say Jesus and Come to Me* (1982), remain the first and most sustained considerations of interracial lesbian relationships not only in the South but in all of U.S. literature. All of these writers are joined by their radical emphasis on feminist, sexual, and racial liberation, building on a tradition of outspoken Southern women's writing that reaches back to the work of Chopin, Dunbar Nelson, and even Evans and Southworth. Shockley's explicitly lesbian fiction makes further interventions in the tradition of writing that depicts intimate relations between black and white women. Lane von Herzen's *Copper Crown* (1991), which Sharon Monteith describes as "an eco-utopian romance,"[16] similarly foregrounds the homoerotic bonds between her white and black protagonists, and together these queer works open suggestive possibilities for rereading the interracial female intimacies in Hellman's and Porter's work, as well as Willa Cather's *Sapphira and the Slave Girl* (1940), Ellen Douglas's *Can't Quit You, Baby* (1988), Minrose Gwin's *The Queen of Palmyra* (2010), and even Kathryn Stockett's popular yet problematic *The Help* (2009).

Building on the innovations of these forebears and the success of the lesbian-feminist publishing house, Naiad Press, which was based in Tallahassee, Florida, Dorothy Allison's stories, essays, poems, spoken-word pieces, and two novels, *Bastard out of Carolina* (1992) and *Cavedweller* (1998), infuse tender depictions of poor and working-class white Southerners with a unique and uncompromising focus on female homoeroticism, sexual abuse, feminist agency, and sadomasochistic pleasure. Yet Allison's work is also doubly compelling for the way she that avoids tying her characters to a simplistic model of lesbian identity. Similar interests in sadomasochism and (homo)sexual liberation can be found in the short stories collected in Jay Quinn's two *Rebel Yell* anthologies and the fiction and poetry of Charles Nelson, Roy F. Wood, and Jeff Mann, all of which explore the relationships between male homosexuality, religion, race, and class in the rural South and beyond. As the first book-length meditation on gay male life in Appalachia, Mann's memoir *Loving Mountains, Loving Men* (2005) belongs with other key works of queer Southern memoir, particularly Mab Segrest's *Memoir of a Race Traitor* (1995), Pratt's *S/HE* (1995), Kevin Sessums's *Mississippi Sissy* (2007), and Reynolds Price's *Ardent Spirits* (2009). And these works should be read alongside the growing body of sociological and historical studies about the queer South written by James T. Sears, John Howard, Daneel Buring, E. Patrick Johnson, Wesley Chenault, Stacy Braukman, Brock Thompson, and others.

A recent focus of literary criticism has been the use of postmodern parody to (de)construct the "post-Southern," whereby writers play with claims of truth and authenticity by self-reflexively referencing the images, tropes, signs, and symbols of Southern culture from earlier works. Some authors have made queerness central to their postmodern revisions of familiar Southern genres, including John Kennedy Toole's subversive *A Confederacy of Dunces* (1980); Suzan-Lori Parks's rewrite of Faulkner, *Getting Mother's Body* (2003); Edward P. Jones's neo-slave narrative *The Known World* (2003); and

Valerie Martin's unsettling plantation novel *Property* (2003). But other writers trouble this turn to the postmodern and post-Southern because they often have a political stake in using their queer characters to validate the feelings and experiences of queer-identified people living in the South. Striking a balance between naturalistic portrayals of gay or lesbian characters and queer destabilization of norms and identities, these writers weave stories of sexual minorities into narratives of Southern history and culture while still avoiding preexisting myths and stereotypes. June Arnold's *Sister Gin* (1989) and Lisa Alther's *Original Sins* (1981) and *Other Women* (1985) challenge religious, political, and social forms of homophobia by exploring the tender and complex love affairs shared by Southern women. Blanche McCrary Boyd combines powerful depictions of feminist and antiracist alliances with comic explorations of lesbian sexuality both in her early writing and in her popular *The Revolution of Little Girls* (1992), which rewrites the coming-of-age story with the tale of a high-school beauty queen who rejects the mystique of the Southern belle and comes out as a lesbian. Cris South's *Clenched Fists, Burning Crosses: A Novel of Resistance* (1984) offers a direct condemnation of Southern racism, sexism, and homophobia in her lesbian protagonist's fight against the beatings, lynchings, and rapes (including her own rape) perpetrated by the Ku Klux Klan. Alice Walker's *The Color Purple* (1982) imagines a sexual relationship between rural African-American women that evokes the queer sexual and gender ambiguity of early Blues singers. Harlan Greene's elegiac *Why We Never Danced the Charleston* (1985) and *What the Dead Remember* (1992) try to locate a place for gay male identities within the contexts of Southern myth and history. Daniel Black's *Perfect Peace* (2010) uses the setting of a rural black community in Arkansas to tell the story of Paul, who is raised as a girl named Perfect for the first eight years of her/his life. Finally, Reynolds Price weaves male homosexuality into highly meditative and symbolic works about kinship, religion, race, identity, and love, particularly in the three novels of the epic family cycle, *A Great Circle: The Surface of Earth* (1975), *The Source of Light* (1981), and *The Promise of Rest* (1995). Perhaps more than any other Southern writer, Price includes homosexuality and other nonnormative desires within a broader exploration of the lives of common, everyday Southerners, white and black. He also refuses to limit homosexuality to a political identity and instead imbues same-sex eroticism and love with the complexity and dignity of any other form of human intimacy. *The Promise of Rest* also describes the death of the young Wade Mayfield to AIDS and transforms the pain of loss and betrayal into a life-affirming story of courage and loyalty.

Allan Gurganus also writes about AIDS in *The Practical Heart* (2001), which, like *Plays Well with Others* (1997), weaves homosexuality into darkly comic stories of social absurdity and genuine tragedy. Horton Foote's play *The Young Man from Atlanta* (1995) makes a Williams-esque exploration of homophobia, suicide, and the meaning of family by perversely keeping the presence of the homosexual body permanently offstage. Jim Grimsley, in his plays and novels such as *Dream Boy* (1997) and *Boulevard* (2002), focuses extensively on the ways that urban and rural Southern settings create unique opportunities and problems for gay men. And Randall Kenan's *A Visitation of Spirits* (1989) and *Let the Dead Bury Their Dead* (1992) arguably provide the most sustained literary examination of what it means to be gay and black in the South. Set in North Carolina, Kenan's stories explore the joys and troubles of black gay men who are forced to confront issues of homophobia, cross-racial desire, religious prejudice, family loyalty, racism, rural poverty, and the ubiquitous influence of late-twentieth-century pop culture. Like Kenan, Craig S. Womack has helped expand the boundaries of both queer and nonwhite literary canons with *Drowning in Fire* (2001), in which a Muskogee Creek man comes to terms with his homosexual desires among the pressures of tribal history, family memory, and conservative Christianity. Although set in Oklahoma, this novel amplifies the possibilities for remapping the racial, ethnic, and sexual boundaries of what we think of as "the South" in the twenty-first century.

Over the last few decades, Southern forms of queerness have also become more visible in popular culture. In *Southern Ladies and Gentlemen* (1975), Florence King played up the comic image of flamboyant gay men who can live openly in the South because they do not threaten the social order. Although focused primarily on female characters, the Atlanta-based television show *Designing Women* (1986–1993) and the hit play and film *Steel Magnolias* (1987–1989) became gay classics, not only because they openly discussed social issues surrounding homosexuality, but also for their camp, almost drag-queen-like parodies of Southern femininity. The wildly popular two-actor comedy *Greater Tuna* (1981) and its three sequels, also adapted for television, dealt with issues of perversion, hypocrisy, and prejudice in small-town Texas through lighthearted satire and farcical performances of cross-dressing, as did the cult film *Sordid Lives* (2000). In popular fiction, the novels *The Deal* (2004) and *Three Fortunes in One Cookie* (2005), coauthored by Timothy J. Lambert and Becky Cochrane, make gay romance central to their stories of Southern identity, love, and family. Fannie Flagg's *Fried Green Tomatoes at the Whistlestop Café* (1987), adapted into a massively popular film in 1991, subtly imagines a love affair between two women in the 1930s alongside the story of a contemporary woman trying to renew her sense of identity and purpose. Anne Rice's *Feast of All Saints* (1979) includes a sympathetic yet narrow portrayal of a free man of color's homosexuality in antebellum New Orleans, and the male homoeroticism in *Interview with a Vampire* (1976) enriches her rewriting of the vampire genre. Poppy Z. Brite's *Exquisite Corpse* (1996) follows the exploits of a gay serial killer in New Orleans. And Charlaine Harris's Sookie Stackhouse novels weave gay characters and subplots into her stories of Southern vampires and werewolves, a dynamic that scriptwriter and producer Alan Ball has made even more explicit in his television adaptation, *True Blood*. Finally, Howard Cruse's graphic novel *Stuck Rubber Baby* (1995) depicts a young white man's growing involvement in the civil rights movement in the 1960s at the same time that he comes to terms with his homosexuality, while Mat Johnson's *Incognegro* (2008) gives his story of racial passing and the fight against lynching a surprising plot twist involving gender transitivity.

This wide-ranging collection of literary and popular works demonstrates that queer forms of sex, gender, and sexuality in the South are by no means limited to the familiar categories of "lesbian" and "gay." While it is crucial not to lose sight of the importance of same-sex eroticism in challenging the limits of the "normal," critics must remain sensitive to other dynamics of intimacy and identity that rupture traditional models of gender, race, and family in Southern culture. Writers interested in white and black Southern masculinities reveal the extent to which queer and "deviant" forms of gender and desire are both necessary for, and integral to, historical constructions of male identity, even when those constructions seem exceptionally patriarchal and conservative. Where many white Southern women writers have imagined, even fantasized about, intimate friendships between white and black women, the potential for homoerotic or lesbian forms of intimacy brings to the fore the precarious political dynamics involved in representing any kind of cozy interracialism. Yet queer writers like Shockley and Kenan who have explicitly depicted interracial homosexual relationships also reveal that queer forms of desire can serve as productive models for renegotiating the limits and possibilities of cross-racial unions. Lesbian writers from the 1970s onward have mobilized feminist politics in ways that make it possible to trace the queer resistance expressed in earlier works of Southern women's writing without misconstruing those earlier works as progressive or liberationist in the exactly same sense. Finally, the rise in "out" gay, lesbian, and queer-of-color voices in Southern writing not only corresponds to the rise in interest in multiculturalism beginning in the mid-to-late twentieth century, but also calls new attention to the rich diversity of Southern voices that have shaped Southern literature from colonialism to the present.

Interestingly, however, the popularity and canonical status of many of these queer texts also indicate that same-sex relations have not always been completely marginalized or demonized in the South. Indeed, the complexity of these works dispels several myths about the region and highlights the need for more queer studies. First, the fact that so many examples of Southern queerness can be traced from the colonial period onward weakens the myth that the South is the most conservative, homophobic region in the nation. While not disregarding the South's indisputable histories of racism, religious fundamentalism, and intolerance, these works show that Southern writers often charted the boundaries of Southern regionalism by opening up, rather than condemning, the push and pull between deviance and normalcy. Queer Southern work also dispels common assumptions about rural geographies and the figure of the closet. The conventional narrative about nonhetero-sexual identities assumes that people grow from an early period of silence and confusion to a more liberated adult life out of the closet, and this narra-tive often includes a geographic corollary in which queer people must move from the country to the city before they can experience sexual freedom. While there is unquestionably some truth to this model – particularly where social conservatism and intolerance dominate rural, small-town, and sub-urban Southern spaces – the works discussed throughout this chapter also reveal that queerness is inextricable from even the most traditional-looking forms of Southern culture. A narrative arc from secrecy to openness cannot entirely explain the interwoven strands of gothicism, humor, eroticism, and gender play in Southern writing since at least the 1700s. Nor should we expect that greater openness about sexuality in the twenty-first century will limit the shapes and significance of queerness to more homogeneous forms that have little to do with the particular contours of Southern culture. As long as homophobia and violence remain problems in the South (as in the nation), and as long as the myths and meanings attached to Southern culture continue to evolve, Southern writers will always weave provocative, new forms of queerness into their works, pushing the discourses of sexuality in unexpected directions.

NOTES

1 Michael Warner, Introduction to *Fear of a Queer Planet: Queer Politics and Social Theory*, ed. Michael Warner (Minneapolis: University of Minnesota Press, 1993), p. xxvi.
2 Eve Kosofsky Sedgwick, *Tendencies* (Durham, NC: Duke University Press, 1993), p. 8.
3 Andrea Smith, "Queer Theory and Native Studies: The Heteronormativity of Settler Colonialism," *GLQ* 16: 1–2 (2010), p. 44.
4 See K. J. H. Berland, "William Byrd's Sexual Lexicography," *Eighteenth-Century Life* 23:1 (February 1999), pp. 1–11.
5 Michael Kreyling, *Figures of the Hero in Southern Narrative* (Baton Rouge: Louisiana State University Press, 1987), pp. 9–29.

6 I am indebted to Emily E. VanDette for this interpretation.
7 Ronald G. Walters, "The Erotic South: Civilization and Sexuality in American Abolitionism," *American Quarterly* 25:2 (May 1973), pp. 177–201.
8 See John Saillant, "The Black Body Erotic and the Republican Body Politic, 1790–1820," in *Sentimental Men: Masculinity and the Politics of Affect in American Culture*, eds. Mary Chapman and Glenn Hendler (Berkeley: University of California Press, 1999), pp. 89–111; and P. Gabrielle Forman, "Sentimental Abolition in Douglass's Decade: Revision, Erotic Conversion, and the Politics of Witnessing in *The Heroic Slave* and *My Bondage and My Freedom*," in *Sentimental Men*, pp. 149–162.
9 Eric Lott, *Love and Theft: Blackface Minstrelsy and the American Working Class* (New York: Oxford University Press, 1995), pp. 161–168.
10 See Valerie Rohy, "Ahistorical" *GLQ* 12:1 (2006), pp. 61–83.
11 See Siobhan Somerville, *Queering the Color Line: Race and the Invention of Homosexuality in American Culture* (Durham, NC: Duke University Press, 2000).
12 Linda A. Morris, *Gender Play in Mark Twain: Cross-Dressing and Transgression* (Columbia: University of Missouri Press, 2007), p. 2.
13 See Caroline Gebhard, "Reconstructing Southern Manhood: Race, Sentimentality, and Camp in the Plantation Myth," in *Haunted Bodies: Gender and Southern Texts*, eds. Anne Goodwyn Jones and Susan V. Donaldson (Charlottesville: University Press of Virginia, 1997), pp. 132–156.
14 Mary Biggs, "'*Si tu savais*': The Gay/Transgendered Sensibility of Kate Chopin's *The Awakening*," *Women's Studies* 33 (2004), p. 146.
15 Valerie Rohy, *Impossible Women: Lesbian Figures and American Literature* (Ithaca, NY: Cornell University Press, 2000), pp. 91–116; Gary Richards, *Lovers and Beloveds: Sexual Otherness in Southern Fiction, 1936–1961* (Baton Rouge: Louisiana University Press, 2005), pp. 62–93.
16 Sharon Monteith, *Advancing Sisterhood? Interracial Friendships in Contemporary Southern Fiction* (Athens: University of Georgia Press, 2000), p. 77.

14

NAHEM YOUSAF

Immigrant Writers: Transnational Stories of a "Worlded" South

When writers of different ethnic heritages and histories write Southern fiction and explore the changing demographics of the U.S. South, they open up a literary tradition long established as primarily white, and sometimes black as the result of African-American writers having been neglected in the critical exposition of the Southern canon. As Thadious Davies has emphasized in *Southscapes* (2011), no analysis of Southern literary production in its local and global contexts – or, indeed, Southern culture – can ignore the centrality of African Americans, or of their counter-narratives, to an exclusionary story of the region. If Southern literature is racially overdetermined for readers who still expect to find stories raced only as black and white, immigrants and Southern-born writers whose heritage draws on other places tell about the South in new ways and open up "typical" concerns, such as the plantation South and labor on the land, civil wars, and civil rights, to new scrutiny. This essay examines some of the writers whose works extend our understanding of regional identity through their emphasis on the transnational and the global in a more "worlded" South. They include Lan Cao, Susan Choi, Gustavo Pérez Firmat, Monique Truong, and Marcos Villatoro, as well as established Southern writers whose plots and characters contribute to a literary exploration of individuals and groups living according to what are still regarded as "different" cultural traditions in an albeit multicultural South.

Such fictions project the regional studies model outward to forge spatial connections across more fluidly conceptualized landscapes – or ethnoscapes. In Arjun Appadurai's definition, the ethnoscape is an always shifting space insofar as "tourists, immigrants, refugees, exiles, guest workers, and other moving groups and individuals constitute an essential feature of the world and appear to affect the politics of (and between) nations to a hitherto unprecedented degree."[1] In fiction refugees and newly arrived immigrants act as witness characters whose first impressions of the region afford writers the opportunity to consider how the experience of migration impacts myths of continuity and how individuals outside and alienated from the imagined community fare. Fiction is beginning to identify rhizomic communities outside of delimiting ideas of nation-state or regional local color, even though most stories remain decidedly transnational and few intervene creatively in the ideas of globalization that social scientists and anthropologists examine.[2] Stories also reflect and sometimes comment politically on the plight of submerged ethnic groups whose presence in the South is the direct result of their labor but this is most apparent in investigative journalism and documentary film. Stephanie Black's *H-2 Worker* (1990), exposing the plight of migrant and seasonal Jamaican sugarcane harvesters in Florida, and Charles Thompson's *The Guest Worker* (2005), focusing on migrant farm workers in North Carolina, are clear examples of this trend. Such films begin to explore how Jamaicans, Haitians, and Mexican immigrants have taken the place of Southern blacks in the plantation economy.[3]

The twenty-first century has seen a sharp increase in anti-immigration bills in the South and measures to monitor undocumented and illegal aliens have become more draconian, with the Southern Poverty Law Center declaring new laws, like Alabama's HB 56, a humanitarian crisis because it has unleashed vigilantism against the state's Latino population, regardless of immigration status, and "harkens back to the bleakest days of Alabama's racial history"[4] Fiction takes a while to catch up even with such dramatic changes, if writers elect to engage them. There are few examples of what we might call agenda-driven fiction, perhaps because the fear of being topical is almost as powerful as the fear of being political, or of having one's fiction read as sociological, although Tom Wolfe's *A Man in Full* (1998) includes a fearless depiction of Chamblee, Atlanta as a "Chambodia" of legal and illegal immigrants in overcrowded housing, with a Vietnamese labor force tied to a chicken-processing factory. Novels that do expose the harsh realities of migrant labor are revealing, and Martyn Bone notes that Wolfe creates a "sobering example" of "the less glamorous edges of the postsouthern metropolis [where] traditionally 'southern' manual labor is still being performed."[5] David Eggers's *What Is the What* (2006) is one such narrative, a fictionalized autobiography of Valentino Achak Deng, in which the Sudanese refugee is attacked and robbed in his Atlanta apartment by African-American con artists, after having found refuge there, and Deng imagines himself telling his story to each African-American character he encounters in an effort to understand it and to cleave his experience to theirs in an act of historical affiliation. Much more usually in Southern fiction, there are echoes of political events and debates current at the time in which novels are set: the Japanese attack on Pearl Harbor in Augusta Trobaugh's *Sophie and the Rising Sun* (2001); the Korean War and the McCarran-Walter Immigration

Act in Susan Choi's *The Foreign Student* (1998); the aftermath of the U.S. war in Vietnam in Lan Cao's *Monkey Bridge* (1997) and Monique Truong's *Bitter in the Mouth* (2010). Remarkable therefore is Madison Smartt Bell's trilogy of novels on the Haitian Revolution – *All Souls Rising* (1995), *Master of the Crossroads* (2000), and *The Stone that the Builder Refused* (2004) – which, while outside the scope of this essay, is the most sustained evocation of the Caribbean South by a white Southern writer.

White and black Southern writers have, of course, depicted immigrants. Joel Chandler Harris's slave in *The Story of Aaron (So Named) The Son of Ben Ali* (1896) is the son of an Arab slave trader sold into slavery; Flannery O'Connor's Polish immigrant Mr. Guizac in "The Displaced Person" (1955) is killed by a community threatened by his foreignness; and Tennessee Williams's interest in immigrant characters in a changing South is evident across his plays, as Robert Rae reveals in *Globalism in the Southern World of Tennessee Williams* (2010). Early-twentieth-century immigration patterns led to immigrant writers being represented in American letters, but the idea of the South as monocultural persisted as a hard-won myth. This is the image Roy Hoffman critiques in *Chicken Dreaming Corn* (2004), a novel that follows a family from 1916 to 1945 through two world wars, its title a Southern twist on a Romanian saying. As Morris Kleinman sweeps the steps of his store on the morning of a Confederate Veterans' parade, he gazes across the center of Mobile, Alabama, to "the Lebanese clothing store and Syrian pressing shop ... [and] the Greek bakery," across Upper Dauphin Street to the storefronts of Habeeb and Zoghby and Kalifeh, and to Lower Dauphin and businesses run by German Jewish merchants Greenbaum and Leinkauf.[6]

Literature that explores a multicultural South is amassing with writers as different as Robert Olen Butler, Tom Wolfe, Anne Tyler, Cynthia Shearer, and even John Grisham, beginning to explore immigrant experiences. In *Digging to America* (2006), Tyler imagines the adoption of Korean girls by two Baltimore families, the white Donaldsons and the Iranian-American Yazdans, who have very different views on cultural identity and assimilation. Grisham, best known for Mississippi-set legal thrillers, explores tensions between Mexican migrant farmworkers and locals in *A Painted House* (2000), a semi-autobiographical novel he sets in Arkansas. Shearer's *The Celestial Jukebox* (2005) is the most detailed depiction of an ethnically diverse small town. At the center of fictional Madagascar in the Mississippi Delta is Angus Chien's Celestial Grocery situated between an African-American man's property on one side and a white man's on the other. Different plot strands follow Boubicar, newly arrived from Mauritania, who comes to work at the grocery, as well as Mexican laborers and a Honduran family. While a summary impression makes the novel seem an exceptional fetishization of a "multi-culti" South, Shearer's depiction of an imagined community in the Delta may be read as a palimpsest landscape, according to the model in cultural geography that investigates places for their known heritages but also for their least tangible characteristics. Her fiction rests on documented foundations that remain largely unknown outside the region: Chinese laborers migrated to the Delta around 1870, with many setting up groceries for free blacks during Reconstruction, and now comprise the largest Chinese population in a Southern state. The Lebanese became established in the Delta in the 1870s, as Viviane Doche-Boulos detailed in *Cedars by the Mississippi: Lebanese-Americans in the Twin-Cities* (1978); rarely has either group been the topic of fiction, although in *Go Down, Moses* (1942), Faulkner's Isaac McCaslin, ruminating on the Delta, asserts: "*Chinese and African and Aryan and Jew all breed and spawn together until no man has time to say which is which nor ... cares.*"[7]

Robert Olen Butler's Pulitzer Prize–winning stories of Vietnamese communities in Louisiana in *A Good Scent From a Strange Mountain* (1993) were paradigm-setting. While the ethnic group he explores had already spent some twenty years in Louisiana, a Miss Giàu meditating on exile, observes "We are not a community. We are all too sad perhaps, or too tired.... Maybe that's just me saying that. Maybe the others are real Americans already." The idea of an organic community so central to nostalgic conceptions of the region is thrown into sharp relief when writers focus on what is putative and contingent about it. The production of such communities in fiction is dependent on cultural practices and memories shared by some authors and researched by others. Butler served in Vietnam as special agent for U.S. forces but later as a translator, and is attentive to linguistic nuance, as when Miss Giàu explains to her new friend Mr. Cohen that with the voice falling her name means "wealthy" but when he pronounces it like a question, as Giau, she becomes "Miss Pout." Her misinterpretation of Mr. Cohen is the more telling, however, when she assumes that "this very American man" will be celebrating Christmas like all Americans; when she discovers that as a Jew he will not be celebrating this makes him seem to her "not an American really." Having discovered a commonality she deems "strange," Miss Giàu and Mr. Cohen plan to begin the New Year by exploring their affiliation.[8] In the 1996 collection, *The Future of Southern Letters*, Jefferson Humphries, praising Butler's stories, observed in an aside that "surely this community will be speaking in its own voice shortly and we will need critics who know how to properly hear it."[9] Lan Cao, the first Vietnamese American to assay this task, published *Monkey Bridge* a year later, her semi-autobiographical novel exemplifying that sometimes new immigrants find place in fiction before they are studied as a social phenomenon. For Cao, translation is a painful exercise that puts pressure on the mother-daughter relationship that is the novel's focus. Mai chooses not to release her mother's words but to muffle them; reinterpreting her mother for their new surroundings, the English-speaking child navigates life in the South for the parent.

Stereotypes of the insularity of Southern literature are proved untenable when fictions equate the region with other "Souths": South Vietnam in *Monkey Bridge* and in African-American Tony Grooms's novel *Bombingham* (2001), or a journey from South Korea to Charleston, South Carolina and on to South Vietnam in Joe Porcelli's *The Photograph* (1995). Novels emphasizing transnational and diasporic connections are discussed in collections of criticism including *South To A New Place* (2002) and *Look Away! The U.S. South in New World Studies* (2004), where connections are made with East Germany, Italy, Ireland, the Caribbean, and Central and South America. The dual-location fiction or transnational story is becoming one of the South's necessary fictions, with critically acclaimed and new writers recasting it on different continents, and with white writers beginning to pursue African connections to the U.S. South once seemingly only acknowledged by African-American writers. Barbara Kingsolver's *The Poisonwood Bible* (1998) focuses on a family of missionaries leaving the pine-covered Georgia hills for the jungle of the Belgian Congo in the 1950s, and Kathleen Coskran's *The High Price of Everything* (1988) mixes stories set in her birthplace of Georgia with others set in Ethiopia.

So far, however, the South's relation to near neighbors Latin America and the Caribbean has dominated scholarship on Southern literature, via conceptualizations such as "New World Studies," "Calypso Magnolia," the "Neuvo South," and the "American tropics" defined as an "extended Caribbean," which includes the U.S. South, the Atlantic littoral of Central America, the Caribbean islands, and northern South America.[10] Cuban-born and Miami-raised Gustavo Pérez Firmat whose *Life on the Hyphen: The Cuban-American Way* (1994) opened up discussion of "hyphenated" identities, and Martinique's Edouard Glissant who places the South firmly within the plantation and post-plantation cultures of the Americas in his essay in *Look Away!*, have helped extend literary studies beyond the triptych of Edward Said, Homi Bhabha, and Gayatri Spivak underpinning so much theorizing of postcolonial spaces. Bhabha's thesis on the "location of culture," discovering agency in marginality and seditious mimicry, continues to be revealing when used, as Scott Romine posits in *The Real South* (2008), to "resignify" the Southern past. Bhabha's qualification of nationhood and community rests on the idea that those who exist at the margins of the modern nation "disturb the ideological manoeuvres through which 'imagined communities' are given essentialist identities"[11] Melanie Benson pursues such ideas in *Disturbing Calculations: The Economics of Identity in Postcolonial Southern Literature, 1912–2002* (2008), along with "the temporality of repetition" through which marginalized subjects create a "collective agency."[12] Firmat's works, like the poem "Carolina Cuban" (1985) and short story "My Life as a Redneck" (1992), navigate dual identities and play off the cultural adaptability of bilingual writers. Glissant's *Faulkner, Mississippi* (1996) in its unbounded openness to the novelist and the region, and, indeed, Tierno Monénembo's "Faulkner and Me," an inquisitive memoir-styled critical assessment of why West African writers are fascinated by Faulkner, may be read together as a counter-narrative to V. S. Naipaul's *A Turn in the South* (1989) because, as Leigh Anne Duck concludes, where Naipaul ultimately "backs away," Glissant's foray into fictional as well as factual Souths "insists on negotiation."[13]

As Douglass Sullivan-González and Charles Reagan Wilson's *The South and the Caribbean* (2001) shows through insightful comparative analysis, there is no easy consensus between historians, let alone imaginative writers, as to the legacies of plantation slavery that crisscross the Caribbean South. George Handley's "new hemispheric geography" of Plantation America understands the plantation as a transnational phenomenon that challenges myths of exceptionalism, as underlined by Antonio Benítez-Rojo's contention that a plantation society has proliferated as "a repeating island," in a meta-archipelago, replicating a mechanistic and systemically brutal form of economy. Tracing out-migration from plantation economies reveals forms of "new slavery" that disturb ideas of a "post-slavery" present, as demonstrated most recently in Cindy Hahamovitch's *No Man's Land* (2011). Handley's "diasporic poetics of the Americas" is a template for comparative literary studies and may be usefully read alongside the critical work of Deborah Cohn, whose Faulkner-inflected study of "Two Souths" (1999) argues that the "sense of place" that has undergirded Southern critical history is most valuable when "associated with neighboring spaces that share a history" or " some communicable tradition and idiom."[14]

Broad position pieces debating the growing significance of fiction by immigrants are relatively few but include Yousaf and Monteith's "Making an Impression: New Immigrant Fiction in the Contemporary South" (2004) and Martyn Bone's "The Transnational Turn in the South: Region, Nation, Globalization" (2004). Among the crucial foundations that go to build a scholarly archive on the ways in which the global and local intersect in Southern literature are "Postcolonial Theory, the U.S. South, and New World Studies," a special issue of *Mississippi Quarterly* edited by Jon Smith, Kathryn McKee, and Scott Romine, the journal *The Global South* inaugurated in 2007, and McKee and Annette Trefzer's special issue of *American Literature*, titled "Global Contexts, Local Literatures: The New Southern Studies."[15] Until relatively recently, then, in new directions forged by scholars in New Southern Studies, immigrants usually remained quietly outside of Southern literary criticism; not quite black but not white either in a racially bipolar South, they could neither be identified with the segregated status quo nor with the various aspects of pastoral idealism that textured criticism by writers as different as apologists for slavery, opponents to Reconstruction, the Southern Agrarians, and the editors of *The History of Southern Literature* (1985). Augusta Trobaugh sets *Sophie and the Rising Sun* in a pastoral landscape in rural Georgia against whose backdrop gardener Mr. Grover Cleveland Oto, named after the Progressive-era president, is viewed as an eccentric in 1938 but by 1941 as an enemy sympathizer or spy, as were all Japanese-Americans, many of whom were interned in camps in the South. At first, puzzled attempts are made to force this "strangest-looking" man into the racial matrix that is Salty Creek's status quo. "I think he's a colored man. At least he's certainly very dark," allows one white lady, while another admits, "Why, no one in this town had ever seen anything like him." However unobtrusive middle-aged Mr. Oto makes himself, and despite his perfect tending of the symbolic Southern garden, he cannot make a home there during World War II, and certainly not with Sophie, the white lady with whom he falls gently and completely in love and who thinks of him as just Grove, "a peaceful green place." At the end of the novel, without either of them there, the town returns to "normal" with only Miss Anne, whose first-person narrative this is, keeping the couple close in her memories, as testament to her dream that somewhere their love may overcome xenophobia and spite.[16]

While Mr. Oto may be the protagonist in Trobaugh's romance, immigrants have traditionally been auxiliary characters in a narrative's subplot. Consequently, the risk is that he or she will be (under)read as simply one more displaced person in a literary tradition where misfits are legion. Stories that focus on migrants or exiles, imagining a single immigrant in one time and place, are redolent of postcolonial themes of anxiety and displacement but also consigned to a fictional timelock: a solitary foreigner enters the South in a bygone decade, safely historicized and largely invisible unless an event like the Japanese attack on Pearl Harbor thrusts them into view. Susan Choi sets *The Foreign Student* in Tennessee, at the University of the South in Sewanee, where her father became the first Asian student to attend in 1955. But she grapples in interesting ways with protagonist Chang's invisibility, especially when charged by his religious sponsors to explain the war he fled in South Korea to congregations in a very different South: "'Korea is a shape just like Florida. Yes? The top half is a communist state and the bottom half are fighting for democracy!' He would groundlessly compare the [38th] parallel to the Mason-Dixon line, and see every head nod excitedly." Chang's explanation is diminished simile by simile: "This is like, if the war is all over Florida, and our side are trapped in Miami," and MacArthur's landing at Inchon helps Chang present a morally unambiguous story to appreciative listeners.[17]

Chang is a casualty of a civil war but also of the liminal zone in which he exists already, caught in Korea between his father's acculturation to Japanese colonizers and identification with his friend whose politics as a student subversive could not be more different. Chang is an outsider with no place in Korea's new dispensation, and with the arrival of the U.S. State Department, he is renamed Chuck because even his monosyllabic name is too difficult for his boss, from North Carolina, to deal with, and begins to act as a conduit for cultural imperialism. Working for the U.S. Information Service, he translates features from *Time* for Korean news, thereby contributing to the ideology of regime change. In this way he feels that he has crossed over to become "translation's unnatural byproduct" (84), an image that reflects his provisional status as well as his service role. Once in Tennessee, Chang's presence is equally unusual because most immigration around the Korean War comprised of war brides and war orphans, and the McCarran-Walter Immigration Act of 1952, in place until the 1965 Immigration and Nationality Act, allowed only one hundred Koreans a year entry to the United States. Between 1952 and 1965, Korean immigrants were numerically so small, and so scattered geographically, that they represented a hidden minority. Foreign students such as Chang would not have been returned in census figures either. The Committee on Friendly Relations Among Foreign Students organized by the Y in 1911 had stopped sponsoring most student organizations by 1947 and hence stopped keeping count.[18] Chang should therefore be understood as an exceptional figure to stand at the center of a Southern novel.

Nor can Chang acclimatize: he is morosely introspective. In the United States he cannot sleep in an unlocked room and withdraws into cramped places, reiterating his hiding out in a stair cupboard (its width too short to lie down and its height too low for him to kneel) from members of the Korean People's Army who take possession of his family home. His discomfort in Tennessee is also conveyed as an inevitable consequence of the nomad's interregnum, caught and held in a middle space, the U.S. South itself becoming interstitial in this narrative.

Quiet and tentative in the relationships he forges at Sewanee, Chang is most perplexed by the color line. Alone over the Christmas holiday, Chang is expected to dine with Sewanee's black servants, men he greeted with hand-shakes when they met, a breach of protocol the foreign student fails to com-prehend. He retreats, not wanting to be served and aware that his presence spoils their holiday. However, by the end of the novel, he is working with the same group of men to pay his student debts and in their company finally gains a contentment and even friendship. The most revealing of his relation-ships, however, crosses the color line in the other direction: his romantic involvement with Katherine, the young "companion" of a professor thirty years her senior. Accompanying Chang to Jackson, Tennessee, when he gives a talk on Korea, she is mistaken for a Northerner because as a Southern lady she would not be expected to travel alone with him. It is precisely their inability to conform that draws one to the other; Katherine prefers Chang to his "American" name Chuck. The relationship Choi imagines is borne out of pain and loneliness. Katherine suffers an "unmoored feeling" from child-hood when her involvement with Chang's English professor splits her from her family when she is just fifteen. Her relationship has arrested her emo-tional development: for Katherine, a lover to be cherished will inevitably be a man her mother will disapprove of.

The stranger, of course, is a trope in U.S. literature, notable in African-American writing from slavery through civil rights; from Olaudah Equiano's *Interesting Narrative* (1789) to James Baldwin's "Stranger in the Village"(1955), the stranger marks the boundaries of each community he enters. The immigrant as stranger is an interloper that Southern writ-ers deploy to critique tropes such as parochialism and hospitality. Chang is subjected to biting and banal questions, like "Do Koreans live in trees" and "How did you people like the war we had for you?", the same kind of paro-chialism that leads Salty Creek to refer to Mr. Oto as "Miss Anne's Chinese gardener" and an "*ugly, dried up yellow foreigner,*" and a teacher in Boiling Springs, North Carolina to blame a child, Vietnamese immigrant Thuy Mai, for the Japanese attack on Pearl Harbor in Monique Truong's short story "Kelly" (1991).[19] At other times the stranger is figured as a catalyst for a Southern character's understanding, as in Connie May Fowler's 1960s-set *Sugar Cage* (1992), where Haitian guest worker Soleil Marie is instrumental in her white boyfriend's beginning to understand what the civil rights move-ment is fighting for when he "hadn't paid much attention" before meeting her on his uncle's plantation near St. Augustine, Florida.

Multiethnic characters further dispel the myth of a static racial landscape. Writers have used genre fiction to filter new Southern protagonists into pop-ular forms to which readers return for familiarity, like police procedurals and family romances. Marcos McPeek Villatoro's Romilla Chacón is a homicide detective of Salvadoran descent who transfers from Atlanta to Nashville. In

Home Killings (2001), she becomes "the newest Nashville hero" after being
wounded in action while "bringing peace to our city." Chacón is by necessity
finely attuned to her surroundings, assessing each police officer's willingness to work with her, meeting facile assumptions about her background
with barbed wit, and facing down the reason she has been hired in the first
place: "It only takes a couple of cases in which language differences become
an issue in order for someone like [her boss] to throw up his hands and
beg for help."[20] Carolina Garcia-Aguilera's private eye Lupe Solano based
in Miami's Little Havana and Michiro Naito's Alabama-based investigator
Koji Suda combine with Villatoro's Chacón in gaining a foothold in the
genre that its critics conclude illuminates the South as much as the South
illuminates the detective.[21]

Limiting understanding of ethnic marginality, however, can obscure the
racist tensions new immigrants face, as in Toni Morrison's diminution in
1993 of the violent struggle between Texan and Vietnamese shrimpers in her
contention that immigrants will always measure themselves against African
Americans as the only "real aliens" in the United States and that "a hostile
posture toward resident blacks must be struck at the Americanizing door."[22]
It is a view that recalls Malcolm X in the 1960s but inhibits recognition of
the globalizing connections that bring new immigrants to labor in the United
States and fails to allow that acknowledging multiracisms does not equate
to diluting the significance of the brutal history of African-American oppression or resistance to it, as Ishmael Reed has shown in *MultiAmerica* (1997).
Writers and critics of new immigrant stories go some way toward breaking
such assumptions by personalizing immigrant lives in the rural South and
exposing the resentment new communities can suffer. Assumptions about
a black-white continuum unravel when racial segregation is located within
a broader context of meaning: the gradual de-Europeanization of the U.S.
population following World War II, or the fallout of U.S. intervention in
East Asia, the Free Trade movement, political coalitions between African
Americans and Latinos and demonstrations like the 2007 strike of Indian
shipyard "guest workers" in Pascagoula, Mississippi, which included singing civil rights anthem "We Shall Overcome" in Hindi and marching on
Washington.

What has received less attention is how a bicultural aesthetic informs
and provides alternative perspectives on narrative conventions, scripted
stories, and regional imagery, as when Miss Giàu working in the Chinese
restaurant Plantation Hunan thinks, "[T]his plantation house must feel like
a refugee. It is full of foreign smells, ginger and Chinese pepper and fried
shells for wonton."[23] Poetry is often the form in which immigrant writers first explore the emotional vulnerability of living so far from home in

semi-autobiographical modes, with witness figures couched as interlocutors for others living with difference. In *The Arkansas Testament* (1987), Derek Walcott recalls a sojourn in the South in 1958 that was stark, bleak, and lonely. Racial segregation in Fayetteville forces him to seek out "my own area" in restaurants and leads to speculation on Southern progress from "Sherman's smoking march to Atlanta" through "the march to Montgomery," despite which the narrator feels, "I was still nothing. A cipher/in its bubbling black zeros, here." He compares the experience to apartheid South Africa when every "candle-struck" face in the restaurant "stares into the ethnic abyss," and thinks back on the Indian Wars, the Underground Railroad, and "the tinkle of ankle chains running north." In this starkly anti-pastoral testament, his motel room smells of detergent pine, the rug is "pine-needled" shag, and the houses opposite are "Confederate grey." When sunshine floods the cold day, his poetic meter "drop[s] its limp," but for all the poet sees and feels, the only muse available to him is "a toothless sybil in garage tires" that hisses at him: "Your shadow still hurts the South, / like Lee's slowly reversing sword." The poem's persona can only conclude that the Caribbean poet will inevitably "STAY BLACK AND INVISIBLE TO THE SIRENS OF ARKANSAS."²⁴

In the same decade in which Walcott published his memories of the segregated South, Pakistani-born Aurangzeb Alamgir Hashmi took the reader on an imagistic tour of the United States in *My Second in Kentucky* (1981). The title poem evokes the nostalgia the poet feels on a stormy Friday night in "my neighborhood" in his new Kentucky home. Sure that "all mosques are asleep in Lahore," he gazes, "lonely as God," at windows bright with family life and "grunts, Allah."²⁵ A shift from utter dislocation to locating oneself in a Southern neighborhood is apparent, even though the poet remains lonely. Subsequent shifts toward identifying as Southern are signaled in poetry by Firmat for whom affinity to the South looms large (Fermat wrote "Carolina Cuban" on the night his son was born), and in fiction by Monique Truong who in the commentary on her first published short story admits she identifies with Southern writers rather than Asian-American writers, and is most influenced by Faulkner because "I understood his narrative climate better than [Maxine Hong] Kingston's."²⁶

In Truong's first novel, *The Book of Salt* (2003), Vietnamese Binh, a wanderer since being cast off by his homophobic father, becomes the chef to Gertrude Stein and Alice B. Toklas in Paris in 1934 where he embarks on a love affair with a Dr. Lattimore, a biracial Southerner passing for white in Europe. This is surely a sly allusion to Frances E. W. Harper's *Iola Leroy* (1892), in which mixed-race Dr. Lattimore identifies firmly with the black community, refusing to pass even in the post-Reconstruction era. In contrast to his lover, who is a cipher of a racialized South but invisible in France,

Binh is the embodiment of France's colonial history; his "yellow skin … fla-grantly tells my story, or a compacted distorted version of it …. Foreigner, *asiatique*, and, this being Mother France, I must be Indochinese … general-ized and indiscriminate." In Paris, Binh finds his ethnicity amplified, tasted like an exotic cuisine: "They crave the fruits of exile, the bitter juices, and the heavy hearts. They yearn for the taste of the pure sea-salt sadness of the outcast whom they have brought in to their homes." Even when Stein writes about him in her "Book of Salt," casting him in the most elemental of roles, he remains unnamed as the "Little Indochinese."[27] Truong's novel *Bitter in the Mouth* extends such themes and also revisits her first published story, "Kelly." One of Truong's salient literary preoccupations involves the impetus to push Vietnamese characters through the vernacular of silence that surrounds their lives – to create figures caught in specific historical moments and to return to their formative moments, in childhood or ado-lescence, as immigrants or refugees. Binh and Thuy Mai, Truong's speaking protagonist in "Kelly," are subalterns who tell their own stories. Truong radically reworks her central premise of immigrant estrangement in *Bitter in the Mouth*, structuring the novel around a revelation over two days in August 1998 that Truong reels out very slowly: first-person narrator Linda Hammerick, whose Southern family narrative this is, was born Linh-Dao Nguyen in Vietnam. For most of the book she seems totally unaware of this fact because her memories only begin in the summer of 1975 when, aged seven, she is adopted into a Southern Baptist family and welcomed to Boiling Springs, North Carolina by Kelly who becomes her best friend. Linda's grandmother's death-bed warning that "*[w]hat I know about you, little girl, would break you in two*"[28] taunts her with the vital clue that she must trace back into her past to find the truth about herself. Truong deploys a metafictional metaphor whereby the sentences that "land" between Linda and the reader fall like playing cards, with images and events recognizable from her previous works: "The only way to sort out the truth is to pick up the cards again, slowly, examining each one" (5).

Bitter in the Mouth is a brilliantly imaginative work that marks debts to and departures from "classically" Southern literature and comments with gentle irony on the thematically driven enclaves into which some crit-ics risk constraining the rich and heterogeneous breadth of Southern fic-tion. It takes its epigraph from *To Kill A Mockingbird* (1960), specifically the scene in which Atticus points out to daughter Scout that most people, even the poor white Ewell family, are "real nice … when you finally see them." The trope of non-seeing or selective blindness characterizes fiction set in the region. Here the white population of Boiling Springs seems to make a pact of not seeing Linda who comprises "the blind spot" in an otherwise "20–20 field of vision" that distinguishes black from white (170). Linda sees her lawyer father as Atticus and the first boy she likes as Dill but she comes to feel more like the hidden specter and recluse Boo Radley than Scout, although the irony of his unnaturally white skin is not lost on a girl plagued by epithets "gook" and "Jap" throughout elementary school. While adults seem to look past or around her, she suffers a heightened visibility for peers eager to pounce on anyone they deem strange, simultaneously vividly present and opaque. That she suffers secretly from auditory-gustatory synesthesia means she is painfully attuned to the bitter taste of every word spat at her.

A "modern, slightly modified representative of the family" (13), Linda follows generations of Hammerick men to Yale and the attempts she makes to understand herself through her studies may be read as an ironic comment on how critics may locate this novel. She chooses a sophomore psychology class on "The American Family at the end of the 20th Century" subtitled "Dysfunction, What's Your Function?", a Literature seminar on "Dysfunctionalia: Novels of Misspent Southern Youths and their Social Context," as well as a cross-listed Literature and Sociology class "Alienation/ Alien Nation" that teaches her that an aberration is "a mirror that failed to produce an exact image" (133). Truong also interweaves two Southern stories with Linda's that are both "aberrant" and representative: the legend of orphan Virginia Dare, the "first child of our state" raised by Indians, and the story of George Moses, a slave poet. The emotional attachment Linda has to the story of each echoes her coming to consciousness that her own story is also that of an orphan.

While the writer herself may enjoy access to cultural traditions originating outside the region, in her fictions Truong explores gaps in family histories even though protagonists Thuy Mai and Linda identify almost completely with the South as home. Her fiction marks a shift from what Mai in *Monkey Bridge* calls the "anthropologist's eye" she develops to scrutinize the habits of the Vietnamese community in Falls Church, Virginia, to which she belongs but from which she seeks to distinguish herself, even as she acknowledges that such a position exaggerates her own precarious foothold in Southern culture: "one step backwards ... and the entire apparatus of American normalcy could fall right out of synch."[29] While identifying as Southern is precarious and insecure in Truong's "Kelly," in *Bitter in the Mouth* Linda has no such doubts about her homeplace and learns to survive her sense of alterity in a family that refuses to tell her who she once was. The tragedy that makes of her a Hammerick may be compared to Mai's inheritance of Vietnam in *Monkey Bridge* where she discovers her family history is a fiction, a protective veil drawn over her by a mother who seeks to shield her from the truth, namely that her beloved grandfather was a Vietcong agent from whom they escaped to Virginia and that "false lives" and "alternate versions" hide "a family history of sin, revenge and murder" (227, 252). The tragedy of her parents' suspicious deaths in a trailer fire, and of her rescue, is hidden from Linda in an effort to protect her on the part of her adopted father whose first love was her mother Mai-Dao; she is the child they could have had, but in his benevolence he erases her past. After his death, and at the conclusion of the novel, Linda is sitting at the kitchen table at home in Boiling Springs with her white adopted mother DeAnne, his wife, each forgiving the other for what they cannot change. This scene in a southern kitchen acts as a reminder of the ways in which southern women's writing is continually shaken up, as Minrose Gwin has signaled: "anything can happen, anything is possible: new recipes are being formulated ... a kind of fermentation is taking place which is transformative, radical and profoundly woman-centered."[30]

This essay began by reading novels in which isolated and damaged refugee protagonists enter Southern communities. In a global and generically fluid era of Southern studies, narratives by and about immigrants are changing from outsider to insider status, but even the most utopian stories cannot be other than politically charged when read against anti-immigration bills and a post-911 backlash. If some of the most marginal and transitional of Southerners have been immigrants of ethnic heritages who have formed a buffer zone between blacks and whites, by the late twentieth century they became significant characters in Southern literature. In the first decades of the twenty-first century, new immigrants are not only writing themselves into the previously proscribed narratives of Southern identity but amending those scripts by contributing to a shared story of evolving genealogies in the region. Traditionalists may find evidence of the continuity they seek in their stories, but readers and scholars pursuing the New Southern Studies will acknowledge the trajectories the fictions map across post-plantation economies and how they expose the social effects of U.S. colonial incursions. They will read them for the ways in which, to paraphrase Bhabha, they contribute to unpacking the ideological maneuvers through which "Southern literature" was once imagined as distinctively regional, and for what they bring to our evolving apprehension of a more worlded South.

NOTES

1 Arjun Appadurai, *Modernity at Large: Cultural Dimensions of Globalization* (Minneapolis: University of Minnesota Press, 1996), p. 33.

2 Deleuze and Guattari define the rhizome and in *A Thousand Plateaus*, trans. B. Massumi (Minneapolis: University of Minnesota Press, 1987), pp. 20–28.

3 For a detailed reading of Black's film, see my essay, "A Sugar Cage: Poverty and Protest in Stephanie Black's *H-2 Worker*," in *Poverty and Progress in the U.S. South since 1920*, eds. Suzanne Jones and Mark Newman (Amsterdam: VU Press, 2006), pp. 155–166.

4 "Alabama's Shame: HB 56 and the War on Immigrants," Southern Poverty Law Center at http://www.splcenter.org/alabamas-shame-hb56-and-the-war-on-immigrants. See, for example, features such as Kathy Lohr's "In Southern States, Immigration Law Battle Rages On," NPR, March 28, 2012, and posts such as "Southern States: Immigration's New Battlefield," *New American Media*, July 18, 2007, at http://news.newamericamedia.org/news/view_article.html?article_id=b2d00dcf68061446b673f55963acf6a8 (accessed January 12, 2012).

5 Martyn Bone, *The Postsouthern Sense of Place in Contemporary Fiction* (Baton Rouge: Louisiana State University Press, 2005), p. 212.

6 Roy Hoffman, *Chicken Dreaming Corn* (Athens: University of Georgia Press, 2004), pp. 3–4.

7 William Faulkner, "Delta Autumn," in *Go Down, Moses and Other Stories* (London: Chatto and Windus, 1960), p. 258.

8 Robert Olen Butler, "Snow," in *A Good Scent from a Strange Mountain* (London: Minerva, 1993), pp. 134, 129.

9 Jefferson Humphries, "Introduction," in *The Future of Southern Letters*, eds. Jefferson Humphries and John Lowe (Oxford: Oxford University Press), p. 16.

10 For example, Jon Smith and Deborah Cohn's Introduction to *Look Away! The U.S. South in New World Studies*, eds. Smith and Cohn (Durham, NC: Duke University Press, 2004), pp. 1–24; John Lowe, "'Calypso Magnolia': The Caribbean Side of the South," *South Central Review* 22.1 (2005): 54–80; the American Tropics project was based at Essex University at http://www.essex.ac.uk/lifts/American_Tropics/index.htm

11 Homi Bhabha, "DissemiNation," in *Nation and Narration*, ed. Homi Bhabha (London: Routledge, 1990), p. 300.

12 Bhabha, *The Location of Culture* (New York: Routledge, 1994), p. 199.

13 Monénembo in *Global Faulkner*, eds. Annette Trefzer and Ann J. Abadie (Jackson: University Press of Mississippi, 2009), pp. 174–183; Duck, "Travel and Transference: V.S. Naipaul and the Plantation Past," in *Look Away!*, p. 169.

14 George B. Handley, *Postslavery Literatures in the Americas: Family Portraits in Black and White* (Charlottesville: University Press of Virginia, 2000); Antonio Benítez-Rojo, *The Repeating Island: The Caribbean and the Postmodern Perspective* (Durham, NC: Duke University Press, 1996); Deborah Cohn, *History and Memory in the Two Souths: Recent Southern and Spanish American Fiction* (Nashville, TN: Vanderbilt University Press, 1999).

15 Nahem Yousaf and Sharon Monteith in *Forum for Modern Language Studies* 40:2 (2004): 214–224; Bone in *Transnational America: Contours of Modern US Culture*, eds. Clara Juncker and Russell Duncan (Copenhagen: Museum Tuscalanum, 2004), pp. 217–235.

16 Augusta Trobaugh, *Sophie and the Rising Sun* (London: Time Warner, 2002), pp. 21, 87.

17 Susan Choi, *The Foreign Student* (New York: Harper, 1998), pp. 51–52.

18 Liping Bu, "The Challenge of Race Relations: American Ecumenism and Foreign Student Nationalism, 1900–140," *Journal of American Studies* 35:2 (2001), pp. 217–237.

19 Yousaf and Monteith, "'I was Pearl and my last name was Harbor': Ethnic Southern Memory and Monique Thuy-Dung Truong's 'Kelly'," *North Carolina Literary Review* special issue "Ethnic North Carolina," ed. Margaret Bauer (2004), pp. 113–122.

20 Marcos McPeek Villatoro, *Home Killings* (Houston, TX: Arte Publico Press, 2001), pp. 241, 16.

21 J. K. Van Dover and John F. Jebb, *Isn't Justice Always Unfair?: The Detective in Southern Literature* ([Bowling Green, OH: Bowling Green State University Press, 1996), p. 360.

22 Toni Morrison, "On the Backs of Blacks," *Time*, December 2, 1993.

23 Butler, p. 126.

24 Derek Walcott, *The Arkansas Testament* (New York: Farrar, Straus and Giroux, 1987), pp. 104–117.

25 Alamgir Hashmi, *My Second in Kentucky* (Lahore, Pakistan: Vision Press, 1981), pp. 22–23.

26 Monique Thuy-Dung Truong, "Kelly," *Amerasia Journal* 17:2 (1991): 41–49].

27 Monique Truong, *The Book of Salt* (London: Chatto and Windus, 2003), pp. 152, 19.

28 Monique Truong, *Bitter in the Mouth* (London: Chatto and Windus, 2010), p. 12. Subsequent references are included in parentheses.

29 Lan Cao, *Monkey Bridge* (New York: Penguin, 1997), p. 212. Subsequent references are included in parentheses.

30 Minrose Gwin, "Sweeping the Kitchen: Revelation and Revolution in Contemporary Southern Women's Writing," *Southern Quarterly* 30 (Winter-Spring 1992): 54–55.

FURTHER READING

Region and Genre

Cox, Karen L. *Dreaming of Dixie: How the South Was Created in American Popular Culture*. Chapel Hill: The University of North Carolina Press, 2011.

Greeson, Jennifer. *Our South: Geographic Fantasy and the Rise of National Literature*. Cambridge: Harvard University Press, 2010.

Guterl, Matthew Pratt. *American Mediterranean: Southern Slaveholders in the Age of Emancipation*. Cambridge, MA: Harvard University Press, 2008.

Handley, George. *Postslavery Literatures in the Americas: Family Portraits in Black and White*. Charlottesville: University Press of Virginia, 2000.

Inge, M. Thomas and Ed Piacentino, eds. *Southern Frontier Humor: An Anthology*. Columbia: University of Missouri Press, 2010.

Johnson, Sherita L. *Black Women in New South Literature and Culture*. New York: Routledge, 2009.

Jones, Paul Christian. *Unwelcome Voices: Subversive Fiction in the Antebellum South*. Knoxville: The University of Tennessee Press, 2005.

Ladd, Barbara. *Nationalism and the Color Line in George W. Cable, Mark Twain, and William Faulkner*. Baton Rouge: Louisiana State University Press, 1996.

Piacentino, Ed. "New Explorations of Antebellum Southern Humor." *Mississippi Quarterly* 64.3-4 (2011): 597–610.

Romine, Scott. *The Narrative Forms of Southern Community*. Baton Rouge: Louisiana State University Press, 1999.

Rubin, Louis D. *Edge of the Swamp: A Study in the Literature and Society of the Old South*. Baton Rouge: Louisiana State University Press, 1989.

Rubin Jr., Louis D., Blyden Jackson, Rayburn S. Moore, Lewis P. Simpson. and Thomas Daniel Young eds *The History of Southern Literature*. Baton Rouge: Louisiana State University Press, 1985.

Simpson, Lewis P. *The Brazen Face of History: Studies in the Literary Consciousness in America*. Baton Rouge: Louisiana State University Press, 1980.

Weaks, Mary Louise, and Carolyn Perry. *Southern Women's Writing: Colonial to Contemporary*. Gainesville: University of Florida Press, 1995.

Wilson, Charles Reagan. *Baptized in Blood: The Religion of the Lost Cause, 1865–1920*. Athens: The University of Georgia Press, 2009.

Slave and Neo-Slave Narratives

Andrews, William L. *To Tell a Free Story: The First Century of Afro-American Autobiography, 1760–1865*. Urbana: University of Illinois Press, 1986.

Andrews, William L., Frances Smith Foster, and Trudier Harris, eds. *The Oxford Companion to African American Literature*. Oxford: Oxford University Press, 1997.

Beaulieu, Elizabeth Anne. *Black Women Writers and the American Neo-Slave Narrative: Femininity Unfettered*. Santa Barbara: Praeger, 1999.

Bell, Bernard W. *The Afro-American Novel and Its Tradition*. Amherst: University of Massachusetts Press, 1987.

Davis, Charles T. and Henry Louis Gates Jr., eds. *The Slave's Narrative*. Oxford: Oxford University Press, 1985;

Dubey, Madhu. *Signs and Cities: Black Literary Postmodernism*. Chicago: University of Chicago Press, 2003.

Fisch, Audrey A., ed. *The Cambridge Companion to the African American Slave Narrative*. Cambridge: Cambridge University Press, 2007.

Graham, Maryemma, ed. *The Cambridge Companion to the African American Novel*. Cambridge: Cambridge University Press, 2004.

Keizer, Arlene B. *Black Subjects: Identity Formation in the Contemporary Narrative of Slavery*. Ithaca: Cornell University Press, 2004.

Mitchell, Angelyn. *The Freedom to Remember*. New Brunswick: Rutgers University Press, 2002.

Rody, Caroline. *The Daughter's Return. African and Caribbean Women's Fictions of History*. Oxford: Oxford University Press, 2001.

Rushdy, Ashraf H. A. *Neo-Slave Narratives. Studies in the Social Logic of a Literary Form*. Oxford: Oxford University Press, 1999.

Remembering Generations: Race and Family in Contemporary African American Fiction. Chapel Hill: University of North Carolina Press, 2001.

Ryan, Tim A. *Calls and Responses: The American Novel of Slavery since* Gone with the Wind. Baton Rouge: Louisiana State University Press, 2008.

Sekora, John and Darwin T. Turner, eds. *The Art of Slave Narrative: Original Essays in Criticism and Theory*. Macomb: Western Illinois University Press, 1982.

Sievers, Stephanie. *Liberating Narratives. The Authorization of Black Female Voices in African American Women Writers' Novels of Slavery*. Hamburg: Lit Verlag, 1999.

Spaulding, Timothy. *Re-Forming the Past : History, the Fantastic, and the Postmodern Slave Narrative*. Columbus: Ohio State University Press, 2005.

Literature and the Civil War

Bernath, Michael T. *Confederate Minds: The Struggle for Intellectual Independence in the Civil War South*. Chapel Hill: University of North Carolina Press, 2010.

Blight, David. *Race and Reunion: The Civil War in American Memory*. Cambridge, MA: Harvard University Press, 2001.

Bonner, Robert E. *Mastering America: Southern Slaveholders and the Crisis of American Nationhood*. New York: Cambridge University Press, 2009.

Carnes, Mark C., Ted Mico, John Miller-Monzon, and David Rubel, eds. *Past Imperfect: History According to the Movies*. New York: Henry Holt and Co., 1995.

Fahs, Alice. *The Imagined Civil War: Popular Literature of the North and South, 1861–1865*. Chapel Hill: University of North Carolina Press, 2001.

Fahs, Alice, and Joan Waugh, eds. *The Memory of the Civil War in American Culture*. Chapel Hill: University of North Carolina Press, 2004.

Fields, Annie A., ed. *Life and Letters of Harriet Beecher Stowe*. Whitefish: Kessinger Publishing, 2004.

Foote, Shelby. *The Civil War*, 3 vols. London: Pimlico, 1992.

Fuller, Randall. *From Battlefields Rising: How the Civil War Transformed American Literature*. New York: Oxford University Press, 2010.

Hutchison, Coleman, *Apples & Ashes: Literature, Nationalism, and the Confederate States of America*. Athens: University of Georgia Press, 2012.

Kaufman, Will. *The Civil War in American Culture*. Edinburgh: Edinburgh University Press, 2006.

Lang, Robert, ed. *The Birth of a Nation*. New Brunswick: Rutgers University Press, 1994.

Loewen, James W. and Edward H. Sebesta, eds. *The Confederate and Neo-Confederate Reader: The "Great Truth" about the "Lost Cause."* Jackson: University Press of Mississippi, 2010.

McPherson, James M. *Battle Cry of Freedom: The Civil War Era*. New York: Oxford University Press, 1988.

Nickels, Cameron. *Civil War Humor*. Jackson: University Press of Mississippi, 2010.

Panabaker, James. *Shelby Foote and the Art of History: Two Gates to the City*. Knoxville: University of Tennessee Press, 2004.

Toplin, Robin Brent, ed., *Ken Burns's The Civil War: Historians Respond* New York: Oxford University Press, 1996.

Warren, Craig A. *Scars to Prove It: The Civil War Soldier and American Fiction*. Kent: Kent State University Press, 2009.

Watson, Jay. *Reading for the Body: The Recalcitrant Materiality of Southern Fiction, 1893-1985*. Athens: University of Georgia Press, 2012.

Literature and Reconstruction

Blight, David. *American Oracle: The Civil War in the Civil Rights Era*. Cambridge: Belknap Press of Harvard University Press, 2011.

Brodhead, Richard. *Cultures of Letters: Scenes of Reading and Writing in Nineteenth Century America*. Chicago: University of Chicago Press, 1993.

Du Bois, W. E. B. *Black Reconstruction in America: An Essay toward a History of the Part Which Black Folk Played in the Attempt to Reconstruct Democracy in America, 1860–1880*. Oxford: Oxford University Press, 2007.

Fulton, Joe B. *The Reconstruction of Mark Twain: How a Confederate Bushwhacker Became the Lincoln of Our Literature*. Baton Rouge: Louisiana State University Press, 2010.

González, John Morán. *The Troubled Union: Expansionist Imperatives in Post-Reconstruction American Novels*. Columbus: The Ohio State University Press, 2010.

Griffin, Martin. *Ashes of the Mind: War and Memory in Northern Literature, 1865-1900.* Amherst: University of Massachusetts Press, 2009.

Guterl, Matthew Pratt, *American Mediterranean: Southern Slaveholders in the Age of Emancipation.* Cambridge: Harvard University Press, 2008.

Kaplan, Amy. "Nation, Region, Empire." In *The Columbia History of the American Novel: New Views,* ed. Emory Elliot. New York: Columbia University Press, 1991.

Leiter, Andrew. *In the Shadow of the Black Beast: African American Masculinity in the Harlem and Southern Renaissances.* Baton Rouge: Louisiana State University Press, 2010.

Schmidt, Peter. *Sitting in Darkness: New South Fiction, Education, and Rise of Jim Crow Colonialism, 1865-1920.* Jackson: University Press of Mississippi, 2008.

Silber, Nina. *The Romance of Reunion: Northerners and the South, 1865-1900.* Chapel Hill: University of North Carolina Press, 1993.

Taylor, Melanie Benson. *Reconstructing the Native South: American Indian Literature and the Lost Cause.* Athens: University of Georgia Press, 2012.

Woodward, C. Vann. *The Strange Career of Jim Crow.* New York: Oxford University Press, 1957.

Poetry and Song

Blotner, Joseph. *Robert Penn Warren: A Biography.* New York: Random House, 1997.

Burt, Stephen. *Randall Jarrell and His Age.* New York: Columbia University Press, 2003.

Dickey, James. *Self-Interviews.* New York: Doubleday and Company, 1970.

Jones, Meta DuEwa. *The Muse is Music: Jazz Poetry from the Harlem Renaissance to Spoken Word.* Champaign: University of Illinois Press, 2011.

Lofaro, Michael, ed. Agee at 100: *Centennial Essays on the Works of James Agee.* Knoxville: University of Tennessee Press, 2012.

Moffett, Joe. *Understanding Charles Wright.* Columbia: University of South Carolina Press, 2008.

Salvaggio, Ruth. *Hearing Sappho in New Orleans: The Call of Poetry from Congo Square to the Ninth Ward.* Baton Rouge: Louisiana State University Press, 2012.

Turner, Daniel Cross. *Southern Crossings: Poetry, Memory, and the Transcultural South.* Knoxville: University of Tennessee Press, 2012.

Underwood, Thomas A. *Allen Tate: Orphan of the South.* Princeton: Princeton University Press, 2000.

Warren, Robert Penn. "The Art of Fiction No 18." Interview conducted with Ralph Ellison and Eugene Walter. *Paris Review.* Spring/Summer 1957, no. 16: 112–140.

Watkins, Floyd C. and John T. Hiers. *Robert Penn Warren Talking: Interviews, 1950–1978.* New York: Random House, 1980.

Wright, Charles. *Quarter Notes: Improvisations and Interviews.* Ann Arbor: University of Michigan Press, 1988.

Modernists and Modernity

Baker, Houston. *Turning South Again: Re-Thinking Modernism/Re-Reading Booker T.* Durham: Duke University Press 2010.

Bartley, Numan V. *The New South, 1945–1980: The Story of the South's Modernization*. Baton Rouge: Louisiana State University Press, 1995.

Brooks, Cleanth, and Robert Penn Warren. *Understanding Fiction*. New York: F. S. Crofts, 1943.

Cash, W. J. *The Mind of the South*. New York: Vintage, 1991.

Dolinar, Bryan. *The Black Cultural Front: Black Writers and Artists of the Depression Generation*. Jackson: University Press of Mississippi, 2012.

Duck, Leigh Anne. *The Nation's Region: Southern Modernism, Segregation, and U.S. Nationalism*. Athens: University of Georgia Press, 2006.

Gray, Richard. *The Literature of Memory*. Cambridge: Cambridge University Press, 1977.

Guinn, Matthew. *After Southern Modernism*. Jackson: University Press of Mississippi, 2000.

Kreyling, Michael. *Inventing Southern Literature*. Jackson: University Press of Mississippi, 1998.

Ladd, Barbara, *Nationalism and the Color Line in George W. Cable, Mark Twain, and William Faulkner*. Louisiana State University Press, 1996.

Twelve Southerners. *I'll Take My Stand: The South and the Agrarian Tradition*. Baton Rouge: Louisiana State University Press, 2006.

Watts, Trent. *One Homogenous People: Narratives of White Southern Identity, 1890-1920*. Knoxville: University of Tennessee Press, 2010.

Poverty and Progress

Ciuba, Gary M. *Desire, Violence, and Divinity in Modern Southern Fiction*. Baton Rouge: Louisiana State University Press, 2007.

Clabough, Casey. *Inhabiting Contemporary Southern and Appalachian Literature: Region and Place in the Twenty-First Century*. Gainesville: University Press of Florida, 2012.

Fite, Gilbert C. *Cotton Fields No More: Southern Agriculture, 1865–1980*. Lexington: University Press of Kentucky, 1984.

Godden, Richard and Martin Crawford, eds. *Reading Southern Poverty Between the Wars, 1918–1939*. Athens: University of Georgia Press, 2006.

Gray, Richard. *Southern Aberrations: Writers of the American South and the Problems of Regionalism*. Baton Rouge: Louisiana State University Press, 2000.

Harrington, Michael. *The Other America: Poverty in the United States*. London: Penguin, 1969.

Jones, Jacqueline. *The Dispossessed: America's Underclasses from the Civil War to the Present*. New York: Basic Books, 1992.

Jones, Suzanne and Mark Newman, eds. *Poverty and Progress in the U.S. South since 1920*. Amsterdam: VU University Press, 2006.

Pimpare, Stephen. *A People's History of Poverty in America*. New York: The New Press, 2008.

Trezer, Annette. *Disturbing Indians: The Archaeology of Southern Fiction*. Tuscaloosa: University of Alabama Press, 2007.

Wray, Matt. *Not Quite White: White Trash and the Boundaries of Whiteness*. Durham: Duke University Press, 2006.

Wray, Matt and Annalee Newitz, eds. *White Trash: Race and Class in America*. New York: Routledge, 1997.

The Southern Renaissance and the Faulknerian South

Bradbury, John M. *Renaissance in the South: A Critical History of the Literature, 1920–1960*. University North Carolina Press, 1963.

Brinkmeyer, Robert H., Jr. "The Southern Literary Renaissance." In *A Companion to the Literature and Culture of the US South*, eds. Richard Gray and Owen Robinson. Oxford: Wiley-Blackwell, 2004.

Fowler, Doreen. *Drawing the Line: Boundary Negotiation from Faulkner to Morrison*. Charlottesville: University of Virginia Press, 2013.

Fowler, Doreen and Ann J. Abadie, eds. *Faulkner and the Southern Renaissance*. Jackson: University Press of Mississippi, 1981.

Godden, Richard. *Fictions of Labor: William Faulkner and the South's Long Revolution*. Cambridge: Cambridge University Press, 1997.

Jones, Anne Goodwyn. "The Work of Gender in the Southern Renaissance." In *Southern Writers and Their Worlds*, eds. Christopher Morris and Steven G. Reinhardt. College Station, TX: A&M Press, 1996.

King, Richard H. *A Southern Renaissance: The Cultural Awakening of the American South, 1930–1955*. New York: Oxford University Press, 1982.

Leiter, Andrew B. *In the Shadow of the Black Beast: African American Masculinity in the Harlem and Southern Renaissances*. Baton Rouge: Louisiana State University Press, 2010.

Manning, Carol S. "Southern Women Writers and the Beginning of the Renaissance." In *The History of Southern Women's Literature*. Baton Rouge: Louisiana State University Press, 2002.

Matthews, John T. *William Faulkner: Seeing Through the South*. Oxford: Wiley-Blackwell, 2009.

Millichap, Joseph. *A Backward Glance: The Southern Renascence: The Autobiographical Epic, and the Classical Legacy*. Knoxville: University of Tennessee Press, 2009.

Mishkin, Tracy. *The Harlem and Irish Renaissances: Language, Identity, and Representation*. Gainesville: Florida University Press, 1997.

Polk, Noel. *Children of the Dark House: Text and Context in Faulkner*. Jackson: University Press of Mississippi, 1998.

Richards, Gary. "'With a Special Emphasis': The Dynamics of (Re)Claiming a Queer Southern Renaissance." *Mississippi Quarterly* 55 (Spring 2002): 209–229.

Rubin, Louis Jr. and Robert D. Jacobs. *Southern Renascence: The Literature of the Modern South*. Baltimore: Johns Hopkins University Press, 1953.

Sundquist, Eric. *Faulkner: The House Divided*. Baltimore: Johns Hopkins University Press, 1983.

Woodward, C. Vann. "Why the Southern Renaissance?" In *The Future of the Past*. New York: Oxford University Press, 1991.

Southern Women Writers

Brown, Carolyn J. *A Daring Life: A Biography of Eudora Welty*. Jackson: University Press of Mississippi, 2012.

Claxton, Mae Miller. *Conversations with Dorothy Allison*. Jackson: University Press of Mississippi, 2012.

Dyer, Joyce, ed. *Bloodroot: Reflections on Place by Appalachian Women Writers*. Lexington: University Press of Kentucky, 1998.

Gordon, Sarah, ed. *Flannery O'Connor: In Celebration of Genius*. Athens, GA: Hill Street Press, 2000.

Henninger, Katherine. *Ordering the Façade: Photography and Contemporary Southern Women's Writing*. Chapel Hill: University of North Carolina Press, 2007.

Inge, Tonette, ed. *Southern Women Writers: The New Generation*. Tuscaloosa: University of Alabama Press, 1990.

Jones, Anne Goodwyn. *Tomorrow Is Another Day: The Woman Writer in the South, 1859–1936*. Baton Rouge: Louisiana State University Press, 1995.

Jones, Gayl. *Liberating Voices: Oral Tradition in African American Literature*. Cambridge, MA: Harvard University Press, 1991.

Jones, Suzanne, *Race Mixing*. Baltimore: Johns Hopkins Press, 2006.

Lewis, Nghana Tamu. *Entitled to the Pedestal: Place, Race, and Progress in White Southern Women's Writing, 1920–1945*. Iowa City: University of Iowa Press, 2007.

Magee, Rosemary M., ed. *Friendship and Sympathy: Communities of Southern Women Writers*. Jackson: University Press of Mississippi, 1992.

Manning, Carol S., ed. *The Female Tradition in Southern Literature*. Urbana: University of Illinois Press, 1993.

McHaney, Pearl Amelia, ed. *Eudora Welty: Writers' Reflections upon First Reading Welty*. Columbia: University of South Carolina Press, 2010.

Mills, Fiona, and Keith Mitchell, eds. *After the Pain: Critical Essays on Gayl Jones*. New York: Peter Lang, 2006.

Monteith, Sharon. *Advancing Sisterhood? Interracial Friendships in Contemporary Southern Fiction*. Athens: University of Georgia Press, 2000.

Perry, Carolyn, and Mary Louise Weaks, ed. *The History of Southern Women's Literature*. Baton Rouge: Louisiana State University Press, 2002.

Pollack, Harriet, ed. *Eudora Welty, Whiteness, and Race*. Athens: U of Georgia P, 2013.

Polk, Noel. *Faulkner and Welty and the Southern Literary Tradition*. Jackson: University Press of Mississippi, 2010.

Prenshaw, Peggy Whitman, ed. *Women Writers of the Contemporary South*. Jackson: University Press of Mississippi, 1984.

Prenshaw, Peggy Whitman, ed. *Conversations with Eudora Welty*. Jackson: University Press of Mississippi, 1984.

Prenshaw, Peggy Whitman. *Composing Selves: Southern Women and Autobiography*. Baton Rouge: Louisiana State University Press, 2011.

Scott, Neil R., and Irwin H. Streight, ed. *Flannery O'Connor: Contemporary Reviews*. Cambridge: Cambridge University Press, 2009.

Shloss, Carol. *Flannery O'Connor's Dark Comedies: The Limits of Inference*. Baton Rouge: Louisiana State University Press, 2012.

Tate, Linda. *A Southern Weave of Women: Fiction of the Contemporary South*. Athens: University of Georgia Press, 1994.

Yaeger, Patricia. *Dirt and Desire: Reconstructing Southern Women's Writing, 1930–1990*. Chicago: University of Chicago Press, 2000.

Hollywood South

Barker, Deborah and Kathryn McKee, eds. *American Cinema in the Southern Imaginary*. Athens: University of Georgia Press, 2011.

Boon, Kevin Alexander, *Script Culture and the American Screenplay*. Detroit: Wayne State University Press, 2008.

Brooker-Bowers, Nancy. *The Hollywood Novel and Other Novels about Film, 1912–1982: An Annotated Bibliography*. New York: Garland, 1985.

Campbell, Edward D. C., Jr. *The Celluloid South: Hollywood and the Southern Myth*. Knoxville: University of Tennessee Press, 1981.

Couchman, Jeffrey. *The Night of the Hunter: A Biography of a Film*. Evanston: Northwestern University Press, 2009.

Cripps, Thomas. *Making Movies Black: The Hollywood Message Movie from World War II to the Civil Rights Era*. Oxford: Oxford University Press, 1993.

Dick, Bernard F. *Hellman in Hollywood*. Rutherford: Fairleigh Dickinson University Press, 1982.

French, Warren, ed. *The South and Film*. Jackson: University Press of Mississippi, 1981.

Graham, Allison. *Framing the South: Hollywood, Television and Race During the Civil Rights Struggle*. Baltimore: Johns Hopkins University Press, 2001.

Graham, Allison and Sharon Monteith, eds. *New Encyclopedia of Southern Culture, Volume 18: Media*. Chapel Hill: University of North Carolina Press, 2011.

Heider, Karl G., ed. *Images of the South: Constructing a Regional Culture on Film and Video* Athens: University of Georgia Press, 1993.

Kreyling, Michael. *The South that Wasn't There: Postsouthern Memory and History*. Baton Rouge: Louisiana State University Press, 2010.

Lurie, Peter. *Vision's Impermanence: Faulkner, Film, and the Popular Imagination*. Durham: Duke University Press, 2003.

McPherson, Tara. *Reconstructing Dixie: Race, Gender, and Nostalgia in the Imagined South*. Durham: Duke University Press, 2003.

McWhirter, David B. "Eudora Welty Goes to the Movies: Modernism, Regionalism, Global. Media." *Modern Fiction Studies* 55.1 (2009): 68–91.

Palmer, R. Barton and William Robert Bray. *Hollywood's Tennessee: The Williams Films and Postwar America*. Austin: University of Texas Press, 2009.

Price, Steven. *The Screenplay: Authorship, Theory and Criticism*. London: Palgrave Macmillan, 2010.

Romine, Scott. *The Real South: Southern Narrative in the Age of Cultural Reproduction*. Baton Rouge: Louisiana State University Press, 2008.

Civil Rights Fiction

Dabbs, James McBride. *Civil Rights in Recent Southern Fiction*. Atlanta: Southern Regional Council, 1969.

Haddox, Thomas. "Elizabeth Spencer, the White Civil Rights Novel, and the Postsouthern." *Modern Language Quarterly* 65.4 (2004): 561–581.

Harris, Trudier. "The Power of Martyrdom: The Incorporation of Martin Luther King and His Philosophy into African American Literature." In *Media, Culture and the Modern African Freedom Struggle*, ed. Brian Ward. Gainesville: University Press of Florida, 2001.

King, Richard H. "The Discipline of Fact/ The Freedom of Fiction?" *Journal of American Studies* 25 (1991): 171–188.

King, Richard. H. "Politics and Fictional Representation: The Case of the Civil Rights Movement." In *The Making of Martin Luther King and the Civil Rights Movement*, eds. Brian Ward and Anthony Badger. London: Macmillan, 1996.

Melosh, Barbara. "Historical Memory in Fiction: The Civil Rights Movement in Three Novels," *Radical History Review* (Winter 1988): 64–76.

Metress, Christopher. "Making Civil Rights Harder: Literature, Memory, and the BlackFreedom Struggle," *The Southern Literary Journal*, 40.2 (Spring 2008): 138–150.

Monteith, Sharon. "Revisiting the 1960s in Contemporary Fiction: 'Where Do We Go From Here?'" In *Gender and the Civil Rights Movement*, eds. Peter Ling and Sharon Monteith. New Brunswick: Rutgers 2004.

"'The 1960s Echo On': Images of Martin Luther King as Deployed by White Writers of Contemporary Fiction." In *Media, Culture and the Modern African Freedom Struggle*, ed. Brian Ward. Gainesville: University of Florida Press, 2001.

"SNCC's Stories at the Barricades." In *From Sit-Ins to SNCC: Student Civil Rights Protest in the 1960s*, eds. Philip Davies and Iwan Morgan. Gainesville: University of Florida Press, 2012.

Richardson, Riché. *Black Masculinity and the U.S. South: From Uncle Tom to Gangsta*. Athens: University of Georgia Press, 2007.

Walker, Melissa. *Down from the Mountaintop: Black Women's Novels in the Wake of the Civil Rights Movement, 1966 – 1989*. New Haven: Yale University Press, 1991.

Southern Drama

Andreach, Robert J. *Understanding Beth Henley*. Columbia: University of South Carolina Press, 2006.

Avery, Laurence G. ed. *A Paul Green Reader*. Chapel Hill: University of North Carolina Press, 1998.

Dunlap, William. *A History of American Theatre from Its Origins to 1832*. Urbana: University of Illinois Press, 2005.

Fesmire, Julia A., ed. *Beth Henley: A Casebook*. New York: Routledge, 2002.

Griffin, Alice. *Understanding Tennessee Williams*. Columbia: University of South Carolina Press, 2011.

Griffin, Alice, and Geraldine Thorsten. *Understanding Lillian Hellman*. Columbia: University of South Carolina Press, 2010.

Hampton, Wilborn. *Horton Foote: America's Storyteller*. New York: Free Press, 2009.

Hutchisson, James M. *DuBose Heyward: A Charleston Gentleman and the World of Porgy and Bess*. Jackson: University Press of Mississippi, 2000.

Leverich, Lyle. *Tom: The Unknown Tennessee Williams*. New York: Crown, 1995.

Lott, Eric. *Love and Theft: Blackface Minstrelsy and the American Working Class*. New York: Oxford University Press, 1995.

McDonald, Robert, and Linda Rohrer Paige, eds. *Southern Women Playwrights: New Essays in History and Criticism*. Tuscaloosa: University of Alabama Press, 2002.

Miller, Tice L. *Entertaining the Nation: American Drama in the Eighteenth and Nineteenth Centuries.* Carbondale: Southern Illinois University Press, 2007.

Richards, Jeffrey H. *Early American Drama.* New York: Penguin, 1997.

Saddik, Annette J. *The Politics of Reputation: The Critical Reception of Tennessee Williams' Later Plays.* Madison: Farleigh Dickinson, 1999.

Savran, David. *Communists, Cowboys, and Queers: The Politics of Masculinity in the Work of Arthur Miller and Tennessee Williams.* Minneapolis: University of Minnesota Press, 1992.

Seniors, Paula Marie. *Beyond Lift Every Voice and Sing: The Culture of Uplift, Identity, and Politics in Black Musical Theater.* Columbus: Ohio State University Press, 2009.

Stempel, Larry. *Showtime: A History of the Broadway Musical Theater.* New York: Norton, 2010.

Watson, Charles S. *The History of Southern Drama.* Lexington: University Press of Kentucky, 1997.

Queering the South

Berland, K. J. H. "William Byrd's Sexual Lexicography," *Eighteenth-Century Life* 23.1 (February 1999): 1–11.

Bibler, Michael P. *Cotton's Queer Relations: Same-Sex Intimacy and the Literature of the Southern Plantation, 1936–1968.* Charlottesville: University of Virginia Press, 2009.

Biggs, Mary. "'*Si tu savais*': The Gay/Transgendered Sensibility of Kate Chopin's *The Awakening*," *Women's Studies* 33 (2004): 145–181.

Brantley, Will. *Feminine Sense in Southern Memoir: Smith, Glasgow, Welty, Hellman, Porter, and Hurston.* Jackson: University Press of Mississippi, 1993.

Brasell, R. Bruce. "'The Degeneration of Nationalism': Colonialism, Perversion, and the American South," *Mississippi Quarterly* 56.1 (Winter 2002–2003): 33–54.

Gebhard, Caroline. "Reconstructing Southern Manhood: Race, Sentimentality, and Camp in the Plantation Myth." In *Haunted Bodies: Gender and Southern Texts*, eds. Anne Goodwyn Jones and Susan V. Donaldson. Charlottesville: University of Virginia Press, 1997.

Howard, John. *Men Like That: A Southern Queer History.* Chicago: University of Chicago Press, 1999.

Howard, John, ed. *Carryin' On in the Lesbian and Gay South.* New York: New York University Press, 1997.

Johnson, E. Patrick. *Sweet Tea: Black Gay Men of the South.* Chapel Hill: University of North Carolina Press, 2008.

McRuer, Robert. *The Queer Renaissance: Contemporary American Literature and the Reinvention of Lesbian and Gay Identities.* New York: New York University Press, 1997.

Morris, Linda A. *Gender Play in Mark Twain: Cross-Dressing and Transgression.* Columbia: University of Missouri Press, 2007.

Poteet, William Mark. *Gay Men in Modern Southern Literature: Ritual, Initiation, and the Construction of Masculinity.* New York: Peter Lang, 2006.

Richards, Gary. *Lovers and Beloveds: Sexual Otherness in Southern Fiction, 1936–1961.* Baton Rouge: Louisiana University Press, 2005.

Rohy, Valerie. *Impossible Women: Lesbian Figures and American Literature.* Ithaca: Cornell University Press, 2000.

Saillant, John. "The Black Body Erotic and the Republican Body Politic, 1790–1820." In *Sentimental Men: Masculinity and the Politics of Affect in American Culture,* eds. Mary Chapman and Glenn Hendler. Berkeley: University of California Press, 1999.

Sears, James T. *Rebels, Rubyfruit, and Rhinestones: Queering Space in the Stonewall South.* New Brunswick: Rutgers University Press, 2001.

Sedgwick, Eve Kosofsky. *Tendencies.* Durham: Duke University Press, 1993.

Somerville, Siobhan. *Queering the Color Line: Race and the Invention of Homosexuality in American Culture.* Durham: Duke University Press, 2000.

Walters, Ronald G. "The Erotic South: Civilization and Sexuality in American Abolitionism." *American Quarterly* 25.2 (May 1973): 177–201.

Wilson, Angelia R. *Below the Belt: Sexuality, Religion and the American South.* London: Cassell, 2000.

Wise, Benjamin E. *William Alexander Percy: The Curious Life of a Mississippi Planter and Sexual Freethinker.* Chapel Hill: University of North Carolina Press, 2012.

Immigrant Writers and Transnational South

Appadurai, Arjun. *Modernity at Large: Cultural Dimensions of Globalization.* Minneapolis: University of Minnesota Press, 1996.

Bhabha, Homi, ed. *Nation and Narration.* London: Routledge, 1990.

Benson, Melanie R. *Disturbing Calculations: The Economies of Identity in Postcolonial Southern Literature, 1912–2002.* Athens: University of Georgia Press, 2008.

Bone, Martyn. *The Postsouthern Sense of Place in Contemporary Fiction.* Baton Rouge: Louisiana University Press, 2005.

Clifford, James and George E. Marcus. *Writing Culture: The Poetics and Politics of Ethnography.* Berkeley: University of California Press, 1986.

Cohn, Deborah. *History and Memory in the Two Souths: Recent Southern and Spanish American Fiction.* Nashville: Vanderbilt University Press, 1999.

Davis, Thadious M. *Southscapes: Geographies of Race, Region, & Literature.* Chapel Hill: University of North Carolina Press, 2011.

Hahamovitch, Cindy. *No Man's Land: Jamaican Guestworkers in America and the Global History of Deportable Labor.* Princeton: Princeton University Press, 2011.

Hobson, Fred, ed. *South to the Future: An American Region in the Twenty-First Century.* Athens: University of Georgia Press, 2002.

Hollinger, David. *Postethnic America: Beyond Multiculturalism.* New York Basic Books, 2000.

Humphries, Jefferson, and John Lowe, eds. *The Future of Southern Letters.* New York: Oxford University Press, 1996.

Juncker, Clara, and Russell Duncan, eds. *Transnational America: Contours of Modern US Culture.* Copenhagen: Museum Tuscalanum, 2004.

King, G., 1996. *Mapping Reality: An Exploration of Cultural Geographies.* London: Macmillan, 1996.

Lowe, John. "'Calypso Magnolia': The Caribbean Side of the South," *South Central Review* 22.1 (2005): 54–80.

Lowe, Lisa. *Immigrant Acts*. Durham: Duke University Press, 1996.

Peacock, James L., Harry L. Watson, and Carrie R. Matthews, eds. *The American South in a Global World*. Chapel Hill: University of North Carolina Press, 2005.

Ryan, Maureen. "Outsiders with Inside Information." In *South to a New Place: Region, Literature, Culture*, eds. Suzanne W. Jones and Sharon Monteith. Baton Rouge: Louisiana State University Press, 2002.

Smith, Jon and Deborah Cohn, eds. *Look Away! The U.S. South in New World Studies*. Durham: Duke University Press, 2004.

Wood, Joseph. "Vietnamese American Place Making in Northern Virginia," *Geographical Review* 87.1 (1997): 58–72.

Yousaf, Nahem. "A Sugar Cage: Poverty and Protest in Stephanie Black's H-2 Worker." In *Poverty and Progress in the US South since 1920*, eds. Suzanne Jones and Mark Newman. Amsterdam: VU University Press, 2006.

Yousaf, Nahem and Sharon Monteith. "Making an Impression: New Immigrant Fiction in the Post-War South," *Modern Language Forum* 60.2 (2004): 214–224.

"'I Was Pearl and My Last Name Was Harbor': Ethnic Southern Memory and Monique Thuy-Dung Truong's 'Kelly'," *North Carolina Literary Review* (2004): 113–122.

Butler, Octavia, 4, 28, 29
Kindred (1979), 29, 32–33
Butler, Robert Olen, 8, 206
A Good Scent From a Strange Mountain
(1993), 207, 213
Byrd II, William, 190

Cable, George Washington, 4, 65
The Entomologist (1899), 193
"The Freedman's Case in Equity"
(1885), 64
The Grandissimes (1880), 22–23, 63–64,
193
John March, Southerner (1894), 64
Caldwell, Erskine, 120, 124, 154, 169
God's Little Acre (1933), 94–95, 97–98
Journeyman (1935), 101
Tobacco Road (1932), 8, 94–95, 106, 108,
110, 179
You Have Seen Their Faces (1937) with
Margaret Bourke White, 99, 105, 107
Cao, Lan, 8, 204
Monkey Bridge (1997), 206, 207–208,
216–217
Capote, Truman, 153, 154, 196–197
"A Diamond Guitar" (1950), 196
Other Voices, Other Rooms (1948), 196
Cash, W.J., *The Mind of the South* (1941),
100
Caudill, Harry M., *My Land is Dying*
(1971), 110
Chesnutt, Charles, 22, 23–24
The Conjure Woman (1899), 23–24
The Marrow of Tradition (1901), 92, 100
Choi, Susan, 8, 204
The Foreign Student (1998), 206, 210–212
Chopin, Kate, 19, 125, 137, 194
The Awakening (1899), 19, 194
civil rights literature, 5, 7, 159–173, 201,
212, 214
civil rights movement, the 5, 108, 111, 159–
166, 186, 213
as a second Civil War, 163
as a second Reconstruction, 69, 162–163
and voter registration, 160–161
Civil War, the (1861–65), 1, 2, 12, 19, 36–37,
39–53, 55, 57, 58, 69, 92, 93, 100,
102, 124, 130, 177
the Confederacy and Confederates,
1, 40–41, 43, 47, 48, 50, 64, 92,
101, 206
Daughters of the Confederacy, 40
slavery as the primary cause of, 40, 49

reconciliation romances about, 3,
42–43, 56
See also Silber, Nina
anti-reconciliation literature, 43–45, 48
as the "Lost Cause," 1, 4, 11, 20–21,
23–24, 42–46, 56–57, 92, 96, 101,
124, 133
and civil rights, 50, 163
and the Vietnam War, 50–51
class issues, 104–113, 122
Cleage, Pearl, 172, 183
Bourbon at the Border (1997), 164
Cofer, Judith Ortiz, 7, 140–141
and Flannery O'Connor, 140
colonial drama, 174–175
comedy, 134–137, 152, 165, 170, 182, 191,
196, 199–200
satire, 147–151, 165, 200
Southwestern/frontier humor, 15–23,
25n10, 190–191
Cooper, Anna Julia, *A Voice From the South*
(1892), 25n13, 124
cotton, 2, 88, 97–98
as a subject for fiction, 93–95
Cox, Karen, *Dreaming of Dixie: How the
South Was Created in American
Popular Culture* (2011), 12
Crews, Harry, 109
Childhood: The Biography of a Place
(1978), 111
Cripps, Thomas, 152–153
cross-racial relationships, 112
Cruse, Howard, *Stuck Rubber Baby* (1995),
201
Cruz, Nilo, 183–184
Custis, George Washington Parke
The Indian Prophesy (1827), 176
Pocahontas; or the Settlers of Virginia
(1830), 176

Dabbs, James McBride, 161–162, 165
Dargan Olive Tilford (aka Fielding Burke),
Call Home The Heart (1932),
97–98, 122
Davenport, Doris, 197
Davis, Ossie, *Purlie Victorious* (1961), 165
Davis, Thadious, 112
*Southscapes: Geographies of Race,
Region, and Literature* (2011), 204
De Forest, John William, 4
The Bloody Chasm (1881), 56
*Miss Ravenel's Conversion From Secession
to Loyalty* (1867), 56, 63

Cambridge Companions to...

AUTHORS

TOPICS